M000301611

A Saga

of

Texas Land &
Oil Law

By Edgar Freeman Smith

Copano Bay Press

2011

Originally published in 1940 under the title *A Saga of Texas Law*.

Copano Bay Press Edition
Copyright 2011

ISBN 978-0-9829828-7-7

"The Constitution declares that might does not make right, and that the voice of the majority shall never be loud enough, nor the power of government strong enough, to destroy or restrict the just liberties of the humblest citizen. By the light of this constitutional philosophy, the dark places of the world have been illumed. Our people, in that hope, that ambition that springs from freedom, went forth to conquer, to build, to sow and to reap, to live and enjoy. In the lifetime of two generations they have conquered a continent, and placed not only the necessities but the luxuries of life in more homes and before more people than obtains in all the balance of the world combined."

—Judge C. M. Cureton

"An attorney who measures up to the highest standards of his profession must not only be learned in jurisprudence, but must be ever alert to encourage, and even to urge upon his clients, the recognition of moral obligations, as well as a compliance with statutes as interpreted by decisions. The lawyer who knows only the law, and not the principles of righteousness and justice upon which law should be founded, fails to realize that with intellect, but without conscience, he cannot discharge his duty as a member of that profession which peculiarly requires a clear conception of the great fundamental distinctions between right and wrong, whenever a moral question is involved."

—Judge Edwin L. Garvin

"The practice of the law changes with the conditions which surround it. The rules of evidence, the rules of decisions, the point of view of the legislator, the principles of constitutional construction, are changing with the rapidly expanding growth of society, and it is our place to keep accurately, and from a not unsympathetic point of view, in touch with the new life. To a certain extent, we are breaking away from precedent, and from principles hitherto thought to be unchangeable, and he that would live in this new life must understand it and be a part of it."

—Judge Hiram M. Garwood

Contents

Publisher's Note

I'm honored to have had the opportunity to work with the writings of a man so humble, dedicated, competent and human as Edgar Freeman Smith. While this book is fundamentally about law and some landmark cases that changed the lives of Texans, it is also full of life lessons...it extolls the virtues of hard work, scholarship, frugality and doing the right thing (or at very least that which you believe to be right at the time.) It's a good thing that young E. F. Smith never realized that he was poor and didn't have much chance of becoming a lawyer. Had he struck upon this realization, Texas may well have been short one good lawyer and one really good book. No substantial changes have been made to the original text in preparing this edition. None were needed.

-Michelle M. Haas, Managing Editor
Windy Hill

PREFACE

The great lawyer is the supreme artist. From the rough tone of apparently unrelated and unmeaning facts he carves the living truth. Upon the canvas of the mind, under his touch, grow visions beautiful and sublime. Liberty, law, and human rights are his creations. All history, all literature, all life are his materials. The artist himself is soon forgotten.

Unless the great lawyer at some time in his life holds high public office his name is seldom, if ever, known to fame. If he holds high office, he is known to posterity by reason of that fact and not because of the supreme intellectual power that made him great in the most competitive of all professions.

How many people outside the legal profession know anything about William Pinkney, possibly America's greatest lawyer, of Luther Martin, Reverdy Johnson, James Innes, William Wirt, Rufus Choate, Jeremiah Black, Charles O'Connor, William M. Evarts and James C. Carter? What do we of today know of that amazing man, Sergeant Smith Prentiss, who was "more eloquent than Webster"? We are told that his arguments were poems of beauty framed in unanswerable logic, but his efforts were expended in courtrooms. And today, with one or two exceptions, all we have are a few fragments of his masterly arguments.

It has been my good fortune to know many of the great lawyers of Texas and to observe them in action in the trial of important and strenuously contested lawsuits where, in some instances, the amounts involved could be calculated only in astronomical figures. Many of these men were artists, but they painted no picture on canvas and wrote no poem on paper. They dealt with the minds and emotions of men.

The right of men and women to life, liberty, property, and the pursuit of happiness is affected by the law, and its administration. I wanted to write a book that would tell a factual story of the law and how it is administered. I tried to write the book in the third person. It could not be written that way.

The law governs and controls the rights of men from the period of gestation until the death taxes have been paid. The law and the lawyer are inseparable. The law is not perfect; lawyers are not saints; judges are human and frequently err. "How," I asked myself, "can I write the story of the law that I want to write without telling the story of the lawyer and how he works?"

If the story I wanted to tell was to have any value, it must make the law, the lawyer, and the lawyer's work as real as life itself. "Then," I asked myself, "why not write of life itself?" The conclusions a man forms in his mind, the things that govern his actions, that make him behave as he does, are usually the result of three things: his environment, training, and heredity. The lawyer that I know best always wanted to be a lawyer. Without any apparent opportunity of ever becoming a lawyer, he did become one. He participated in the trial of many famous and celebrated lawsuits that made history in the empire that is Texas. Sometimes he was associated with, and sometimes opposed by, great lawyers, some of whom became nationally famous. On the pages of this book the attempt is made to show these men in action.

While the book is autobiographical, it is only incidentally so. The purpose of the book is to tell a story showing how the law actually functions. To effect the purpose of the book, I have told the story of many lawsuits and of the lawyers and judges who participated in the trial of these lawsuits. Deep human interests were involved in all these lawsuits; the lives, liberties, and fortunes of men and women were at stake in some of these lawsuits, and the welfare of all the people of Texas was at issue in others. As a participant in these battles of the courtroom, I was, of course, a partisan. Since these lawsuits were tried, there has been what lawyers refer to as a "cooling time." As a historian reporting what happened, and why and how it happened, I have attempted to state the facts fairly and impartially. The reader may draw his own conclusion as to what was right and just, or unjust and wrong. Such comment as I have made is kept severely apart from the facts.

Lawsuits are not pink teas; they are battles. The lawyer is a soldier, a hired soldier. His talents, ability and experience are for sale. He reserves, however, the right to reject any tendered employment. The true lawyer is not a mercenary soldier.

Most lawyers, once they are employed, are faithful to their employment. This faithful, even devoted, service to the cause of his client becomes a part of the life of the lawyer. A lawyer will work to the point of physical and mental exhaustion in his effort to win a lawsuit even when he has formed, since his employment, a strong personal dislike for his client. A lawsuit is a contest. Most men like to win. It is essential to the welfare of the lawyer for him to win. His fame as a lawyer and his hope of future employment depend in no small degree upon his ability to win lawsuits.

The honorable lawyer, and most lawyers are honorable men, without the slightest hesitation and at financial loss to himself, will advise a prospective client not to bring a suit when the lawyer is of the opinion that his prospective client has no cause of action. This advice, however, is not predicated on any abstract theory of right or wrong. It is based entirely on the opinion of the lawyer that the prospective client does not have a legal cause of action. Lawyers learn that law and justice are not always, unfortunately, one and the same thing.

The law is not, the assertion of some law school teachers to the contrary notwithstanding, an exact science. How can it be? In a jury trial disputed issues of fact are settled by a verdict of twelve men chosen at random from those living in the county where the case is tried. The law of the case is first determined by the trial judge, and upon appeal, by the judges of one or more appellate courts. These judges come from different environments and have formed different opinions from their experiences as lawyers. The result is that these judges often disagree as to what the law is, or what the law should be, when applied to a particular set of facts.

Most young lawyers begin their careers as lawyers with fine ideals, high enthusiasms, and as champions of the right or what they think is the right. When I had been in the practice for only a few years and was having a miraculous run of luck winning lawsuits, it was my proud boast that I could win any lawsuit, provided my client was in the right. This was a beautiful dream and about as unreal as are most dreams. With the passing years I became sadly disillusioned. I do not recall ever having tried a lawsuit that I was not convinced, at the time of the trial, that my client was right. This was not surprising, for prior to the trial I had heard only my client's version of the facts.

There are men in our prisons who should not be there, and who possibly would not be there if they had been defended by able lawyers. Many men have doubtless been acquitted, when tried on a criminal charge, who were guilty and would today be in prison, except for the fact that they were defended by an abler lawyer than the lawyer who prosecuted the case for the government. Many persons have come into court with a just cause of action in a civil case, or a just defense to an outrageous cause of action, and come away the loser. Every courthouse in this country is a house of tragedy. Within their walls have been enacted grim dramas of real life and the villain did not always lose at the end of the last act.

In this book, when the incidents of a lawsuit are told, the story follows the record, a record made in the courts, one that is open to the public. There will not be any disclosure of the secrets of client and lawyer, for the lawyer is obligated by the ethics of his profession and by the code of the gentleman to preserve for all time the secrets confided to him by his client.

E. F. Smith

Austin, Texas

CHAPTER I:
BORN ON THE BUCKHORN

My father was a Presbyterian minister. His church sent him as a missionary to the Chickasaw Indians. The Chickasaws were one of the five civilized tribes. These civilized Indians were compelled by our government to sign treaties, by the terms of which they surrendered their homes and ancestral lands east of the Mississippi, and in exchange therefor were given the country, now a part of the State of Oklahoma, designated as the Indian Territory. This country was originally a part of Louisiana. The United States bought this land from Napoleon, who had neither title nor possession, took it by force from the Comanche and Kiowa Indians, and by force, compelled the Indians of the five civilized tribes to make it their future home.

My father, at the request of his church, removed from Texas to the Chickasaw Nation in 1886. He first located at the Mill Creek Settlement, moving a year later to some land he had leased from an Indian near Buckhorn Stage Station and there, by the side of the road, known as the Whiskey Trail, he built a home. The location of Father's home is about three miles southeast of the present town of Sulphur.

Aided by his two oldest sons, who were then husky boys in their late teens, he built a log home consisting of three rooms and a hall. There were stone fireplaces in two of the rooms. There was no bathroom. Buckhorn Creek was a hundred yards away, and it was the source of the water supply for the family and the stock.

In the summertime this creek was the bathroom. In the winter time the family bathed in the kitchen after first heating water on the kitchen stove, and the bathtub was one of the washtubs. In this home on the Buckhorn I was born. I was the last child of my father's family. The next child was a son, seven years my senior; the next was a daughter, ten years my senior; the next a son, sixteen years my senior: the next a son, eighteen years my senior, and the oldest child was a daughter, twenty years my senior.

In one of the rooms Father had built shelves on each side of the fireplace, running from the fireplace to the corners of the room, and on these shelves he placed his books. This was his library. As a small boy, I read most of these books. Some of the books that I remember were McGuffey's readers and other school books, among them some that Father had studied at Cane Hill College. This was a school in Arkansas, which I believe has ceased to function. I also remember that we had a *Lady of the Lake*, *Rokeby*, and perhaps other books by Scott, Macaulay's *History of England*, a *History of the Southern Confederacy* by Alexander Stephens, the dialogues of Plato, many books on the subject of theology and polemics, books of poetry by Burns, Longfellow, Whittier, Lowell and others, Johnson's *Lives of the English Poets*, "Parson" Weems' *Life of General Washington*, the "Complete" works of William Shakespeare in one volume of very fine print.

There was one adventure book that I read again and again. Its title was *Conquering the Wilderness*. In this book were stories about Kit Carson, Bill Gordon, Jim Bridges, Bill Williams; and I think it was in this book that I first read the story of the "grey-eyed man of destiny," the filibustered William Walker, who fought a duel in San Francisco, then with a band of freebooters, made war on a Mexican territory, invaded Honduras, and was there captured, tried and condemned by a court martial and shot.

My father was a good man. He knew there is a God, and he also knew there is a heaven. He probably believed there is a hell. He concerned himself very little with the affairs of this world. In this he was entirely consistent, because to him this world was only a temporary residing place where men and women could, by faith, prayer and right living, prepare themselves for the joys and pleasures of that permanent, eternal home that God in His goodness has prepared for the faithful. He sought neither fame nor fortune, but in obedience to the command of his Church was happy in his work, a work which he verily believed he had been called by God to do.

Father was not a sociologist; it may be that he did not even know the meaning of the word. To him men were individuals with souls to save. He, in common with most of the frontiersmen of his day, was charitable; of his little he gladly gave to those who were in distress.

My mother was a good woman. She loved and respected Father, and thought the work he was doing very important. Father's work kept him away from home most of the time. At night and just before bedtime, the family would gather in one room, and if Father was at home, he would read a chapter from the Scriptures and then we would all kneel by our chairs while he prayed. To Mother, God was very real, and Jesus was her Savior and personal friend. When Father was absent, she would pray to God in the name of his Son, Jesus, that God would bless the work of her absent husband, protect and keep him well, and return him safely to his loved ones at the expected time. Family prayer at our home was not unlike the family worship recounted by Burns in "The Cotter's Saturday Night."

The Church was poor, and Father's pay was insufficient for even the modest needs of his family, but the land that Father had leased from the Indian was rich, virgin soil, and it produced crops in great abundance. Corn, cotton and oats were the principal crops, and Mother always had a marvelous garden. Father had a few cattle, and these, with the work stock, were permitted to graze on the open range. Mother raised chickens, ducks, geese, and turkeys, not for the market, because there was no market, but for home consumption.

Friends and strangers traveling the Whiskey Trail were welcome to put up for the night at Father's home, and there was never any charge for this hospitality. These travelers brought news from the outside world. Most of the work on the farm was done by the older children, for Father was away from home nearly all the time organizing new churches, and visiting and revisiting churches previously organized by him.

What was once the Chickasaw Nation is a beautiful country. When I was a boy, it was almost primeval, little affected by the activities of men. It was a well-watered country. Every few miles there was a clear river, creek, or spring branch. Along these water courses were fine stands of timber. There were post oak, red oak, hickory, elm, pecan, walnut and ash trees. Between the streams were prairies. There were deer by the hundreds. The woods were full of turkeys, and prairie chickens were so numerous as to be a nuisance.

The Indians were generally poor, and the few white people in the country were no better off than the Indians. The people did not have much money and did not need much, for, with the exception of flour, sugar, and salt, nearly everyone raised his own food. Clothing did not cost much. Boots and hats for the men and shoes for the women had to be bought; but in every home was a crude cobbler's outfit, and the boots and shoes, when they became worn, were half-soled, patched and otherwise repaired, so that a pair of boots or a pair of shoes were made to last a long time. The children, including those in their late teens, went barefoot in the summer time, and it was not uncommon for a married woman, the mother of several children, to go barefoot, but most of the women did not consider this very genteel.

The women did not buy dresses, hats and underthings, and it was not often that a man bought a store suit. The material for these things was bought, and the women folks made the clothes. In his ministerial work, Father was always neatly dressed in a black bought suit, white shirt and collar, black tie, black shoes and a black hat. In my mind is a picture of this frontier preacher. He was a slender man, of medium height, silver hair, and wore a neatly trimmed beard that had become grey, and his eyes were a clear and a fearless blue. He carried himself very erect, for he had served about four years as a soldier in the army of his cousin, General E. Kirby Smith.

When Father could devote a few days to the farm work, he put away his ministerial garments and wore clothes that had been made by Mother—boots and a second-best hat. If he was sent for to conduct a funeral, or if a couple came to his home to be married, he would dress in his best clothes. Sometimes the bridegroom would expostulate: "Brother Smith," he would say, "you need not dress up just to marry us. You are all right as you are."

To this Father would reply: "I think I had better change my clothes. It will not take long. This is a happy day for you, one that you will always remember. I do not want anything that I may do, or fail to do, to mar the beauty of the occasion for you."

Father had a beautiful voice, and the mental picture that I have of him now is that when he preached a sermon, conducted a funeral or performed a marriage ceremony, he created the proper atmosphere required for the occasion. I never heard Father speak unkindly of anyone or lift his voice in anger. I remember him as being calm, serene and untroubled. There may have been about him a little sternness, a quality amounting to a certainty that he had the right to give orders and to have them obeyed, that had become a part of his very being as a result of his years of service in the army. Except that his body was not so robust nor so tall as that of the South's Great Commander, he was not in his personal appearance unlike the familiar picture we see of General Robert E. Lee.

The neighbors and the people Father served, saints and sinners alike, with but few exceptions, addressed him as "Brother Smith." There were a few who addressed him as "Parson."

Each summer Father held in different parts of the nation three or four camp meetings. The people made great plans for these meetings and would come to them from as far away as fifty or sixty miles, which were long distances requiring as much as two days to travel. Father always wanted Mother to attend these meetings with him, and she would go when she could. It was not easy for her to arrange to be away from home. It required all of her time from early in the morning until the bed time hours for her to get her work done. Five-thirty was about the time we would get up in the morning, and we would go to bed about nine o'clock. During these hours, three meals for several persons had to be prepared, and they were prepared over a hot, wood-burning, cook stove; new clothes were made, old ones repaired, and once a week the family washing had to be done, a long, hard day's work. The next day was ironing day, and the irons were heated over the same hot cook stove that was used for cooking purposes. Quilts had to be pieced, then hung in a frame and quilted. Feathers from the geese and ducks were carefully saved, and these, before they were used to make beds and pillows, were placed in a tub filled with limewater, where they remained for three or four days, being frequently stirred. Then they were removed from the limewater, shaken and dried. Goose feathers were better than duck feathers; but Mother, for lack of sufficient geese, had to use both, the duck feathers in the beds and the goose feathers in the pillows. The older children milked the cows, but Mother had to care for the milk. One of my earliest responsibilities was the churning job.

When Mother went to a camp meeting, one of the older children had to remain at home to take care of things; the stock had to be fed, the cows milked, the eggs gathered up, the hog pens cleaned out, and any sick stock looked after. It must have been a great relief to Mother to get away from the responsibilities of her home for one or two weeks. Father generally had to go in advance of his family and get the meeting organized, the arbor repaired, the grounds where the meeting was to be held cleaned up, and everything put in as good shape as possible.

Much preparation had to be made at home by Mother; food to feed several people for the duration of the meeting had to be prepared, cakes and pies were baked, hams and great sides of bacon were brought from the smokehouse and stored in the food box, dozens of loaves of bread were baked, and many jars of fruit were carefully packed in the wagon. The morning of departure was a busy time. The bows were put on the wagon bed and across these a wagon sheet was drawn. Then the wagon was loaded with bedding, food and a trunk or two of clothes, and finally the mules were hitched to the wagon. Mother and one of the older boys would take their places on the spring seat, while we younger children would climb aboard and lounge on the bedding that had been placed in the wagon bed behind the spring seat. The wagon sheet would be rolled about halfway up on each side to afford plenty of ventilation, for it was summer time and very hot. The boy on the spring seat, inflated by his importance, would gather up the lines that guided the team of mules, release the brake and give the formal words of command to the team to move forward. These words for some reason known only to teamsters and mules were "get up," although the mules were not down, but standing patiently hitched to the wagon. When the wheels of the wagon began to turn, our summer vacation had begun.

Most of the people lived isolated lives, seldom seeing anyone other than the members of their own families, and they had the same desire that we have to go somewhere; almost any place would do, where they could see something different from the familiar scenes about their homes, meet old friends, make new acquaintances, hear and discuss the latest news, and have social contacts with their fellow men. The camp meetings supplied a real need of these people, religious and social.

A camp meeting usually lasted for two weeks and was held at some country schoolhouse, which in the winter time was used on Sundays for church and Sunday school purposes. These school buildings were of log construction and had been built and furnished with crude benches, a blackboard, and a table for the teacher, by the voluntary joint efforts of the men residing in that community. There would be a mass meeting once a year, a meeting similar to the New England town meeting, at which there would be a discussion of the community's public affairs and a board of school trustees elected for the next year. There were no other public officials, except the postmaster, who almost invariably kept the neighborhood general store.

There were no local taxes. The roads and bridges were built and maintained by money voluntarily given and labor voluntarily performed. The school board did not employ a teacher. The board would authorize a teacher to teach a "subscription school," which meant that the teacher must contact the parents in the neighborhood, and those who wanted to would "subscribe," that is, sign an agreement, that their children would attend the school for a certain number of months, never more than five and sometimes for not more than three months. The parents paid the teacher direct. The price of tuition for each child was from one to two dollars per month, depending on how far along the child was advanced in his studies.

The men of the community would, by their voluntary action, supply the wood that was used for fuel in heating the school building. The teacher furnished the chalk for blackboard use and was his own janitor. He swept out the building and made the fire in the morning, but during the day he was free to call on any boy to bring in wood or to replenish the fire, or to go to the spring or creek for a bucket of drinking water. The boys always asked for the privilege of doing these things, because it gave them an excuse for escaping from the schoolroom. If the teacher was a woman, she might give an older boy his tuition for sweeping the floor and making the morning fire. After Father's death and when Mother had moved to the town of Sulphur, I was the school janitor, but there we had three rooms, and I was paid, in addition to my tuition, five dollars a month.

The camp meetings were held under a brush arbor, near one of the school buildings. Father's church was not the only church active in the Indian country. The Baptist, Methodist and Christian, then called Campbellites, in honor of the Mr. Campbell who had founded the Christian Church, were also very active. Any of these churches were welcome to use the community school building for church services in the winter time or the brush arbor in the summer time. These churches, with their diverse doctrines and beliefs, had very little friction, but the question of whether baptism should be by immersion or by sprinkling was debated by some of the brethren with much heat. Father did not think it made any difference how a person was baptized. He believed that baptism was a service formulated by the church whereby the person being baptized forsook his allegiance to the world and pledged his allegiance to God and the church, and if the spirit was right, the method used was immaterial.

Father would baptize by immersion or by sprinkling as the person to be baptized might choose. He thought the ceremony of infant baptism one of the most beautiful services of his church, and he tried to make the service an impressive one.

The camp meetings were held near some spring or creek, usually both, and this spring or creek was the source of the water supply for men and stock. Each day Father would preach at eleven o'clock in the morning and again at night. The people attending the meetings, except those living in the immediate community, would be camped near the arbor. Two or more families might form a group for the purpose of cooking their food and eating together. All the cooking was done out of doors and by open fire. When the evening service began, the fires over which the evening meals had been cooked would still be burning, and as the service proceeded, the light from these fires which encircled the arbor would slowly burn down, until at the last there would be only glowing embers twinkling, and then going out.

During the afternoons the older people would gather under the arbor and visit, discussing with each other the health of the children, the condition of the crops, the weather, and the latest news and gossip. If the camp meeting was being held near a creek, and it generally was, the young people after the noon meal would go to the creek, the young men and boys in one group, and the young women and the girls in another. Never did they go together; to do so would have been considered immodest. The young women and girls would bring with them to the camp meeting old calico dresses and old stockings, and wearing these, they would wade and bathe in the creek. The men and boys were not so handicapped. They went into the water wearing only their birthday suits. Father was an excellent swimmer and greatly enjoyed the sport.

Many boys and girls found romance at the camp meetings. Their courting was conducted on the sly, because the older men and women "made fun" of those known to be courting. Most of the men were married by the time they were twenty-one, and a girl was ready for marriage at sixteen and was usually an old woman at forty. A boy of twenty-one was as able as a man of thirty-five to make a living for himself and his wife and for their children, when the children came.

A girl of sixteen knew by experience how to keep house, and most of them had for years been caring for their younger brothers and sisters. If necessary, she could milk the cows, feed the hogs and poultry, make her own and most of her husband's clothing, and often made a hand in the field with her husband.

Children were not economic liabilities, but were assets. By the time a boy was ten, he could earn his cost by the work he did on the farm, and from then until he became twenty-one, his labor became more and more profitable to his father. The same was true, but in a lesser degree, of the girls. When a boy from a family well-to-do, measured by the standards of that time and place, became twenty-one, or married, his father usually gave him a good team, a wagon, and sufficient supplies to last until he could make a crop. The boy and his parents then considered all financial accounts between them settled; unless when the father and mother were old and needed a home, it was understood that the home of any child could be the home of the parents. When a girl married, her parents usually supplied her with a feather bed, pillows, sheets, quilts and sometimes with a cow and a calf.

Conditions in this world do not long remain static. Change is inevitable. The *status quo* can seldom be maintained for any great length of time. The older children of our family married and established homes of their own. Father became an invalid. The lease on the farm expired. He was ill for three years. Asphalt mines had been opened about three miles west of Buckhorn at the mining camp of Gilsonite. There Father built a two-room plank house. The work stock, cattle, hogs and poultry were sold, and Father, Mother and we three younger children moved into the little house at Gilsonite. Father's great Church, in its crusade to Christianize the world, forgot the soldier who had served it so long and so well in one of its outposts. For three years Father was incapacitated. The sister ten years my senior taught a "subscription" school and made a few dollars for a few months each year; the brother seven years my senior went to work in the mines. His wages were one dollar and twenty-five cents a day for a ten-hour day. Then Father died.

It was snowing on the day of the funeral. The neighbors made the best coffin they could. The nearest minister lived at Daugherty, eight miles away, and the storm was too bad to send for him. The coffin, with the body in it, was carried in a wagon through the storm and over the snow-covered and rough road to the Buckhorn burying ground. There other friends had dug the grave. Snow had been shoveled away and a fire built in the cleared space. Around this fire the family and friends gathered in an effort to keep warm while a song or two was sung. No last salute of guns was fired, and no bugle notes of taps were blown, as this once proud soldier of the South was buried, and no burial service of the church was said over the grave of this humble soldier of the Cross.

The Buckhorn burial grounds are closed now. The graves of those who are buried there are surrounded on three sides by a farm, where each year crops are planted, cultivated and harvested; on the fourth side is a modern highway over which motor cars are driven at a speed that enables them to travel farther in an hour than Father could ride in a long day on his horse. Overhead an occasional airplane passes, and each day across his grave the air waves carry beautiful music that is caught by tens of thousands of radios, and enjoyed by millions of people. Father has been dead for only forty-one years, but he never dreamed that such things could be.

At my age, I am living in a world as different from the one that Father lived in when he was the age that I am now, as the world of his age was different from the world in which Plato lived. The home in which I live is air-conditioned. The suggestion of such a possibility to Father would have amused him as a mere fantasy, or perhaps he would have been concerned about the mental condition of the person who would seriously suggest such a possibility.

The frontier of Father's day is gone; other frontiers have been discovered, conquered and left behind us, and in the future are other frontiers, which are unknown now, but which will be discovered and conquered, provided men are left free to exercise their ingenuity and initiative and the incentive for individual effort is not destroyed.

Thirty years after I had left the Indian country I returned for a two-day visit to the scenes of my childhood. During this long absence, I had seen no one, other than the members of my own family, who had ever known my father. While I was in Sulphur my nephew, Miles Wright, and I met an old Indian, Jack Frost. Miles introduced me to Mr. Frost and told him that I was a son of Reverend James J. Smith. The face of the old Indian showed his apparent pleasure at hearing the name of my father, and he made this simple statement: "I knew your father long and well; he was the best man I have ever known."

Chapter II:
A Boy Wants to be a Lawyer

Within a year or two after Father's death, the mines at Gilsonite were closed down. Brother found work in a coal mine at Phillips, a little town between Coalgate and Lehigh, in the then Choctaw Nation. At the end of the school term Mother, Sister and I joined Brother, and that summer I helped Brother dig coal. We were paid by the ton for the coal we dug. We did not make much money. We were paid twice a month, and the little we received, after deducting what we owed to the company store, was paid to us in gold, except the small change.

Mother did not like for us to work in the mine, which was an underground one, and when one day an accident that might have resulted in the death of all the men working in the mine was narrowly averted, she insisted that we find something else to do. Brother was able to get a contract with the mining company for furnishing certain timbers called props and caps used in the mines. That fall and winter Mother, Sister, Brother and I lived in the Boggy River woods. Our living quarters consisted of a one-room log house and a tent.

That winter I mastered the use of a double-bitted ax, and became familiar with the business end of a cross-cut saw. The work was hard and the hours were long, but I had an immense amount of fun. There were deer and wild turkey in the woods; the trees were full of red and grey squirrels, there were plenty of quail, and a few ducks and geese settled on the lake near our home. This was the only winter that I had to miss school, but Sister insisted that I continue my studies under her supervision, and I did so most reluctantly, for I was tired when night came, entirely too tired to study, but not too tired to go on a coon and opossum hunt, as I did many times.

Near our old home on the Buckhorn was a group of sulphur springs, and about a mile from these springs was a bromide spring seeping out of the side of the high bank of Rock Creek. The waters of these springs possess certain medicinal qualities that are claimed to be beneficial to those suffering from various and sundry bodily ailments. A town had been built up around the group of sulphur springs. There were some comfortable and rather commodious hotels and baths erected for the use of those visiting the springs. After our winter in the Boggy River country we moved to Sulphur, where Brother was able to enter business in a small way, and Sister had occasional work as a teacher. I secured the job of janitor at the school, and during the holidays I obtained what work I could at the hotels and bathing places.

The United States Government became interested in the sulphur and bromide springs and decided to include them in a national park. To do this the Government bought the entire town of Sulphur. Immediately there was a building boom, for an entirely new town had to be built, but instead of building one town, the people built two, one on the west side of Rock Creek and another on the east side of the creek. This resulted in a first class town fight that lasted for years.

During the building boom, the Artesian Hotel, a four-story brick structure, was erected on the east side. It was, when completed, the most palatial building that I had ever seen. This building was erected one summer, and I got a job from the contractor as a brick carrier. I was sixteen years old at the time, and never before or since have I had as tough a job as this one. We worked nine hours a day, six days a week, and my wages were twenty cents an hour. In handling the brick, the skin on the inside of my fingers and thumbs was worn to the quick, and from these abrasions the blood oozed.

One day at the noon hour, one of the bricklayers asked me if I wanted to learn the bricklayer's trade, and when I told him I did not, another workman asked me what I did want to be, and I told him I was going to be a lawyer. This statement of mine brought laughter and jeers from some of the men. An older man, and a very kindly one, said: "Son, you can be a lawyer or anything else you make up your mind to be in this country, if you start soon enough, work hard, save your money and keep honest. Trouble with me is, I just drifted along until now it is too late for me to do anything except lay one brick on top of another."

On another occasion, I brought ridicule on myself by making the statement in the presence of the other workmen that someday I would be a guest of the hotel we were building. It was thirty years before I made good my boast. By then the Artesian Hotel had, in my eyes, lost its glory and its grandeur, but nevertheless, for two days and nights I was a guest of the Artesian Hotel.

When I had gone as far as I could in the Sulphur school, I went to Gainesville, Texas, where I found work before and after school hours, and on Saturdays, in the store of a Jew merchant. This enabled me to pay my way while I went to high school. The completion of my high school work was the end of my formal education, but I have never ceased to be a student.

With the passing years I have, when I could, bought good books, and these I have read and studied. I am writing this book in my library at home where I am surrounded by some of the best books ever written. Inside my library walls are hundreds of books which tell the history, the struggle, the valiant efforts, the faults, the glories, the failures of men and nations. There are shelves of books by philosophers, Plato, Kant, Spinoza, Voltaire, Emerson, Schopenhauer and other immortals, not the least of whom, in my opinion, was Erasmus of Rotterdam, and not to be despised is Rabelais, the monk. There are many books on the science and theory of government, and here are the oldest and newest books on the now much discussed subject of economics, with a greater disparity between the theories of Adam Smith and the theories of the moderns than the changes that have occurred in the years between their writings would seem to justify. Other shelves are filled with the writings of the poets of all the ages from the time of the ancients until now. Surrounding me are books of adventure, of fact and of fiction.

One long shelf is filled with books that were written by me, being the bound volumes of the printed briefs that I have written and filed in the Appellate Courts of the Nation, and the State of Texas. Each of these briefs represents a legal battle, some of titanic proportions. Each brief, supported by the record of the case, tells a story of human relations, of avarice or generosity, of love or hate, of hope or despair, and some of these stories are stranger and more bizarre than can be found in any book of fiction on the shelves of my library.

While I was in Gainesville, Sister had married, and Brother and the beautiful girl he was to marry had agreed upon a date for their wedding. Brother had been the principal breadwinner for the family since before Father's death. It was my job to take over his task. Mother, who had become a semi-invalid, and I rented a three-room house for five dollars a month, and there Mother made a cheerful home for me. I obtained work in a store at a salary of thirty dollars a month, and on this we lived, for it was all we had.

I came home one night and found Mother much worse than usual. I walked across town, a distance of more than a mile, to the home of Dr. Ponder, and asked him to come and see Mother. We went together to his barn and hitched his team to the buggy, and then rode together to my home. On this night drive, Dr. Ponder engaged me in conversation and elicited from me the information that my job in the store was paying me thirty dollars a month. Whereupon, he told me that I could not expect to improve my position by continuing to work as a clerk in a store. I replied that I had no intention of being a store clerk all my life. He then asked me what I was planning to do. I told him I was going to be a lawyer. I had always wanted to be a lawyer, but I did not know why. I did not know any lawyers and I did not see a case tried in a courthouse until I was twenty-one years old.

Dr. Ponder was a kindly gentleman, and he was well acquainted with our financial situation. He pointed out to me, with consideration for my feelings, that it would take years of study and preparation before I could become a lawyer, and that young lawyers without influential friends rarely succeeded. He concluded his observations with this statement: "It is much better for an underprivileged boy to learn a good trade than to attempt to be a lawyer."

That was the first time I remember hearing the word "underprivileged." I did not know what the word meant, but I felt that it meant something bad, and that in the opinion of the good doctor I was an underprivileged boy. On the frontier every man and every boy believed he was as good as any other man or boy. I am still of that belief.

Looking backward thirty-five years, I now know that Dr. Ponder was right. I was an underprivileged boy. I thank God that I did not know it then. Such knowledge might have given me an inferiority complex. If such knowledge had been accompanied by a maudlin, more or less sincere, public sympathy for my underprivileged condition, I would in all probability have felt that in some obscure way I was a victim of injustice and commenced feeling sorry for myself. This is a mental condition hard for any boy to overcome. In my home I had been taught, and in my ignorance I believed the teaching to be true, that I could be a lawyer or anything else I might want to be.

A kindly grey-haired old gentleman was the president of a little bank in Sulphur. He had been a lawyer in Arkansas, perhaps a judge of some court, for his friends addressed him as Judge White. I became acquainted with Judge White and talked to him about my ambition to be a lawyer. He encouraged me and loaned me books, and told me of other textbooks I should obtain and study. This was the beginning of my legal studies. I wish I could say that from this beginning I moved steadily forward, never permitting anything to discourage or divert me from my course, until I had reached my goal. Such, however, is not the fact.

Long years were to follow, and I was often discouraged and strongly tempted to give up the effort to become a lawyer. It was not easy to work hard all day and then study at night, and I often needed someone who could explain some of the complex problems.

CHAPTER III:
STRUGGLING IN SNYDER

By the end of the year 1906, the building boom in Sulphur, caused by the building of the new town, was at an end. Times were hard. I had work, but the pay was small and the hours were long. The store opened for business at seven-thirty in the morning and remained open until eight or later at night, except on Saturday night, when it stayed open as long as there was a customer to be served, or any prospect of a customer coming into the store.

A railroad was being built in West Texas. Two men that I knew, Ivan and Sam Richardson, went to West Texas to investigate the prospects. When these men returned, they assured me and many others that the town of Snyder, the county seat of Scurry County, had great prospects of becoming a city. There was plenty of work, so they said, and wages were high. On this report, eight or ten families moved from Sulphur to Snyder, one merchant and a capitalist among the number. The capitalist was worth perhaps $25,000. A third of a century ago, $25,000 was a small fortune in either Sulphur or Snyder. Money could be loaned at an interest rate of ten per cent annually, with the repayment of the loan well secured. Frequently good notes, having ample security, could be discounted so that the rate of interest earned would be twelve or fifteen per cent annually. This rate of interest assured an annual income of $2,000 to a man with $20,000 to loan. Taxes were not high, and a man with an income of $2,000 could, and usually did, save from $500 to $1,000 of his income.

My oldest brother decided that he would go to Snyder. Mother and I discussed the possible advantages and disadvantages of my going to Snyder. Finally it was decided, largely on the advice of my older brother, that I, too, should go to Snyder. Mother could not go. Neither could Brother's family. The two Richardsons had reported that a house to live in could not be obtained in Snyder "for love or money."

On December 31, 1906, the two Richardsons, Brother, and I got on the "jerk water" train at Sulphur. Each of us had been supplied with a shoe box filled with food, enough to last us from the beginning of our journey at Sulphur until we had arrived in Snyder. At Davis, eight miles west of Sulphur, we changed to the Santa Fe for Fort Worth. We arrived in Fort Worth at night. There we had to wait a few hours before we could get on the Texas & Pacific train for Colorado City.

The union depot at Fort Worth, not the present beautiful building, but the one that was replaced by the present building, was filled with people. Never in my life up to then had I seen so many people coming and going as there were that night in the depot. Every thirty or forty minutes the announcer would call some train. The only loudspeaker that he used was the one that God gave him, but he could be heard distinctly for a city block. Finally he called "Al-l-l-l aboa'd-d-d-d! The T & P for Eastland, Baird, Abilene, Sweetwater, Pecos, El Paso and all points west. All aboa'd. Track 3. Train leaves in thirty minutes!"

Immediately there was a rush by the people for the gate leading to Track 3. Everyone, it seemed, was going west. I was sure that we would be unable to get on the train in thirty minutes. To my surprise, we did, with at least twenty minutes to spare.

There may have been one or more Pullman cars on the train. I do not know. I was not even interested. What greater luxury and pleasure could anyone want than to be permitted to ride in a chair car? It was not a chair car, but it was called a chair car, and, therefore, so far as I knew or was concerned, it was a chair car. It did have red, plush-covered seats, and I did not want anything any more comfortable than one of those seats upon which to spend the night. Our train left Fort Worth at about eleven o'clock at night. Some time during the night, a freight train was wrecked ahead of us, and this made us several hours late in arriving at Colorado City and too late to get the stage for Snyder.

The railroad that was being built into Snyder had its origin at Roscoe, a town between Sweetwater and Colorado City on the Texas & Pacific. This railroad would not be in operation for many months. The new railroad was the Roscoe-Snyder & Pacific. Its course from Roscoe was northwest, and presumably, if it was ever to reach the Pacific, its Pacific terminal would be somewhere in the neighborhood of Seattle. It was destined, however, that the northwestern terminus of this railroad was to be Fluvanna, a little town about twenty miles northwest of Snyder.

The next day after we arrived in Colorado City, we rode the stage, a three-seated hack, from Colorado City to Snyder, a distance of thirty miles. Snyder had its origin as a buffalo camp and trading post. When Scurry County was organized in 1884, Snyder became the county seat. At the time of which I am writing, Snyder had a population of about five hundred. There were not more than forty-five hundred people in the entire county. The business center of Snyder was scattered on the four sides of the courthouse square. Most of the business houses were adobe in construction, with two or three plank buildings, and one small two-story brick building on the west side of the square, the ground floor of which was used by the Snyder National Bank, the only bank then in Snyder. Since the depression, it is still the only bank in Snyder.

Scurry County is in the semi-arid section of West Texas and is located about fifty miles south and east of the great staked plains. The only timber in the county is mesquite, with an occasional cottonwood tree growing on the banks of Deep Creek. Primarily, it was a cattle and sheep country. The soil is a rich sandy loam, and when there is sufficient rain, this land can produce and has produced excellent crops of cotton, grain and sorghums. Drouths are not infrequent, and there are years when the crops are a complete failure.

There had been good rains in 1906, and fine crops had been grown on the lands that were farmed during that year. The prosperous farming condition of the country and the possibility that the country might become a fine farming section, together with the fact that the railroad was being built to Snyder, brought on the building boom in Snyder that reached its highest peak early in the year 1907.

When our little party of four arrived in Snyder, work was plentiful, and wages were high. I obtained work that paid me $15 a week. Within a few weeks I was able to rent a new, two-room box house, and Mother came from Sulphur to make a home for me.

Mother and I bought a lot for $50 in one of the many new real estate additions to Snyder. For a few hundred dollars, mostly on credit, we built a four-room box house on our lot. In the fall of 1907 there was a nationwide panic. All new construction ceased in Snyder. Many men were thrown out of employment. Within a month more than one hundred families moved away from Snyder.

Mother and I lost our home, because we could not meet the payments on it when they became due. I was out of work. We disposed of our household furnishings for what a secondhand store would pay for them, and with all of our worldly possessions in three trunks and our hand baggage, we moved to San Antonio. We had $18 when we arrived in San Antonio. We found a place to board for a few dollars a week, and I began the search for work. Sometimes I could obtain a few days' work at low wages, and I accepted whatever work I could obtain and at whatever wages my employer was willing to pay. During the time we were in San Antonio, I walked hundreds of miles in my search for work—any kind of work.

My oldest brother and his family had remained in Snyder. Financial conditions improved, and with improving financial conditions, new construction work commenced there. Brother wrote that he had work for me, and upon receipt of this letter, Mother and I returned to Snyder.

In moving from Sulphur to Snyder and from Snyder to San Antonio, then back to Snyder from San Antonio, I kept my few law books, and studied them when I could.

My experience in losing our home in Snyder in 1907 taught me a lesson, one that I have never forgotten. I concluded then that it is never wise to go in debt for anything, that when I could not pay for anything I wanted, I would do without until I was able to pay for it. Hard times were to come again and again while I lived in Snyder, times when work could not be had. When these times came, Mother would stay with the family of my oldest brother while I went away in search of work.

Chapter IV:
Admitted to the Bar

On the 24th day of September, 1913, Miss Bessie Buchanan of Snyder, and I were married. In a rented house, she made a home for me and a home for my invalid mother, until Mother died in 1918.

I had never at any time given up the idea of becoming a lawyer. After my marriage, Mrs. Smith encouraged me to continue with my legal studies. In November, 1914, I took the bar examination. The examination consisted of hundreds of written questions which had to be answered in writing. It took me five days to take the examination. Many weeks were to pass before I was to learn the result. In January, 1915, a letter came from the Clerk of the Court of Civil Appeals giving me my grades on the many subjects on which I had been examined. All of my grades, except two, were above ninety. The Clerk advised that I had passed the examination, and that upon receipt of five dollars, he would issue and mail to me my law license. The day I received this letter was one of the happy days of my life. I was a lawyer!

I had my license to practice law, but I did not have any clients. The lawyer cannot ask for legal work. The ethics of the profession forbid his doing so. The young lawyer must obtain work with some established law firm, or he must open his own office and wait for clients to come to him. The waiting is often long and expensive. I was not financially able to open a law office and wait for clients, because I had to earn a living. I was very fortunate, however, in that I secured work as manager of the Scurry County Abstract Company.

The title of "manager" sounds very impressive, but there were only two employees in the office of this abstract company, a young lady and I. In accepting this work, it was understood and agreed that I could, in addition to my abstract work, give such time as was necessary to attend to any legal work that might come to me to do. During my first six months as a lawyer, I was employed to examine a few abstracts, write a few deeds, contracts, deeds of trust, and was employed in three cases in the court of the Justice of the Peace and had two probate cases in the County Court.

One day a man, who lived near Fluvanna, came into the office and wanted to employ me to defend him against three complaints that had been filed against him in the County Court of Borden County. Borden County joins Scurry County on the west. This man had been driving along the public highway in his wagon in Borden County, when he met two men, one of whom he disliked and with whom he had had a previous quarrel. At this meeting, which occurred on the public highway, the quarrel between these two men was renewed. All three men got out of their wagons, and my client cursed his enemy, finally drew his pistol and with it struck, but did not injure, his opponent. The County Attorney of Borden County filed three complaints against my client, one for disturbing the peace, one for using profane and abusive language in a public place, to-wit, on a public highway, and the third complaint charged my client with the commission of an aggravated assault.

My client was guilty of all these offenses. The offenses of disturbing the peace and of using profane and abusive language in a public place are minor misdemeanors; but the offense of aggravated assault is a very serious misdemeanor, and a person guilty of the commission of such an offense is subject to the payment of a very substantial fine, and to imprisonment in the county jail. My fee in these three cases was twenty-five dollars.

After I had been employed, I began to search the law books to see if I could find a way to save my client in whole or in part from the penalties of the law. I found what I thought was a possible way for my client to escape the more serious consequences of his unlawful conduct, provided the County Attorney did not suspect what my purpose was and prevent me from carrying it out.

The average law-abiding citizen, so long as he himself has not inadvertently gotten into serious trouble, is disposed to think that a person who violates the law should be punished for his offense in the manner and to the extent provided by law. I have known some excellent people who were of this opinion until they themselves got into trouble with the law, and then they were very anxious to find a lawyer who could get them out of their trouble. It is the duty of a lawyer when employed in a criminal case to use all lawful means to obtain an acquittal for his client. When the criminal lawyer resorts to unlawful acts in the defense of his client he ceases to be a criminal lawyer and becomes a lawyer criminal. Sometimes the statement is made that a man is acquitted of a criminal charge on a technicality of the law. A lawyer may be a technician in the science or art of practicing law, but strictly speaking there is no such thing as a technicality of the law. Either a thing is the law or it is not.

On the day that the three cases against my client were set for trial at Gail, the county seat of Borden County, I was up at five o'clock in the morning in order to make the thirty-mile drive from Snyder to Gail, so as to be in Gail at the time court opened. When my client and I arrived in Gail, the County Attorney, the prosecuting witness, and the other witness, who had been present at the time of the alleged controversy, were at the courthouse and ready for trial. I suggested to the County Attorney that my client was willing to plead guilty to the charge of disturbing the peace, provided that he and the County Judge would agree that his punishment for that offense should be the lowest penalty fixed by law.

"What about the two other complaints?" the County Attorney asked.

"My client will not plead guilty to either of the other two complaints," I told the County Attorney. "He will agree that both of these cases may be taken up and disposed of immediately after the charge of disturbing the peace is disposed of."

The County Attorney agreed to my suggestion, and the County Judge, upon the recommendation of the County

Attorney, agreed to impose the lowest penalty. The case was called and my client pleaded guilty, and a formal judgment of conviction was entered against my client upon his plea of guilty. After the necessary entries were made showing how the case had been disposed of, and the costs computed, my client paid his fine and costs, amounting in all to about twenty dollars. When these things had been done, the County Judge called the aggravated assault case against my client.

"What says the defendant?" the Judge asked.

I stood and said: "The defendant wishes at this time to file with the clerk of this court his sworn plea of *autro fois convict*."

I handed the clerk my plea of *autro fois convict*, and when it had been filed, I read it to the judge. The plea consisted of a written statement, duly verified by the defendant, setting forth the fact that if the defendant had struck his enemy with the pistol as charged by the State of Texas, his act in doing so was a part of the same transaction and occurred at the same time that the defendant was charged with disturbing the peace; that the State of Texas had carved out of the several offenses charged to have been committed by the defendant at the same time and place and as a part of one and the same transaction, the offense of disturbing the peace, and had tried the defendant for that offense, and the defendant had been, upon his plea of guilty, convicted; that this trial and conviction had placed the defendant in jeopardy, and that he could not be lawfully tried for any other offense growing out of the same transaction and occurring at the same time when he had committed the offense of disturbing the peace, for which he had been tried and convicted.

I then read to the court the law as declared by the courts and as stated by law textbook writers that a defendant, who has formerly been convicted of a crime, cannot be tried a second time for the same offense because the Constitution of the United States and the Constitution of the State of Texas provide that no person shall be twice put in jeopardy for the same offense.

The County Attorney contended that the defendant was not being tried a second time for the same offense; that the offense of disturbing the peace was one crime and the offense of aggravated assault was an entirely distinct and different crime. The County Attorney argued that the defendant had been placed in jeopardy in his trial for disturbing the peace, but had not been placed in jeopardy for the crime of aggravated assault.

In reply to this argument, I directed the attention of the court to the established law of Texas, as declared by its Court of Criminal Appeals, the court of last resort in criminal cases in Texas, that where a citizen is charged with committing more than one offense at the same time and where all the offenses are a part of one and the same transaction, and the State elects to try the defendant for one of these offenses, and the defendant is either convicted or acquitted, the State cannot thereafter try the defendant for another offense growing out of the same transaction and which occurred at the same time, provided the facts in support of the two or more offenses are the same.

The court sustained my client's plea of *autro fois convict*, and the case of aggravated assault and the case of using profane and abusive language were both dismissed.

My law practice increased to such an extent that in about eighteen months from the time I obtained my license to practice law, I was able to give up my abstract work. I rented two rooms on the second floor of one of the new bank buildings, and there I opened my law office. My office rent was six dollars per month. The building was not steam heated, and there was no janitor service.

In the winter time my first job at the office each morning was to take the ashes out of the stove and build a fire. Then I would sweep the floor and dust the furniture. Sometimes I used a shovel in cleaning the floor of my offices. Snyder is in the edge of the dust bowl. I have seen sand storms in Snyder at three o'clock in the afternoon when the blowing sand was of such density that it was necessary for motorists driving their automobiles on the streets of the town to turn on the driving lights of their cars in order to see the street in front of them. After one of these sand storms, the dust on the floors of our home and on the floor of my office would be very deep.

When Mrs. Smith and I married, she owned a city lot. We traded this lot for a small law library. Most of these law books had at one time been owned by Martin Littleton, the Texas boy who, it is said, worked as a section hand on the railroad at Weatherford, Texas, when he was a young man, but who was afterwards to become one of the nation's great trial lawyers, with his office in New York City and his home on Long Island.

There had been shelves in the abstract office on which I could place my law books. There were no shelves in my new law office. I was not financially able to buy bookcases for my books, so I bought lumber at one of the lumber yards, borrowed tools, and made my own bookshelves. As fast as I could, I added new books to my library, and I was, of course, a subscriber for the *Southwestern Reporter* which published all of the opinions of the appellate courts of Texas, Arkansas, Missouri, Kentucky and Tennessee. I also bought books other than law books, when I could, to read and study at home. These books were the beginning of my present home library.

I did not employ a stenographer. I knew how to operate an Oliver typewriter, and I did my own stenographic work. The fees that I earned were small, but living expenses were not high. In my third year as a lawyer, I earned and collected $2,252 in fees. To earn this amount in small fees, I had to do, and did do, an immense amount of work. Acting as my own stenographer, it took me from eight to twelve hours a day to get my work done.

One day a client gave me his check for $150 in payment of certain legal services. Before depositing this check, which represented the largest fee I had up to that time received, I took the check home and showed it to Mrs. Smith. I wanted that young lady to know that she had married a man who was a financial success. The check for $150 was ample proof of that fact to Mrs. Smith and to me.

After our second year of married life, Mrs. Smith and I held a financial council of war, and then and there determined that from then on, out of whatever I earned, however little, we would, unless prevented by sickness, save something. We religiously adhered to our program. I do not know whether this was wise or unwise. I know that we missed much of the pleasure and fun that other young people enjoyed. In lieu of the fun and pleasure that we missed, we had our dreams. We dreamed and planned for a time when we would have plenty to satisfy our modest requirements; of a time when we would have a lovely home with a library well filled with good books; and of the many places of interest at home and abroad that we would visit.

We had fun with our plans and our dreams, and when our plans matured and our dreams became realities, we were not disappointed. We were in our forties when we first had time and opportunity to play; then we attempted to make up for the playtime we had missed when we were young. To do this, we had to hurry, for the physical incapacity that comes with old age would soon slow us down. Perhaps when old age comes, it will bring to us its compensations. Of one thing I am convinced, and that is, that the playtime that rightfully belongs to the young cannot, if missed, be regained in later life. Perhaps Mrs. Smith and I should, when we were young, have lived more in the present and less in the future. I knew the ugliness and the cruelty of poverty. I may have been obsessed by fear of poverty; perhaps I had a poverty complex. Mrs. Smith and I had our choice. We could easily have spent all that I earned the first few years after we married. We elected to do without then, in order that we might have more when we were older. We planned for an old age of security, tranquillity and peace.

CHAPTER V:
MAYOR OF SNYDER

Not long after I was admitted to the bar, an old lawyer told me that there were two times in a lawyer's life when he should hold public office. The first of these was when the lawyer was young and needed the compensation and the prestige of the office, and the opportunity it would give him to make friends. The other time when a lawyer should hold office, he said, was when the lawyer was old, had acquired a competence and a rich experience, and was in a position to serve the state or the nation without any thought of his own interest.

The town of Snyder was in debt, for it had voted bonds to build and install a water and sewerage system. At a special election, a majority of the voters had authorized the issuance of additional bonds for the purpose of securing money with which to pay for paving the public square. There was some question as to the legality of this election. The streets on the four sides of the square were well graveled, as were the two principal streets of the town.

The town of Snyder was in an independent school district. Bonds had been voted, issued and sold by the school district to pay for the erection of a high school and two ward school buildings. Taxes were assessed and collected on the property in Snyder for the support of the schools and for the support of the city government. These taxes had to be sufficient to maintain and operate the schools and the city government, pay the interest on the bonded indebtedness of the town and the school district, and provide a sinking fund with which to pay the principal of the debts represented by the bonds, when the bonds became due. Snyder at this time had a population of about three thousand. There were perhaps six hundred people in the town gainfully employed. My taxes were only a few dollars a year, for I owned very little property.

In the spring of 1917, I determined to act on the advice given me by the older lawyer, and I became a candidate for the office of mayor of the town of Snyder.

Many influential men in Snyder favored a street paving program that would include the public square and several miles of streets. To carry out the proposed paving program, the town would have to issue and sell a large amount of bonds. Before this could be done, the qualified tax-paying voters at a special election held for that purpose must authorize the issuance of the bonds. The special election could not be held until authorized by the city council. If and when these paving bonds were issued, provision would have to be made for a sinking fund to pay the bonds at maturity, and for the payment of the interest each year on the bonds.

The people favoring the street paving program persuaded a fine gentleman, a prosperous businessman, to become a candidate for mayor, and persuaded other good men who favored the street paving program to become candidates for aldermen from each ward in the town. One of these men was a Republican and had some connection with the Republican Executive Committee of the State, district or county.

Those opposed to the street paving program put out an opposition ticket for the offices of mayor and for aldermen from each of the three wards in the town. I was the candidate for mayor on the opposition ticket.

The *Snyder Signal* was an excellent newspaper published at Snyder. This newspaper favored the street paving program and gave much front page publicity to the pro-paving ticket; never mentioning the anti-paving ticket, except to refer to us collectively as the representatives of that small group of conservatives who had no vision and who were without faith in the future of Snyder. The candidates on the pro-ticket were referred to by this newspaper as forward-looking, progressive men of vision, who wanted to keep the City of Snyder in its rightful place, which was, of course, in the lead of all the progressive cities and towns of West Texas.

I do not know why it is that men who believe in a large public debt and extravagant spending of the public money are always referred to as progressives and liberals, and the men who want their governments, national, state and municipal, to live within their respective incomes, are designated as conservatives, reactionaries and even tories.

I thought of myself as a liberal, because I believed in the right of the individual to live his own life as he wished, entirely free from all governmental restraint, except that he should be compelled to keep the peace, fulfill his contracts and be prohibited from interfering with the equal rights of other men, and made to bear his just share of the expenses incident to maintaining an economically administered government. I believed that the men who made our nation had a great fear of the power of any government, and that in the Constitutions of our nation and state, a sincere effort had been made to hold in check the dangers to the individual that are inherent in every government. These ideas of mine about government, I thought, must be liberal, because they were the ideas of General Washington and Mr. Jefferson.

The only publicity the anti-paving ticket could get in the *Snyder Signal* was adverse publicity, except by paid advertisements. I was opposed to paying the newspaper to do something for us, when it was giving away the same thing to our opponents. We had several hundred election cards printed. These cards were five inches long and three inches wide. On one side of these cards appeared the words "Progressive Democratic Ticket," and under this heading were the names of our candidates and the respective offices they sought. On the other side of the card appeared "Our Platform," which had been written by a lawyer in Snyder who had at one time been the Secretary of a United States Senator. Our platform read as follows:

We are progressive—and we are all DEMOCRATS.

Nobody brought us out; we want to be elected and we announced ourselves.

We have no connection whatever with the Republican Executive Committee of the County, District or State.

We believe in a bigger SNYDER, and a better Snyder, although we think we have the best city in West Texas now.

We advocate extension of the water works; reduction of the insurance rate by improving the fire department and water system.

We believe in extension of the sewerage system.

We believe in putting the city on a business basis and conducting the business of the city in a business manner.

We believe in the extension of the present utilities to serve all tax payers before incurring further indebtedness.

The majority of the voters have declared in favor of paving the square.

IT WILL BE DONE, if it can be done legally.

After our printed cards had been distributed, our opponents referred to our ticket as the "So-called Progressive Ticket." For whatever the designation "progressive" was worth, it was ours. I was not particularly proud of the statement in "Our Platform" where, by inference, we charged our opponents with being Republicans. To be a Republican in Texas in 1917, was almost a misdemeanor. We knew that only one of our opponents was a Republican, and that he was a good man and an excellent citizen.

There were three wards in Snyder, the north ward, the east ward, and the west ward. Nearly all the bankers, merchants, doctors and lawyers lived in the west ward. These men were the heavy taxpayers. I lived in the north ward. On the night of the election, the returns from the west ward were the first to come in. Our candidate for alderman from the west ward had been defeated by twenty-four votes, and I had lost the ward as a candidate for mayor by forty-nine votes. The east ward was the next ward to report. There, our candidate for alderman had been elected by a majority of thirty-one votes, and I had carried the ward by seventeen votes. Finally, the returns came in from the north ward, and these showed our candidate for alderman to be elected by a majority of thirty-two votes and that my home ward had given me a majority of forty-three votes, which was sufficient to elect me mayor by the small majority of eleven votes.

There were three holdover aldermen and two of these were anti-paving. This gave the anti-paving group four out of six of the city aldermen and the mayor. The aldermen were elected for two years, and I was elected to fill out the unexpired term of the man who had been elected in 1916, and who had resigned. This unexpired term would end in April, 1918.

A short time after the city election of 1917, a member of the school board of the Snyder Independent District resigned. The other members of the board appointed me to serve out his unexpired term. At the first meeting of the school board after I became a member, I was elected president of the board. As mayor and as president of the school board, I was the official errand boy for the entire community.

Our schools were not in a healthy condition, because after we provided the money for the sinking fund to pay off the school bonds at maturity, and to pay the annual interest charges, we did not have sufficient money available to operate our schools properly. We needed more teachers and if we expected to obtain good teachers, we had to pay better salaries than we were paying. The tax rate could not be increased, because it was already as high as the law authorized. I suggested to the other members of the board, that in order to obtain the additional money the schools needed, that we direct the tax assessor for the school district to increase the valuation of all property within the school district twenty per cent above what the property had been valued for the year before. This suggestion was adopted.

The action of the school board in causing the property valuation to be increased was highly displeasing to a number of our good citizens. These men and women seemed surprised, even annoyed, at my action in favoring an increase in their property valuations, in view of my position in the mayoral campaign. Many of these citizens complained to me personally. I explained to them that the reason the valuation of their property had to be increased was because it took such a large part of our tax money to take care of the bonded debt; that we would not have enough money left to operate our schools properly and adequately; that our action in increasing the property valuation was an absolute necessity if we were going to have good schools; and that this was the only legal way that additional funds could be procured. I further explained to them that the increase in the property valuation for tax purposes was equal and uniform and fair to all alike. I doubt if any dissatisfied taxpayer was entirely convinced by my explanation.

The office of town marshal of Snyder was an elective one. For years, the people had elected a splendid man to this office. This gentleman had supported me in my campaign for mayor. The marshal was an elderly man and performed most of his duties on horseback. Automobiles had become commonplace, and some people acted as if they thought our streets were racing tracks. Within a short time after I was elected mayor, there were a number of serious accidents, in which innocent people were injured. There was a state law fixing the maximum speed at which cars could be driven in incorporated cities, and we had a city ordinance containing the same provision as the state law. The state law and the city ordinance were being violated many times every day. A number of merchants and businessmen came to me insisting that the city do something about the hazard to life and property created by the automobiles speeding over our streets.

A person cannot be convicted for driving an automobile at an unlawful rate of speed except upon positive proof that the automobile was being driven at a speed in excess of the maximum speed allowed by law. The one certain way of proving the speed at which an automobile is being driven, other than by the speedometer on the automobile itself, is to have the automobile followed by another machine with a speedometer.

The city marshal could not drive an automobile, and he could not tell how fast an automobile was being driven by sitting on his horse and watching the automobile as it was driven down the street. The city council authorized the employment of a motorcycle officer, whose duty it should be to patrol the streets on his motorcycle and arrest all persons who violated the ordinance against speeding.

The marshal employed a young man and brought him to my office for instructions. I explained to him that he must keep his speedometer in perfect working condition, and that he should not arrest anyone for speeding until he had followed him for at least two blocks and that he should be careful in keeping the distance between his motorcycle and the automobile the same for a distance of at least a block. Then if the speedometer on his motorcycle showed that the automobile was being driven ten miles an hour faster than the ordinance allowed, he was to arrest the offender. I knew that nearly everyone at some time or an other drove his automobile at a speed in excess of that allowed by law. I thought it fair to give them a margin of ten miles.

For two or three weeks after the motorcycle officer was employed, he made many arrests. The offenders pleaded guilty, and I assessed the minimum fine, for, as mayor, I was also the corporation court judge. People began driving more carefully.

The village of Ira is located about fourteen miles southwest of Snyder, and is perhaps the most prosperous farming section in Scurry County. Ira is almost as close to Colorado City, county seat of Mitchell County, as it is to Snyder. There was a keen rivalry between the merchants of Snyder and the merchants of Colorado City for the business of the people living in the Ira community. One of the best-liked and most prosperous farmers of the Ira neighborhood came to Snyder one day and was arrested by our motorcycle officer for speeding. The gentleman from Ira was outraged. When he came to my office, he declared that he was not guilty and would never pay a fine. I explained to him that he had a right to be tried by a jury. He objected to being tried at all, and insisted that I dismiss the case against him. I explained that I could not do that and set his case down for trial on Saturday of the following week.

"If," he said, "this is the kind of treatment the people of Ira are going to receive in Snyder, we will do our trading in Colorado City."

I tried to explain to him that we were at tempting to enforce the law fairly and impartially toward all, and that a citizen of Ira could not expect to enjoy any greater privileges in Snyder than could a citizen from Fluvanna or any other town in Scurry County.

The gentleman left my office and visited his banker and many of his merchant friends, to whom he detailed the outrage that he thought was being committed against him, and threatened that he and his friends would take their business to Colorado City unless the case against him was dismissed. To my office came the banker and the merchants, some of whom only a few weeks before had urged me to do something to curb the reckless automobile driving on our streets, insisting and demanding that I dismiss the case against the Ira farmer. I refused to do so.

On the day of the trial, the defendant demanded a jury, and without the aid of a lawyer, defended himself. The jury, after considering the case for an hour or two, reported to me that they were unable to agree on a verdict. The defendant then demanded that another jury be summoned at once, and that he be tried again without delay. I instructed the marshal to summon a venire of twelve men from whom the jury of six men could be selected.

In the meantime, the defendant employed one of the best lawyers in Snyder to represent him on his second trial. When

I saw the twelve men that the city marshal had summoned, I felt certain that they would bring in a verdict of guilty, for, without exception, these men were the close friends of the marshal, and there was not a merchant or businessman among them. On being examined by the defendant's lawyer, every man on the jury panel assured him that they would give the defendant a fair and impartial trial.

When the jury was selected, the city produced its only witness, the motorcycle officer, who testified that he had followed the defendant's automobile on the motorcycle, and that the speedometer on his motorcycle showed the speed of the defendant's automobile to be thirty-eight miles an hour, which was eighteen miles an hour more than the law authorized. The defendant was his own, and his only, witness. He testified that at the time and place when he was charged with speeding, that he looked at the speedometer on his automobile and that it registered eighteen miles an hour. He further testified that his speedometer was in good working order.

The defendant's lawyer, in his argument to the jury, criticized the motorcycle officer, and intimated that his testimony was unworthy of belief, because "I suppose he receives a certain amount of money for every arrest he makes where the defendant pleads guilty or is convicted."

The lawyer was in error. The city council had very wisely guarded against this very thing by providing that the motorcycle officer should be paid a straight salary for his services.

The jury was out for only a few minutes and then returned a verdict of guilty. The defendant paid his fine. I was delayed for a few minutes in making the necessary entries in the court's record. When I left the city hall, I found a crowd out in the street in front of the hall. Two or three men were holding the lawyer and other men were holding the motorcycle officer. The latter had a long-bladed knife in his hand. I immediately made careful inquiries of those who had witnessed the disturbance, and from the statements of these witnesses, it appeared that the motorcycle officer was outside the door of the city hall when the lawyer came out and had said to him: "No lawyer can call me a liar and get away with it."

The lawyer replied: "I do not want to talk to you," and attempted to walk away. The motorcycle officer had then grabbed the lawyer. The two men had been separated before either had received any injuries.

A day or two later, I instructed the city marshal to employ another motorcycle officer, because Snyder could not use as a peace officer a man who conducted himself as the present motorcycle officer had done. This was very displeasing to the city marshal, and from that time on, he was my active political enemy.

CHAPTER VI:
DEFENDING FIFTY-FIVE MEN

One morning not long after the United States had entered the World War I, I found, when I came downtown, the people greatly excited. No one seemed to know exactly what had happened. It was known, however, that on the night before three farmers, living in Scurry County, and a man who operated a small restaurant in Snyder, had been arrested by Texas Rangers or officers of the United States and immediately taken out of town. Some said they had been taken to Austin; others thought they had been taken to Fort Worth or Dallas. Wild rumors were circulated to the effect that there had been wholesale arrests during the past night throughout West Texas. It said that a well organized plan had been discovered for the overthrow of our government.

There was, others said, a conspiracy on the part of a great many men to kill all public officials and that private citizens who remained loyal to their government were to be murdered. It was asserted that more arrests were to be made. The people were alarmed and afraid.

When the Dallas and Fort Worth daily newspapers came the next day, the front pages of these papers were filled with news of the conspiracy that the diligent officers had uncovered, apparently just in time to prevent the destruction of the government. These newspapers told in detail of the sudden night raid made in many sections of West Texas, and reported that more than fifty persons had been arrested, and that the prisoners, because of the dangerous situation and the widespread conspiracy, had been handcuffed, loaded into waiting automobiles, and taken to the county jail at Dallas. The officers were, according to the newspaper accounts, very mysterious about the whole thing, intimating, however, that the first raid was only a beginning.

It was a case of war hysteria. In Snyder these newspaper stories increased the alarm and fear of the people. If there was a conspiracy to overthrow the government, and few people doubted the existence of such a conspiracy, for more than fifty men had been arrested in one night, then there must be hundreds, perhaps thousands, of conspirators, the people reasoned. Men began to suspect their friends and neighbors.

Some days after these arrests were made, the relatives of the men who had been arrested in Scurry County came to my office for advice and help. These people told me that the only word any of them had received in regard to their loved ones who had been arrested and placed in the Dallas jail was a telegram to the mother of one of the men, asking her to wire $500 to a lawyer in Dallas, so that the lawyer could get the men out of jail. The man's mother had procured the money and had wired it to the lawyer in Dallas. After that no one received any further word, and the men did not return.

From the statement made to me by the relatives of the men who had been arrested in Scurry County, it appeared that these men had recently joined an organization known as the Farmers and Laborers' Protective Association. The relatives of the Scurry County men who had been arrested employed me to go to Dallas and see what, if anything, I could do about obtaining the release of their loved ones from jail.

When I got to Dallas, the officers were permitting the men to see their lawyers. The men, I discovered, had been charged with a seditious conspiracy against their government. There were eight separate counts in the indictment. Fifty-seven men had been indicted. The charges against them included a conspiracy to interfere with and prevent the enforcement of the law which had recently been passed by Congress conscripting men into the Army of the United States.

The prisoners were, without exception, poor men, and in Dallas they were far from home, and by reason of the publicity given to the charges against them, they stood convicted by public opinion of a crime little short of treason. The bond of each prisoner had been fixed at $5,000. I found, upon investigation, that the lawyer in Dallas, to whom the mother of one of my clients had wired the $500, had done nothing, and could do nothing, toward making bond for my clients. I also learned that some of the prisoners were retaining William H. Atwell of Dallas to represent them. Mr. Atwell was and is a Republican, and prior to the election of Mr. Wilson as President, had served sixteen years as United States District Attorney for the Northern District of Texas.

I went to see Mr. Atwell. Through Mr. Atwell I ascertained the name of a man in Dallas who might be willing to become a bondsman for my clients. I saw this man, and he agreed to make bond for my clients, provided they were able to secure him against loss.

I returned to Snyder and reported to the relatives of my clients what I had found out in Dallas. Some of these people owned considerable land, and at their request I prepared deeds of trust on their land in favor of the bondsman. When these deeds of trust had been properly executed, I returned to Dallas, and the bondsman accepted the security that I had brought and made bond for my clients.

I thought I had achieved something very much worthwhile in obtaining the release of my clients from the Dallas jail, and I felt something like a conquering hero when my clients and I arrived in Snyder the next day. As soon as we got off the train, I suffered a great deflation of my egotism. The sheriff of Scurry County was waiting for my clients with a warrant for their arrest for the alleged crime of entering into a conspiracy to kill certain persons. My clients were taken from the depot and locked up in the Scurry County jail.

The financial resources of the prisoners and of their relatives had been almost entirely exhausted in providing security such as would satisfy the Dallas bondsman. It was two or three weeks before bond could be arranged for my clients so that they could be released from the Scurry County jail.

In the meantime, and much to my surprise, I found that the city marshal of Snyder had been circulating a petition asking me to resign as mayor, on the ground that as mayor of Snyder, it was highly improper for me to defend any man charged with a conspiracy against the government. I never did know how many people signed the petition, because the petition was never presented to me. Several of my friends told me that they had been shown the petition, and asked to sign it. I am sure that several good people did sign the petition.

The compensation that I received for my services as mayor never amounted to more than a few dollars a month. I had to depend on my practice as a lawyer for my livelihood. I was glad to be employed to defend these Scurry County men, even though they were charged with being part of a seditious conspiracy against their government, and at a time when their government was at war. Even if they were guilty, they had the right to be defended by a lawyer of their own selection. The fact that I held the office of mayor of Snyder did not in any way disqualify me from accepting the employment.

The men charged with seditious conspiracy were tried in the United States District Court at Abilene, Texas, before Judge George Whitfield Jack of Louisiana, sitting for Judge Edward R. Meek of the Northern District of Texas. The government was represented by W. M. Odell, United States District Attorney, and his assistant, William E. Allen. The chief counsel for the defense was Judge Atwell. Judge Atwell was assisted by C. Nugent of Hamlin, Fred Nickols of Abilene, J. B. Hartwell of Commerce, R. L. Rush of Eastland, and me. Judge Atwell, an excellent lawyer, knew as few men knew, the law of practice and procedure in criminal cases in the United States courts. He had written, prior to this trial, an excellent textbook on this subject of the law. Judge Atwell, a very handsome man, dressed immaculately.

Fifty-five men were tried at one time. Folding chairs were brought in for the defendants to sit on. It took all of the room inside the railing in the courtroom to provide seating space for the government lawyers, the defendants, and the lawyers representing the defendants.

It was war time, and the newspapers had given, prior to the trial, and continued to give during the continuation of the trial, great publicity to the case. Public opinion had been aroused against the defendants. In some of the great daily newspapers of Texas appeared strong and vigorous editorials condemning the alleged conspirators and heaping praise upon the public officials for their diligence in discovering the conspiracy, and for their efforts to stamp it out before the men in the conspiracy had an opportunity to commit any overt acts.

We did not have much choice in the selection of the jury which was to try the defendants. This, however, was immaterial, for a larger choice in the selection of a jury would not have been beneficial. Any twelve men selected to try these defendants would, by the very nature of the case and the wide publicity given to it, have formed an opinion, and an unfavorable opinion, against the defendants.

The trial lasted seven weeks. The government introduced evidence to the effect that two years prior to the time of the trial there began to be organized local lodges of the Farmers and Laborers' Protective Association; that the men who organized the local lodges declared the purpose of the organization was to bring the farmers and laborers into a common organization in order that they might protect themselves in purchasing supplies in the markets. After the initial organization of a local lodge, each member would be given an obligation to keep secret all proceedings and to stand by the members and abide by the rules. Men testified that it was provided by the rules of the organization that, in the event any member failed to keep the secrets, the penalty was to be death. In the initiation ceremonies, so witnesses testified, there would be explained to the initiate the emblems of the organization, which consisted of a strap, a dirk and a pistol. The strap was emblematic of a formerly enslaved condition; the dirk an emblem of self-defense at close range of the laborer against the capitalist; and the pistol had about the same significance.

There was evidence that there was a state meeting of the Farmers and Laborers' Protective Association held at Cisco, Texas, about February 11, 1917, and at this meeting a resolution was offered that would bind the members to do everything in their power to keep the United States from entering the war. There was evidence that certain members of the organization were against conscripting members of the organization, and a resolution was offered binding every member to resist conscription "to the death;" that the delegates attending this state meeting were to go home and organize, and procure ammunition, and arm themselves in order to resist the United States in raising an army; that they were to blow up railroad bridges, tear up the tracks to prevent the government from shipping soldiers, and cut telephone and telegraph wires to prevent communication.

There was evidence that the members of the organization were to provide themselves with high-powered rifles and use forceful opposition to the government; that various members did obtain rifles for this purpose; that others organized a military company in one instance; that one defendant was very active in urging armed resistance to the government; that the real purpose of the organization was to amalgamate with the IWW so as to get the farmers into that organization. Counsel for the government charged that the IWW would provide the members of the F&LPA with guns, since the IWW had three million rifles stored and ready for use when the time came.

There was evidence that a certain member purchased a pistol and exclaimed that he was ready to oppose conscription, and that a red flag of rebellion was raised by the order. There was evidence that one member of the F&LPA spent one-half of his crop money for a rifle and $5 for ammunition, and that he purchased the rifle and ammunition on the 17th day of May, 1917. This member, so it was testified, sought to return the rifle when he learned that members of the order had been arrested. There was testimony that certain members had traveled one hundred miles to hide ammunition in a canyon and entrenched themselves there; that one defendant had secured employment with a railroad and another with a bank as janitor, and that these members reported themselves as being in a position to do harm to the railroad and to the bank.

The evidence of the defendants was to the effect that they joined the F&LPA because they were told that as members of that organization, they would be able to obtain goods and supplies at a cheaper price than they could procure them from their local merchants. Of the fifty-five defendants tried, the evidence was that forty-five of them did not then own a gun and never had owned a gun. Of the other ten, only five owned guns at the time they were arrested.

It was admitted that three of the defendants did go to a certain canyon in West Texas and hide ammunition, but that later these men came and gave up to the United States officials and registered for war service on the 5th day of June, 1917, and were then ready for service in the Army of the United States when called. There was evidence for the defendants that only one of them was a member of the IWW. There was evidence that the resolutions introduced at Cisco by this member of the IWW had been voted down, and in lieu of the unlawful resolution a lawful resolution had been offered and adopted.

When the government and the defendants had introduced all their evidence, Mr. Odell, the United States Attorney, asked the court to dismiss the case against certain of the defendants, seven I believe the number was, because the evidence of the government was insufficient to connect them with the alleged conspiracy. This motion was granted. The defendants filed a motion requesting the court to instruct the jury to return a verdict of not guilty against all the defendants. This motion was overruled by the judge, except as to one defendant. As to this defendant, the judge entered an order dismissing the case of the government against him.

The opening argument to the jury was made by Mr. Allen for the government. He spoke for about two hours. Then came the arguments for the defendants. Five lawyers made arguments for them. My argument lasted one hour. Judge Atwell made the closing argument for the defendants. He spoke for four hours, making a careful and painstaking analysis of the facts, in an effort to show that there was no evidence sufficient to convince the jury beyond a reasonable doubt that the defendants were guilty of the crime with which they were charged. In his final peroration concluding his argument to the jury, Mr. Atwell paid a beautiful tribute to the flag of the United States, and notwithstanding the fact that he knew that most, if not all, of the men on the jury were the sons of men who had served as Confederate soldiers, declared that not any blood kin of his had ever fired a gun against that flag.

Mr. Odell made the concluding argument for the government in a speech which lasted an entire day. He made a powerful summing up, presenting anew all of the most hurtful evidence against the defendants. Frequently he read to the jury from a transcript of the evidence, which had been prepared by the court reporter, the exact statements made under oath by government witnesses. In this way, he hoped to convince the jury that the evidence of the government was sufficient, beyond a reasonable doubt, to justify a verdict of guilty against all of the defendants, except those that had been dismissed from the case.

Captain Bill McDonald, of Texas Ranger fame, was the United States Marshal for the Northern District of Texas. Captain McDonald as a younger man had made a great reputation in Texas as a Captain of the Rangers. He and Colonel E. M. House were friends. After Mr. Wilson was elected President, Colonel House secured a position for Captain McDonald as one of Mr. Wilson's bodyguards. Later, Mr. Wilson appointed Captain McDonald United States Marshal for the Northern District of Texas.

During the trial of the conspiracy case, Captain McDonald and I were stopping at the Grace Hotel in Abilene. We became casually acquainted. The night the arguments were concluded was very warm. I was sitting in a chair on the sidewalk in front of the Grace Hotel, when Captain McDonald came up, spoke to me, and sat down in a chair near me. He asked me how long I thought it would take the jury to reach a verdict. I told him that I hoped they would be able to reach a verdict of not guilty before morning.

"A verdict of not guilty?!" exclaimed Captain McDonald. "The jury is going to convict every one of them."

That the Captain had faith in his statement was evidenced the next afternoon when it was announced that the jury was ready to bring in its verdict, for the Captain was in the courtroom with some of his deputies, and he had a flour sack filled with handcuffs with which to handcuff the defendants in order to take them to jail in Dallas.

The jury found three of the men guilty, and found all of the other defendants not guilty. Among those found not guilty were all of my clients. The three men that were convicted were the president, the secretary, and the organizer of the Farmers and Laborers' Protective Association. The jury evidently had decided that something was wrong, and that someone should be convicted, but were unwilling, in view of the evidence, to convict anyone except the officials of the organization.

I never did know who sponsored the F&LPA. One or more members of the IWW were active in the organization. I suppose the purpose of its sponsor was to make money and to build up a political organization, based on class hatred. Any group of men who has been taught to hate other men for economical, religious or racial reasons is a potentially dangerous group of men. Ignorant men who are taught to hate their fellow men for such reasons are not so much to blame as is the man who, for political or other reasons, teaches them that such hatreds are right and proper.

It is a terrible thing for any man to be charged with a conspiracy against his government in peace time. It is much more terrible to be charged with such an offense in war time. The defendants who were acquitted were very fortunate in that they had Mr. William H. Atwell as their chief counsel. Mr. Atwell did his full duty toward his clients, regardless of what the public might think of him for defending his fellow citizens charged with a conspiracy against their government when their government was at war.

A United States District Judge has great power. When all the evidence is in and the arguments have been made to the jury, the judge can charge the jury without reducing his charge to writing. Perhaps he may charge the jury in a speech lasting an hour or more. When he concludes his oral charge, counsel for the defendant in a criminal case may take their exceptions to his charge. A United States District Judge may, if he is kind enough, prepare a written charge to the jury in advance and submit this charge to counsel for the defendants, in order that they may have time to prepare proper exceptions to the court's charge. Judge Jack was kind enough to prepare his charge to the jury in writing and to furnish a copy of his charge to Mr. Atwell and the other attorneys for the defense in time for them to make their exceptions to the court's charge.

The three defendants that were convicted were sentenced by Judge Jack to serve six years in the penitentiary at Leavenworth. Mr. Atwell appealed from this judgment of conviction, but the judgment of conviction was affirmed and the men went to prison.

When Mr. Harding was elected President, there was a vacancy in the office of United States District Judge for the Northern District of Texas. At that time I was living in Austin, and I had a letter from Mr. Atwell requesting me to endorse him for the position of United States District Judge and to secure, if I could, the endorsement of certain state judges at Austin. I was happy to do this for Mr. Atwell, and while I do not know whether the endorsements that I procured for him had anything to do with his appointment or not, it is a fact that he was appointed United States District Judge for the Northern District of Texas by President Harding and for many years has filled with great distinction that high office.

My clients, while acquitted in the United States District Court of the charge of seditious conspiracy against the government of the United States, were not yet free men. They had been indicted by a state grand jury, wherein they were charged with having entered into a conspiracy to commit the crime of murder. Shortly after their acquittal in the United States District Court at Abilene, they had to stand trial in the state district court at Sweetwater, county seat of Nolan County. For each of my clients I prepared a plea of *autro fois acquit*, wherein I alleged on behalf of each defendant that if the defendant had conspired to kill any person, such conspiracy was a part of the same transaction as the one wherein the government of the United States alleged that the defendants had conspired against the government of the United States. I then alleged that each of the defendants had been tried and acquitted of the conspiracy charge against the United States Government, and that, therefore, to try the defendants in the state court for an offense which was a part of the same transaction as the alleged offense against the United States would be to put the defendants in jeopardy a second time for the same offense, and that this was prohibited by the Constitutions of the United States and the State of Texas.

The pleas of *autro fois acquit* which I filed on behalf of my clients in the state district court at Sweetwater raised certain questions of fact which ordinarily would have to be submitted to a jury. The District Attorney agreed, however, that the facts were exactly as alleged in my pleas. He raised the question, though, that a trial in the federal court did not constitute a bar to a prosecution in the state court for the same offense or for a different offense arising out of one and the same transaction. Judge W. W. Beall of Sweetwater was the District Judge. He took my pleas under advisement, and the next day announced that he would sustain them. He then dismissed the cases in the state court against my clients and finally they were free men.

I believed at the time I filed the pleas of *autro fois acquit* in the state court at Sweetwater that they were good. I think they were good under the law as it had been declared by the courts. Some years subsequent to this time, the Supreme Court of the United States, in an opinion by Chief Justice Taft, held in a prohibition case that a man who sold whiskey in violation of the laws of the United States, and who at the time he made the sale also violated a state law, could be tried and convicted in the state court for violating the state law, and could thereafter be tried and convicted for this same offense in the courts of the United States. Judge Taft rested his opinion upon the proposition that the United States is one government and a state is an entirely distinct and different government; that there can be no such thing as former jeopardy in a United States court based upon a conviction or an acquittal in a state court, because the defendant has never been in jeopardy in the courts of the United States. (United States vs. Lanza, 260 U. S., 377.)

CHAPTER VII:
ASSISTANT TO ATTORNEY GENERAL CURETON

I was a candidate for two offices in the spring of 1918. I asked for re-election as mayor and for re-election as a member of the school board. Many people, and for many different reasons, did not want to see me re-elected to either office. Some who had supported my candidacy for mayor the year before were against me now, and some who had opposed me a year before were for me now.

The school board, by obtaining additional money through increasing the valuation of property for school tax purposes, had given Snyder an excellent school during the year that I had served on the board.

The city by improving its fire-fighting equipment had secured a substantial reduction in the fire insurance rate for Snyder, and this had resulted in a substantial saving to the property owners. By an economical administration of the finances of the town, the city council had paid current expenses and reduced the bonded debt, without any increase in taxes.

A fine old gentleman by the name of J. Z. Noble ran against me for mayor. In this campaign the issue was that I should not, while holding the office of mayor, have accepted employment to defend men charged with a conspiracy against the government in time of war. The good people who were of this opinion overlooked the fact that a jury had found my clients not guilty. There was no provision in any law which prohibited the mayor of Snyder, if he was a lawyer, from defending any man, charged with any crime, in any court, except the corporation court of the town of Snyder. Guilty men have a right to be defended. I had defended men who, according to the verdict of the jury, were not guilty of the offense with which they had been charged. It seemed to me that anyone would concede the right of a lawyer to defend innocent men.

One elderly gentleman, who had retired from business, carried on a very active campaign against my re-election. This man had two daughters who taught in the Snyder schools.

All members of the school board who stood for re-election were opposed. Here the issue was the act of the board in increasing the property valuation so as to obtain more tax money for the support of the schools. In the school election four trustees were to be elected. There were eight candidates. The four candidates receiving the highest number of votes would be elected. In the school election I was high man by eight votes. All the old members of the board were re-elected.

In the city election Mr. Noble received seven more votes in the west ward than I did. In the east ward, I received eighteen votes more than Mr. Noble did. In the north ward, I led Mr. Noble by nineteen votes. I was re-elected by a majority of thirty votes.

A few weeks after the election the school board met to elect teachers for the next school year. We had an excellent school superintendent, and his selection of teachers was final with me. The board had adopted a rule, which may or may not have been a wise rule, whereby we agreed that we would not employ any teacher that for any reason was objectionable to any member of the board.

One of the daughters of the man who had so vigorously campaigned against me in my race for re-election as mayor was the principal in one of the ward schools. The other daughter was a teacher in the other ward school. The superintendent recommended to the board the employment of these young ladies for the next school year for the same positions they then held.

One member of the board, who was the father of several children, some of whom attended school in the ward school where the young lady was principal, opposed her re-employment. I tried to get him to withdraw his opposition. This he at first refused to do, but at my request, agreed that she might be re-employed as a teacher in one of the other schools. Both young ladies were elected as teachers. The superintendent agreed that he would not assign either of them to the ward school where the opposing member's children went to school.

The next afternoon the father of the two young ladies came to my office. I was surprised to see him.

"Mr. Smith," he said, "I owe you an apology."

"For what?" I asked.

"For the evil thoughts I had about you. I have just had a talk with Superintendent Clark, and when he told me that the board refused to re-elect Zada as principal of the west ward school, I said, 'I am not a bit surprised. My only surprise is that they were allowed to teach in Snyder at all. That fellow Smith runs the whole town, and he hates me because I fought him for re-election, and this is his way of getting even with me.' Clark then told me that you did everything you could to persuade the opposing member of the board to agree to Zada's being re-employed for another year as principal, and when he refused to do that, you persuaded him to agree to her employment as a teacher. I have greatly wronged you in my thoughts. You can depend upon my friendship hereafter."

I was, of course, annoyed by this gentleman's activities in trying to defeat me for re-election as mayor, but it never occurred to me to try to revenge myself on him by preventing his daughters from obtaining re-employment in the Snyder schools.

In 1917 West Texas did not get much rain, and crops were poor. In 1918 it rained less than it did in 1917, and there was almost a total crop failure in Scurry County. Many people moved back East, and times were hard. In the summer of 1918 I concluded that I would if I could, leave Snyder, never to return. I was advised that there was a possibility that I could secure permanent employment in a northern city with the world's largest publishing company. In July, I applied for the position.

The year 1918 was a campaign year in Texas. Mr. B. F. Looney was finishing his third term as Attorney General and was not seeking a fourth term. Mr. C. M. Cureton, who had served throughout Mr. Looney's administration as First Assistant Attorney General, was a candidate for the office of Attorney General. This office under the Republic of Texas had been first held by my great-uncle, David Thomas.

I did not know Mr. Cureton, but Mrs. Smith's family knew him and his family well, for his family and Mrs. Smith's family all lived at one time in Bosque County.

Mr. Cureton had two opponents in the Democratic primary. One of these gentlemen lived in Fort Worth, and the other was a former Speaker of the Texas House of Representatives, whose home was in Fisher County, adjoining Scurry County on the east.

I wrote a letter to Mr. Cureton pledging him my support, offering to campaign for him in West Texas, and asking him to send me some of his campaign literature. He sent me the literature. I used all he sent in a few days, and wrote for more. Several times during the campaign, I wrote for and received more campaign literature which I used in many counties in West Texas, and did all that I could do to further his campaign. The election results were satisfactory to Mr. Cureton and his friends, for he received the Democratic nomination for Attorney General, which in Texas, is equivalent to being elected.

The Constitution of Texas provides that each state officer shall, before assuming the duties of his office, subscribe to an oath of office. In taking the oath of office the officer swears or affirms that he has not offered any appointment to office to anyone as a reward for political support. This oath of office applies to the general election as well as to the primary election. Mr. Cureton could not be elected until the general election in November.

In October I received a letter from the publishing company offering me the position that I had applied for in July. This company had finally completed its investigation of my character, reputation, personal habits, etc., and the job that I had applied for was mine, if I wanted to take it. In the meantime, having lost hope of securing the position with the publishing company, I formed the ambition to go to Austin, if I could obtain an appointment as one of Mr. Cureton's assistants. However, I had to accept or reject the offer of employment from the publishing company. My action on this offer would not wait until after Mr. Cureton had been elected Attorney General at the November election.

I decided to go to Austin at once and see Mr. Cureton. I did go, and for the first time met the lawyer and gentleman whom I was to learn to love. I told Mr. Cureton that I was familiar with the terms of the oath of office he would have to take, and I told him about the offer I had received from the publishing company.

The Attorney General is elected for a term of two years. I make this statement so the reader will understand the significance of what Mr. Cureton said to me.

"Smith," he said, "there is a vacant house on Brazos Street in the same block that I live on that is very convenient to the Capitol. If I were you, I would find the owner of that house and lease it for two years, the lease to begin the first day of next January."

The Attorney General would take office on the first day of January. Mr. Cureton had made no promise of any office to me. I acted on his advice, and when I left Austin the next day for Snyder, I had one copy of the document that I had signed leasing the house at 1606 Brazos Street for two years, beginning January 1, 1919.

When I returned to Snyder, I wrote a letter to the publishing company expressing my deep appreciation for the offer of employment. I told the company that I had made my plans to move to Austin and could not accept the offer.

Mr. Cureton was elected Attorney General at the general election in November, and on the day following the election, he wrote me a letter offering me a place as one of his assistants.

Fate weaves peculiar patterns in the lives of men. If Mr. Cureton had been defeated for the Democratic nomination for Attorney General, I do not know what my life would have been. I know that it would have been entirely different from what it has been.

In December, 1918, I resigned from the school board and as mayor of Snyder and arranged to move to Austin. I left Snyder with the good will of the men with whom I had been associated on the school board and on the city council. Without my knowledge, the members of the city council wrote a letter, not to me, but to the public and had it published in the *Snyder Signal*. This letter reads as follows:

To the Public:

We, the undersigned members of the City Council of Snyder, Texas, take this method of expressing our heartfelt appreciation of the services rendered by E. F. Smith, ex-mayor, who worked so much in harmony and in cooperation with us in the conduct of the city's affairs during his term as mayor. He was a congenial executive and used his entire influence in favor of the public welfare. He was competent, efficient and attentive to the duties assigned him. It is with regret we release him account that other duties compelled him to resign. We recommend him to the State of Texas, in his new work, and trust his relation there will be appreciated as much as it is at home.

> T. J. Blackburn
>
> J. J. Taylor
>
> J. J. Burnett
>
> I. W. Boren
>
> W. W. Echols

There may be those who think the office of mayor of a small town and the office of president of the school board of a small school district are insignificant. I did not think so when I held these offices in Snyder, and I do not think so now. Whatever my mistakes were, and I expect I made many, for I was young and without much experience, I did my best to give the school children of Snyder good schools, and the people of Snyder an honest, efficient, and economical city government.

Somewhere there are a number of middle-aged men and women who have among their papers diplomas from the Snyder High School that were signed by me as president of the school board, and by me delivered to them the night of the graduation ceremonies. On the two occasions that I presided at the graduation ceremonies, I made a short address to the graduating class. On these addresses I worked as carefully as the President of the United States does on his state papers. I tried to say something that would be helpful to the boys and girls who had finished one adventure in life and were going forward to further and different adventures. Recently I found among my papers copies of these two addresses, along with others that I have made on greater but no more important occasions.

If anyone of my Snyder friends should happen to read this book, I want him to know that I have not forgotten the kindness of the Snyder people to me, and that I shall always be grateful for the confidence that the people of Snyder had in me. In later years it was my pleasure to participate in lawsuits involving the mineral estates in more than one-half of all the lands of West Texas. For these services I was well rewarded, but one of the compensations that I received that could not be measured in dollars and cents was the thought that perhaps by my labors I had contributed something of value in saving a part of this great wealth to the landowners and homemakers of West Texas.

Chapter VIII:
Becoming a Trial Lawyer

Mr. Cureton, as First Assistant Attorney General, had worked for six years with the lawyers of the Department, knew them to be able and experienced men and wanted to retain them when he became Attorney General. He promoted Judge Walter A. Keeling, one of the assistants, to the office of First Assistant Attorney General. One of Mr. Looney's assistants resigned to enter private practice. The other men were reappointed. There were only two new appointments to make. Mr. W. F. Schenk, an experienced lawyer of Lubbock, and I received these two appointments.

At the beginning of Mr. Cureton's administration, the personnel of his staff consisted of seventeen men and women. Indicative of the growth of Texas in the past two decades and the increase in the functions of government is the fact that the personnel of the Attorney General's office today, less than twenty-two years since the beginning of Mr. Cureton's administration, is about one hundred. During Mr. Cureton's administration the Legislature authorized two new assistants, and there were certain changes in the personnel caused by resignations. I was for a while the youngest lawyer on his staff. Later this distinction was to go to W. W. (Jack) Meachum, a brilliant and ambitious young lawyer from Houston, who was destined to die before he achieved the high place in the legal profession that his natural talents, integrity, and industry would certainly have earned for him. Mr. Meachum was to be supplanted as the youngest lawyer by Walace Hawkins, who came to the Department as Chief Clerk from The University of Texas Law School. Hawkins was soon promoted from Chief Clerk to an assistant attorney general. This youngster must have possessed great talent, for today he is general attorney of the Magnolia Petroleum Company in Texas, with offices in Dallas. He recently told me that he has seventy-one lawyers on his staff.

When I went to work in the Department, I was not only the youngest, but the least experienced, of Mr. Cureton's assistants. I was at first assigned to the opinion desk, and it was my duty to advise, when requested to do so, the heads of certain state departments and the district and county attorneys. The opinions I wrote had to be approved by a departmental conference. Many questions were submitted that were not easy to answer. There was, however, a good law library in the department, and on the second floor of the Capitol was the excellent Supreme Court law library which was available to the members of the Attorney General's Department. The lights were turned out in the Capitol at eleven o'clock at night. I was so anxious to do my work well and to make good with General Cureton that I would come back to the office almost every night and work until the lights were turned out. This was no hardship. I was happy in my work.

My salary was $3,600 a year, and this was more money than I had ever before earned. I had serious doubts at first that my services were worth to the taxpayers of Texas such a handsome compensation as $300 a month. I thought it was my duty to earn, if I could, the salary that I was being paid. After I had been in the department for a few weeks, Mr. Cureton assigned to me the task of trying a lawsuit. I won the case. Soon I was assigned another lawsuit, and I won it. After that it became my duty to try more and more lawsuits. Within a few months, I was transferred from the opinion desk to the land desk, where I had charge of the legal work affecting the public lands of Texas and the interest of the State, if any, in the lands it had theretofore sold.

Great oil discoveries had been made in Texas. Oil was bringing $3 a barrel, and there was no proration. Wells were drilled at a cost of $15,000, $20,000 and $30,000, and this drilling cost would be repaid from some of the great gushers in a week, two weeks or a month's time. The great boom had come to Texas. In a year's time, Texas produced oil having a greater value than all the gold that has been mined in California from 1849 to the present time. It was my job, under the direct supervision of the Attorney General, to protect, if I could, the interest of the State of Texas, as a landowner in this great flow of black gold. Texas, unlike most of the states, reserved its title to all its lands when it surrendered its status as a Republic and became one of the states in the United States. The Attorney General was the attorney for this great landowner, the State of Texas.

My work was not, however, to be limited to land matters. I was having amazing good luck in the trial of cases, and the Attorney General called on me to try many cases that had nothing to do with land.

I was very happy, for here I was, young and ambitious, with one great lawsuit after another to try, with a great man for my boss. I had arrived in my gloryland. The days were too short for me to do all I wanted to do. When the lights would go out in the Capitol, I would stumble out of the building in the dark, annoyed that I must leave my work. Frequently, I took books out of the library and carried them home with me so that I could continue my studies, and I spent most of the Sundays in the office. In the cases I was trying, my opponents were lawyers of great ability, and I felt a compelling urge to win all my lawsuits. I thought that it would be a reflection on Mr. Cureton if I ever lost a case. I could not, I must not, let Mr. Cureton down.

At first I lacked confidence in myself. The trial of an important lawsuit would be coming up, and my opponents were lawyers of whose fame I had heard and read. Their very names filled me with fear. These men were earning more in a day than I was in a month. After I had prepared, with the greatest care I knew how, a case for trial, I would talk to Mr. Cureton about the case. How often I must have bored that kindly and patient man, who was carrying an immense load of work, as well as determining all matters of departmental policy!

One day after I had consulted with Mr. Cureton about a case, he said: "Smith, you have mastered every detail of this lawsuit as you have done in every case you have tried. I have implicit confidence in your ability to properly try any lawsuit. When you do not know what the law is, or when you are in doubt, you study the books until you find out what the law is. I am glad to help you whenever I have the time to do so, but look at my desk! Here is enough work to keep me busy for a month. It is impossible for me to have such familiarity with the details of your lawsuits as to be of much help to you."

What Mr. Cureton said was of great help to me. The confidence which he indicated he had in me gave me confidence in myself. If I was half as good as this great lawyer said I was, then I must be very good indeed. Wise Mr. Cureton! He knew that I needed self-confidence, and he had deliberately given me the thing that I needed. He had put me on my own. He had made me responsible for my lawsuits. It became clear to me that I could not depend on Mr. Cureton to do my thinking for me or to make the decisions that every trial lawyer must make. I must do my own thinking, make my own decisions and be responsible for my mistakes.

Never again did I bother Mr. Cureton with the details of one of my lawsuits. Questions of policy and the general outline of a lawsuit I would, when I could, discuss with him. When victory came at the end of a lawsuit, there was always a telegram or a letter or a few words in the office from Mr. Cureton congratulating me. The joy of winning a lawsuit and the words of praise and commendation from Mr. Cureton were ample rewards for all my labors.

Then there was my salary of $3,600 a year! Out of this Mrs. Smith and I were saving $150 a month. Once while I was in the Attorney General's Department, I made as accurate a calculation as I could of the fees earned by the lawyers who had appeared against me in the cases I had tried during the past year. According to my calculations, which were only an approximation, the aggregate amount of fees earned by my opponents was approximately $200,000. It was then, for the first time since coming to Austin, that I began to give serious consideration to the possibility that some day I might be able to make some real money in the practice of law.

CHAPTER IX:
THE POOL HALL CASES

A wave of morality swept over the State of Texas during the decade of 1910-1920. The fanatics, and what the more liberal-minded people referred to as the witch burners, were in power. Many people seemed to believe that anything capable of producing pleasure and enjoyment must of necessity be an evil thing and should, of course, be prohibited by law. Someone conceived the idea of prohibiting by law the operation of any pool or billiard table for hire in the State of Texas. A bill to this effect, an expertly drawn bill from a legal standpoint, "water-tight in all its compartments," was passed by the Legislature and approved by the Governor. In this law the Legislature found as a fact that the operation of pool and billiard tables for hire was inimical to the peace, prosperity, health, and general welfare of the people of Texas.

At the time this law was enacted in 1919, public pool and billiard halls were operated in all the cities and towns and in most of the villages in Texas. Here was a business in which several million dollars were invested, paying rent on hundreds of buildings, furnishing employment to a great many people, paying thousands of dollars in taxes in the form of license fees and in ad valorem taxes, a legal and legitimate business one day and an illegal and illegitimate business the next day, provided the law prohibiting the operation of pool and billiard tables for hire was a valid law. The pool and billiard people decided not to surrender their business without a fight.

The validity of the pool hall law was attacked in three different suits filed in the district courts of the United States on behalf of the pool and billiard people. These suits were brought by the law firm of Etheridge, McCormick and Bromberg of Dallas. Each of these suits was based on a different factual situation, but all raised the same legal question;

namely, that the anti-pool hall law was contrary to and in violation of the Fourteenth Amendment to the Constitution of the United States. It was the official duty of the Attorney General to represent the defense in these suits. Mr. Cureton assigned to me the task of defending these suits.

Mr. J. M. McCormick was in immediate charge for his law firm of this litigation for the pool hall people. It was his contention that the operation of pool and billiard tables for hire was not harmful physically or morally, but to the contrary was beneficial in that the operation of such tables for hire provided an opportunity for the average man, unable to buy and maintain a pool or billiard table in his home, to play a game which furnished him with physical exercise, mental relaxation and in general a fine form of indoor recreation where he could meet and be associated in a pleasant and social way with his fellow men; that the business of operating pool and billiard halls was a legitimate business not evil within itself, and that the Legislature was without power or authority to prohibit any business not harmful within itself.

If, Mr. McCormick contended, evil existed in the pool and billiard halls operated in the State of Texas, such evil was not inherent in the games of pool and billiards, but was a mere incident in connection with the manner in which the pool and billiard halls were operated, and these evils, if any, incident to the operation of pool and billiard halls could be abolished by proper and reasonable legislation regulating the business of operating pool and billiard halls, without prohibiting the operation of pool and billiard tables for hire.

In support of his contentions Mr. McCormick proposed to take, and did take, the oral depositions of witnesses who lived in many of the large cities of the nation. I went with Mr. McCormick when he took the oral depositions of his witnesses for the purpose of cross-examining his witnesses.

It was my contention that the anti-pool hall law was valid because the Legislature of Texas had, in enacting the law, found as a fact that the operation of pool and billiard tables for hire was inimical to the peace, prosperity, health, and general welfare of the people of Texas, and that the courts could not go behind these findings of fact by the Legislature, for to do so would be to substitute the opinion and judgment of the court for that of the Legislature in a matter over which the Legislature had exclusive jurisdiction and one coming essentially within the police power of the State.

I made the further contention that as a matter of actual fact the operation of pool and billiard tables for hire was harmful to the peace, prosperity, health, and general welfare of the people of Texas. In support of this last contention I proposed to prove that the halls where pool and billiard tables were available to be played on for hire were the gathering places for loafers, gamblers and the tough element in towns and cities; that it was the general, if not the universal, custom of those who played pool and billiards on tables for hire, for the loser to pay for the hire of the table and that this fact made the pool and billiard table used for hire a gambling device and that it had been so held by the Texas Court of Criminal Appeals.

In support of my contention that the operation of pool and billiard tables for hire was as a matter of actual fact harmful to the peace, prosperity, health, and general welfare of the people of Texas, I proposed to take, and did take, the depositions of many district and county attorneys and other public officials. These men testified that the pool halls in Texas were the rendezvous of the criminal element, the gathering place of loafers and the headquarters of the professional gamblers.

Mr. McCormick took the oral depositions of witnesses who resided in the cities of St. Louis, Chicago, Cleveland, Detroit, Buffalo, Rochester, New York, Philadelphia, and New York City. I went with Mr. McCormick and cross-examined his witnesses. Mrs. Smith accompanied me on this trip. It was a great experience for Mrs. Smith and me for it was our first visit to many of these cities. Mr. McCormick was a very fine gentleman and a delightful companion. He had many times been in the cities we visited and was very helpful to Mrs. Smith and me in advising us what places and things in each city were worthwhile visiting and seeing.

In Rochester the pastor of the largest Presbyterian church in the city testified that there were a number of pool and billiard tables in the young people's department of the church, and he had found these tables and the games that could be played on them very useful because they furnished wholesome amusement and recreation that was very attractive to the young people of the church.

In Chicago, Mr. Julius Rosenwald, then the active head of Sears-Roebuck and Company, testified that he was very much interested in the welfare of young people, and that he had participated in furnishing recreation rooms for the use of young people. In many instances, pool and billiard tables were a part of the furnishings in these recreation rooms. Mr. Rosenwald said that in his opinion the games of pool and billiards were not harmful; to the contrary, he believed they were beneficial in that those who played the games obtained some physical exercise and an opportunity for mental relaxation. It was his opinion, he testified, that the games of pool and billiards were a wholesome form of recreation for men and women, old and young alike. He further testified that in his opinion the operation of pool and billiard tables for hire was not necessarily an evil, but was, he believed, as legitimate a business as the selling of groceries, dry goods and hardware.

Mr. McCormick took the deposition of scores of witnesses. The testimony of all these witnesses was to the effect that the games of pool and billiards were not harmful, but beneficial. Many of these witnesses testified, as did Mr. Rosenwald, that in their opinion the operation of pool and billiard tables for hire was a legitimate business.

Mr. McCormick sought to obtain for his clients a temporary injunction, restraining the public officials of Texas from enforcing the anti-pool hall law. Such cases as these, when filed in a district court of the United States, have to be tried by a three-judge court, and one of the judges must be a Justice of the Supreme Court of the United States, or a judge of a United States Circuit Court of Appeals. The other two judges may be United States District Judges. The pool hall cases were tried in Fort Worth before such a three-judge court, with a Circuit Court judge of the Fifth Circuit presiding. On the day of the trial, one table in the courtroom was heaped high with the envelopes containing the many depositions that Mr. McCormick and I had taken in support of our respective contentions.

Upon the trial of the case, I argued that none of the evidence taken by Mr. McCormick was admissible, for the reason that the Legislature of Texas had found as a fact that the operation of pool and billiard tables for hire was inimical to the peace, prosperity, health, and general welfare of the people, and that this finding of fact by the Legislature was final and conclusive, and the courts had neither the power nor the authority to hear any evidence contrary to the findings of fact made by the Legislature, but must accept as true the facts as found by the Legislature.

In support of my argument, I cited to the court many court decisions. Among the cases cited were:

Hall vs. State, 35 Southwestern, 122, where the Texas Court of Criminal Appeals held that men who played pool with the understanding that the loser of the game would pay the table fees, were guilty of the criminal offense of gambling;

Webb vs. State, 17 Texas Court of Appeals, 205, where the Court of Criminal Appeals held that a man who kept a pool table upon which men played pool, with the understanding that the loser would pay for the drinks or cigars to be purchased from the owner of the pool table, was guilty of keeping and exhibiting a game table for the purpose of gaming;

To a long line of cases such as Tarkio vs. Cook, 120 Missouri, 1, wherein the courts drew a clear distinction between those laws which attempt to prohibit a useful business and those laws which attempt to prohibit a business operated solely for the purpose of giving amusement to the people, the courts holding that a useful business may not be prohibited, but that a business operated solely for amusement purposes may be prohibited;

Frowley vs. Christian, 137 United States, 86, where the Supreme Court of the United States held that the fact that the exercise of the police power prevented the enjoyment of individual rights and caused the destruction of privately owned property did not make the law under which such power was exercised unconstitutional. Where, the court held, a person is deprived of an individual right or suffers loss to his property under the enforcement of a police law, he has no cause of action for damage or other relief, for it is the theory of the law that is compensated for his damage by sharing in the general benefits which the police enactments are intended and calculated to secure;

People vs. Denton, 119 New York, 569, where the New York Court of Appeals held that if it cannot be made to appear that a law is in conflict with the Constitution by argument deduced from the language of the law itself, or from matters of which a court can take judicial notice, the law must stand. "The testimony of an expert or other witnesses is not admissible to show that in carrying out a law enacted by the Legislature, some provisions of the Constitution may possibly be violated."

I then cited five different state supreme court decisions holding laws valid which prohibited the operation of pool halls for hire.

Finally I cited to the court and read from a court opinion which I thought was conclusive. This was the case of Murphy vs. People of California, 225 U. S., 623, where the Supreme Court of the United States had held: "That the keeping of a billiard hall has a harmful tendency is a fact requiring no proof, and incapable of being controverted by the testimony of the plaintiff that his business was lawfully conducted, free from gaming or anything which could affect the morality of the community or his patrons."

Mr. McCormick made, as he always did, a powerful and forceful argument on behalf of his clients. The three-judge court refused to consider any evidence and held the anti-pool hall law valid. In its written opinion, the court said:

> It is our view that the people through their Legislature have the power to pass upon this question of fact and to determine for themselves whether they are useful and not harmful, or whether they are vicious, as they are conducted under the conditions here in Texas. On the very face of the bill, it shows that the people of Texas, through their Legislature, have decided that question of fact against the plaintiffs here.

Mr. McCormick appealed the three cases to the Supreme Court of the United States, where the decision of the three-judge court was upheld. Dallas Labor Temple Association vs. C. M. Cureton, 254 U. S., 663; George Russell Hill vs. C. M. Cureton, and Galveston Artillery Club vs. C. M. Cureton, 254 U. S., 664.

The anti-pool hall law has been the law in Texas for more than twenty years, and is one law that is generally well enforced. It has been twenty years since Mr. McCormick and I tried the pool hall cases. I am now of the opinion that these cases, instead of being won by the State of Texas, should have been lost by it. The anti-pool hall law is absurd, even vicious, in that it denies to the average citizen the right to play a fine game of skill, and was destructive of valuable property rights and caused a considerable loss of employment, and I emphatically disagree with what the Supreme Court said in its opinion in the Murphy case, the case that I principally relied on in winning the pool hall cases. There the court said: "That the keeping of a billiard hall has a harmful tendency is a fact requiring no proof..."

There are billiard halls in YMCA buildings and in churches, and the games played on the tables in these halls are games of skill and afford the players some degree of physical exercise and are a wholesome means of pleasure and recreation. How then can it be said that the keeping of a billiard hall has a harmful tendency requiring no proof?

In the Murphy case, the court also said that the keeping of a billiard hall has a harmful tendency is a fact "incapable of being controverted by the testimony of the plaintiff that his business was lawfully conducted, free from gaming or anything which could affect the morality of the community or his patrons."

The court accepted as a fact, without any proof whatever, that the keeping of a billiard hall has a harmful tendency, then declared that this unproved fact cannot be controverted by any testimony offered by the plaintiff. If every priest, minister, and rabbi, and all the good men and women of the community, came forward and testified that the billiard hall "was lawfully conducted, free from gaming or anything which could affect the morality of the community" or the patrons of the billiard hall, such evidence, the court held, must not be considered, because the unproved fact that a billiard hall has a harmful tendency cannot be controverted.

CHAPTER X:
THE CAPITOL SYNDICATE CASE

When the Republic of Texas became one of the states in the United States, it was provided in the treaty between the United States and the Republic of Texas that all lands not privately owned in the Republic of Texas should thereafter belong to the State of Texas. There are 173,000,000 acres of land in Texas, and about 50,000,000 acres were privately owned when the Republic of Texas became the State of Texas. Most of the land owned by Texas was situated in West Texas. "West" Texas is a vague description but is generally understood as including that part of Texas lying west of an imaginary line beginning at Brownsville on the Rio Grande and running north to the Red River.

Texas needed a new capitol building. The State did not have any money, but it had millions of acres of land. The people, in adopting the State Constitution of 1876, appropriated 3,000,000 acres of public domain for the purpose of erecting a new State Capitol at Austin.

The Legislature, by an Act of February 20, 1879, appropriated and set apart for the building of the new capitol the vacant and unappropriated public domain in ten counties in the Panhandle. Provision was made in this law for the surveying of the land, for the making of field notes, and for filing the field notes in the General Land Office at Austin. This law further provided that should any unsurveyed land remain in the bounds of the land so reserved after surveying 3,050,000 acres, the unsurveyed land should cease to be subject to the provisions of the Act, and provision was made in this law for the sale of the 50,000 acres for the purpose of obtaining money to pay the expense of having all of the land surveyed and for carrying out the other provisions of the Act.

The Legislature, by Act of April 18, 1879, authorized the building of a new State Capitol. This law authorized appointment of commissioners who should have authority to select and adopt plans for the building, to advertise for bids for the construction of the capitol and to contract with such responsible bidder as would construct the capitol for the smallest amount of the public domain which had been set apart for that purpose. A contract was made for the surveying of the land, and a survey was made in league tracts to the total number of 693, aggregating, according to the field notes filed in the Land Office, 3,050,000 acres.

On July 1, 1881, after having had plans and specifications for the building prepared, the commissioners advertised for bids for the construction of the capitol, stating that the contract would be awarded to the lowest and best bidder, and payment would be made in lands, and that bids would therefore be "for the smallest quantity of the 3,000,000 acres of land set apart for that purpose."

Mattheas Schnell by his bid proposed to build the new capitol building for "3,000,000 acres of land." His bid was accepted by the commissioners, and on January 18, 1882, a contract for the building of the capitol was made and executed. The contract provided that the contractor would erect the building according to the plans and specifications attached to the contract and that in consideration therefor the State of Texas would "convey to said party of the second part the complete and perfect title to 3,000,000 acres of land situated in the State of Texas and in the counties of Dallam, Hartley, Oldham, Deaf Smith, Palmer, Castro, Bailey, Lamb and Hockley which lands are fully described in a description thereof printed under the direction of the Commissioner of the General Land Office and maps of the same are on file in the General Land Office . . ."

During the course of the construction of the capitol it was ascertained that errors existed in the original survey of a part of the capitol lands. A partial resurvey was made, and it was discovered by the resurvey that the original surveys, through error, had encroached upon the territory of New Mexico to the extent of 16,000 acres. From the resurvey it appeared that after deducting these 16,000 acres, there still remained, by reason of excesses in other leagues, a sufficient quantity of land to supply the 3,000,000 acres. Corrected field notes were made reducing the quantity of land in the excessive leagues, and the surplus thus discovered was consolidated into three surveys, purporting to contain one league each. On January 11, 1887, by a supplemental contract between the commissioners and the contractor, the resurvey was approved, and it was agreed that the three additional leagues should be included in the lands to be patented to the contractor.

By December 12, 1888, patents to 3,000,000 acres of land had been issued by the State of Texas to the contractor, except that a patent to 246 acres out of league 446 was not issued until some time in the year 1890.

The contract for building the capitol was assigned by Mattheas Schnell to Abner Taylor. The patents to the land were issued to Taylor and he in turn immediately reconveyed the land to a group of men known as the Capitol Syndicate. These men organized the Capitol Freehold Land and Investment Company, Ltd., for the purpose of taking over the land and of financing the building of the capitol.

At the time the contract for the building of the capitol was made, the 3,000,000 acres of land that were to be conveyed by the State in payment for the capitol were largely inhabited by Indians and buffaloes. Fifty cents an acre would have been a high price to pay for the land. The building of the new capitol cost approximately $3,800,000. The State, therefore, received approximately $1.25 an acre for the 3,000,000 acres of land that it conveyed in payment for the capitol. Thirty years after the capitol was built, the 3,000,000 acres of land had a value of perhaps $100,000,000.

About 1910, or perhaps sooner, the assertion began to be made by people living in West Texas that the surveys of land that had been conveyed to the builder of the capitol contained much more than 3,000,000 acres. This agitation continued until the Legislature authorized a resurvey of the entire 3,000,000 acres of land. It took three years to make the resurvey. According to this resurvey, the builder of the capitol had received about 3,073,000 acres of land. The Legislature directed the then Attorney General, Mr. B. F. Looney, to file suit for the recovery of this alleged excess. Mr. G. B. Smedley was Mr. Looney's assistant in charge of land matters. Under Mr. Looney's direction, Mr. Smedley brought several suits for the purpose of recovering the alleged excess land. These cases had not been tried when Mr. Cureton became Attorney General. Mr. Smedley retired from the Attorney General's Department, but because of his familiarity with these lawsuits, he was employed by the State to assist the Attorney General in trying these cases. When Mr. Cureton assigned me to the land desk, I inherited these several lawsuits.

In the trial of these cases, instead of Mr. Smedley's assisting me, he actually tried the cases, and I gave him such assistance as I could. Mr. Smedley had filed five suits, four in trespass to try title for an aggregate of 15,117 acres represented by ten different tracts of land. These suits were brought against the persons in possession of the land. The basis of these four suits was that the land sued for had never been surveyed, but was vacant land and had never, in fact, been conveyed by the State of Texas to anyone.

The fifth suit was a partition suit for 55,116 acres against the persons who, it was alleged, were the trustees for the Corporation to whom the land had been reconveyed by Abner Taylor. In this suit the State alleged, in addition "to the matters already mentioned:

> That on account of mistakes and errors made by the surveyors who made the original surveys and by the surveyors who made the resurveys of the land, there was in fact included within the lands of the Capitol Leagues, which were patented for the erection of the capitol, a total of 3,055,116 acres, or an excess of 55,116 acres;

That the patents were issued, delivered, and accepted on the part of the State and the building contractor under the mistaken belief that there was contained within the lands conveyed but 3,000,000 acres, and that the conveyance by the State and the acceptance by the contractor of the 55,116 acres of land in excess of the 3,000,000 acres was through mutual mistake;

That the Capitol Freehold Land and Investment Company, Ltd., had sold to various persons much of the land that it had received from Abner Taylor for building the capitol, but on June 4, 1915, it owned 900,000 acres of this land; that on that date the ownership of said 900,000 acres was changed from a corporation to what is commonly known as a trust and that the change was a change merely in the form of the ownership of the land;

That the trustees had, from June 4, 1915, to the time of the filing of the partition suit, sold certain of the land but still owned 600,000 acres, and the State's petition described this 600,000 acres, and then it was alleged that the State was the owner of an undivided interest in these 600,000 acres to the extent of 55,116 acres. The State asked the court for a decree of partition between the State and the trustees of said 600,000 acres, and that out of said 600,000 acres there be set apart to the State 55,116 acres.

The five suits were consolidated and tried together in Austin before Judge George Calhoun of the 53rd District Court of Travis County.

The Capitol Syndicate Company was represented by Messrs. Horace Kent Tenney and George Rogers, of Chicago, and Judge I. W. Stevens of Ft. Worth, a former Judge of the Court of Civil Appeals at Ft. Worth. Other defendants were represented by the firm of Madden, Truelove, Ryburn and Pipkin of Amarillo, and Cooper and Lumpkin, also of

Amarillo, I. H. Burney of Fort Worth, and G. P. Hamilton of Matador.

In the four suits in trespass to try title, the defendants answered by pleas of "not guilty," which is the statutory form of answer in such suits in Texas, and means that the defendants deny that the plaintiff has the better or superior title to the land sued for. The defense in the partition suit alleged:

That by unexplained acquiescence by the State for more than thirty years after the State had had notice of the alleged excess, the State had waived its alleged right to the land;

That the State's cause of action, as alleged in its petition, discloses a case of *laches* such as bars the relief sought. (The relief sought in a suit for a partition of land is, as a general rule, an equitable action. One who seeks equity must act promptly, and if he too long delays in bringing his suit, he is by such delay guilty of *laches* and will be denied any relief, even though he originally had a good cause of action.);

That the supplemental contract between the State and the contractor of January 11, 1887, constituted a full and complete settlement between the State and the contractor, and that if thereafter there was an excess in the lands, the State must suffer the loss, or if there was a shortage in the lands, the contractor must suffer the loss; that if there were, in fact, more than 3,000,000 acres of land conveyed by the State to the builder of the capitol, and this was denied, the excess was in surveys that the Capitol Company had long since sold, and that there was no excess at all in the surveys still owned by the trustees;

A denial of any mutual mistake between the State and the contractor with reference to the amount of land intended to be conveyed; that all persons connected with the transaction knew that it was impossible to survey the land with mathematical accuracy, and that there might be an excess or a shortage, and that the excess in acreage, if any, was no greater than would naturally result and be expected in a survey made at that time and under those circumstances; and that the excess, if any, was not sufficiently great to have changed the contract or to give rise to any right in favor of the State.

It was then alleged that the land was of small value at the time the contract was made, and had since been improved and greatly increased in value; that the lands were worth no more than $1,500,000 at the time they were conveyed to the builder of the capitol, and that by reason of changes in the plans as the work of building the capitol progressed, the actual cost of building the capitol to the contractor was $3,744,630.60.

We were thirteen weeks in the trial of these five lawsuits, which had been consolidated and were tried as one case. Weeks were spent in examining and in cross-examining the surveyor who had made the resurvey as authorized by the Legislature. By the surveyor, Mr. Smedley and I were able to show that most of the lands described in the trespass to try title suits had not been included in the original survey of the lands and had not, therefore, ever been conveyed by the State to anyone and that those in possession of the lands under deeds from the Capitol Company had no title thereto. As against the Capitol Company, the evidence showed an excess in almost every league. These excesses, when added together, amounted to the total excess in acres that we had sued for.

When all the evidence had been introduced, the lawyers in the case made oral arguments to Judge Calhoun lasting about five days. The points made by the attorneys for the Capitol Company and the answering arguments made by Mr. Smedley and me may be summarized as follows:

Counsel for the Capitol Company contended that the constitutional provision setting aside 3,000,000 acres of land for the building of the capitol was not a limitation upon the amount of land that could be used for that purpose, but was merely a declaration of a duty on the part of the Legislature to provide for the disposition of at least 3,000,000 acres for that purpose.

To this argument Mr. Smedley and I replied that the courts had often held, citing and reading from the cases, that where the Constitution specifies a certain and definite amount of money to be applied for a certain use, the specification of such amount is a limitation upon the power of the Legislature, and that the Legislature cannot apply a larger amount to that purpose. The same principle, we argued, is applicable when the specification in the Constitution is of a certain and definite amount of land.

Counsel for the Capitol Company contended that it was the purpose of the law to convey a certain tract of land in payment for the building of the capitol. In support of this contention, they stressed the fact that the laws appropriating the land and providing for its survey had alluded to the land as a "reservation" and had directed the surveyor to mark the exterior corners of the "reservation," and that the words "reservation" and "three million acres" were synonymous.

This contention, Mr. Smedley and I pointed out, ignored the express terms of the written contract for the building of the capitol. The building contract made no reference to the lands as a "reservation," but provided that the contractor should receive 3,000,000 acres of land in payment for building the capitol. It could not be true that the words "reservation" and "three million acres" were synonymous, because there were concededly more than 3,000,000 acres in the "reservation," and no attempt had been made to convey all the land in the "reservation" but only so much of said land as it took to make exactly three million acres. The provision of the Constitution, and the two legislative acts with reference to the capitol lands, limited the quantity of land that could be conveyed in payment for the capitol to three million acres.

Counsel for the Capitol Company contended that the land had been surveyed by the State, and when it attempted to convey three million acres of land, according to its own survey, it ran the risk and the hazard of there being more than three million acres in the surveys.

To this contention Mr. Smedley and I replied that in an ordinary case the seller of land may hazard a small excess, where the amount of land sold is computed by surveys, but there could not have been a hazard in the excess of lands sold unless there was a like hazard of a loss on the part of the purchaser; that it was this hazard of a shortage or loss on the part of the purchaser that constituted the consideration the purchaser pays for the excess, and when that consideration is wanting, the purchaser must rely on his express contract if he would claim excess. Since, we argued, the contractor did not hazard the loss of an acre, as the matter was handled, the State certainly did not hazard the existence of an excess.

Counsel for the Capitol Company contended that the State could not recover from the trustee out of the 600,000 acres still unsold, but should have sued George W. Littlefield, or those holding under him, for the recovery of the leagues last patented to the contractor and which had been sold by the Capitol Company to Mr. Littlefield. The basis of this ingenious argument was that once the State had conveyed three million acres to the contractor, the conveyance of any additional acres was void. Therefore, if there was an excess, the lands that had been last patented to the Company and containing the lands over and above the three million acres, were the lands that the State must recover, and these lands, so the Capitol Company contended, had been sold by it to Mr. Littlefield. Therefore, the State, it was argued, was attempting to recover from the trustee for the Capitol Company something neither the trustee nor the Company possessed.

To this Mr. Smedley and I replied that the contention ignored the fact that the excess was not caused by too many leagues of land having been conveyed, but because there was more land in each league than there should be by reason of the fact that the distances between the marked corners of each league were excessive, and this excess land in each league was, according to the testimony of the surveyors who had resurveyed all of the leagues, scattered with fair uniformity throughout all the leagues.

Counsel for the Capitol Company contended that when the land was patented to Abner Taylor, it was not patented to him as the representative of the Capitol Freehold Land and Investment Company, Ltd., and that it was Abner Taylor, and not the trustee of the Capitol Company, from whom the State should seek to obtain relief.

To this contention Mr. Smedley and I answered that the formation of the Capitol Company was a plan of the promoters for the raising of funds for the building of the capitol; that under an agreement between Taylor and the Capitol Company, the Company furnished the money for building the capitol, and as soon as patents were issued for the land, the Company became entitled to the land; that the lands constituted the capital stock of the Company. It was our contention that in a transaction of this kind, the court should ignore mere forms and ascertain what was in truth the substance of the transaction; that the question of the real ownership of these lands should not be determined by the form in which the title apparently rests.

Counsel for the Capitol Company contended that there had been a real change in ownership to the 600,000 acres out of which the State sought to recover 55,116 acres as excess. Taylor had, they contended, conveyed the land to the Company, and the Company had conveyed the land to George Findley and others, as trustees, and the State could not recover the alleged excess from the trustees.

To this contention Mr. Smedley and I replied that it was the Capitol Company that had financed the building of the capitol and received the land in payment, and that this same Company, in the form of the present trust estate, was in possession of the 55,116 acres of excess land.

Counsel for the Capitol Company contended that the State could not recover, because it had been guilty of *laches* by reason of its long delay in bringing the suit.

To this contention Mr. Smedley and I replied that *laches* is never imputable to the government, because it is contrary to sound public policy.

At the conclusion of the long oral arguments, Judge Calhoun took the case under advisement, and later decided the case as follows: In the four trespass to try title suits, he rendered judgment for the State for 11,360 acres of the 15,116 acres sued for. In the partition suit, Judge Calhoun held as a matter of law:

1. That the officers of the State were without authority to convey more than three million acres in payment for building the capitol.

2. That the contract for building the capitol was for a definite and certain number of acres; namely, three million acres.

3. Under the contract it was not intended that the State should hazard an excess in acreage, or that the contractor should hazard a shortage in acreage.

4. That the State was entitled to relief on account of mutual mistake of the parties as to the acreage patented in payment for the capitol.

5. The Capitol Company was, in legal effect, the real purchaser from the State and the real patentee of the lands patented in payment for the construction of the capitol.

6. The conveyance from the Capitol Company to the trustees was a change in the form of ownership only, and worked no real change in the ownership of the lands.

7. That the trustees were not the actual owners of the 600,000 acres of land or of any interest in the same.

8. The State, after the delivery of the patents to the capitol leagues patented in payment for the capitol, was the owner of an undivided interest in all of

said lands so patented, to the extent of the excessive acreage within the bounds of the same above three million acres.

9. The Capitol Company and the trustees, having taken possession of and asserted claim to all of the land so patented, including the excessive acreage, and having sold and conveyed to others various portions of said land, and the State, having elected by this suit to acquiesce in such conveyance and to claim its lands out of the land now remaining in the hands of said defendants, the State is the owner of an undivided interest in the lands now remaining in the hands of said defendants to the extent of the excessive acreage, and which excessive acreage is 55,089 acres, and the State is entitled to have partitioned and set apart to it out of said lands remaining in the hands of the defendants the said excessive acreage.

Under the judgment in all five suits, the State recovered a total of 66,449 acres of land. Commissioners were appointed to make a fair and impartial partition of the 600,000 acres, setting aside for the State 55,089 acres. The Capitol Company appealed, and on appeal, the Austin Court of Civil Appeals affirmed the judgment of the trial court. (238 Southwestern, 956.) The Supreme Court, after granting writ of error, affirmed the judgment of the Court of Civil Appeals and of the District Court.

Chapter XI:
Martial Law at Galveston

To Galveston, the beautiful island city where the oleanders bloom, ships come from all the nations of the world. The merchandise that comes to Galveston in these ships is transported by the railroads to the cities and towns of Texas and other states in the Southwest. In the spring of 1920, a strike of the longshoremen at Galveston interrupted the normal course of business. The merchandise that came by ships to Galveston could not be moved. The owners of perishable goods suffered heavy losses. Merchants could not obtain the merchandise they had ordered and had to take losses, and the people for whose use the goods were intended were deprived of things they needed. It was reported that serious disorders and public disturbances occurred when any attempt was made to employ men to replace the longshoremen who were out on strike.

Governor W. P. Hobby declared martial law at Galveston and sent about nine hundred soldiers to that city to enforce his declaration, with Brigadier General Jacob F. Wolters in command. When General Wolters asked the Attorney General for a legal adviser, Mr. Cureton gave the assignment to me.

One of my first duties was to defend a suit brought in one of the state district courts at Galveston by certain citizens, wherein it was sought to restrain, by injunction, Governor Hobby and General Wolters from enforcing the Governor's declaration of martial law.

The day this case was tried, the courtroom was crowded with people, most of whom were strikers, or their sympathizers. The case was tried before Robert G. Street, then an elderly man, who, I was told, had been, when a young man, a Colonel in the Confederate Army. The men on strike, their relatives, friends and sympathizers constituted a very large part of the population of Galveston, perhaps a majority of the voters of Galveston County, and were apparently well organized.

To the injunction suit I filed a plea to the jurisdiction of the court. This meant that the defendants asserted that the court did not have the power to enjoin the Governor and the Commanding General from enforcing the Governor's declaration of martial law. In support of the jurisdictional plea, I relied on the following legal propositions:

1. Section 7, Article 4 of the Constitution of Texas provides that the Governor shall be Commander-in-Chief of the military forces of the State, except when they are called into the actual service of the United States, and further provides that the Governor "shall have the power to call forth the militia, to execute the laws of the State, to suppress insurrection, repel invaders..."

2. Section 10, Article 4 of the Constitution provides that the Governor "shall cause the laws to be faithfully executed ..."

3. Necessarily, I argued, the Governor, and he alone, must determine when a rebellion, insurrection or invasion has occurred, and when it is necessary to call out the militia to execute the laws of the State, and that he, and he alone, must determine when the laws are not being "faithfully executed." The courts cannot substitute their judgment in these matters for the judgment of the Governor.

4. The State Government, under the Constitution, consists of three departments, each supreme in its own sphere and entirely independent of the other departments. If, I argued, a case is being tried in a court, neither the Governor nor the Legislature may compel the court to decide the case in a certain way, because, under the Constitution, that is a matter left entirely to the judgment of the court; the courts and the Governor cannot compel the Legislature to legislate in a certain

way, because, under the Constitution, decision as to what laws shall or shall not be enacted is vested solely and exclusively in the Legislature. I then argued that the people of Texas in the Constitution had vested in the Governor the power to call forth the militia to enforce the law whenever, in his judgment, such action was necessary, and that no court could prohibit or restrain the Governor from exercising the power so vested in him. If he exercises his power unlawfully, he is answerable to the people; and if by his unlawful action, he injures any citizen in his person or property, he is personally liable in a civil action to such citizen for damages.

The attorney for the plaintiff was a lawyer of ability and a real orator. He made an argument lasting more than an hour. It was an argument that had great appeal for the partisan crowd that was in the courtroom. When this gentleman had concluded his argument, I arose to reply.

Judge Street waved me back to my seat and said: "One minute, Mr. Smith; it is not necessary for you to make any reply to the argument made by counsel for the plaintiff. This court is convinced beyond any shadow of a doubt that it does not possess the power to enjoin Governor Hobby and General Wolters from enforcing the Governor's declaration of martial law. The plea to the jurisdiction of this court is sustained, and the suit is dismissed."

Plaintiffs gave notice of appeal, but never did perfect the appeal. The action of Judge Street was typical of the old-time courageous judge. Judge Street, at the time he decided this case, was a candidate for re-election. His decision was very unpopular with a great many people, who, within a few months, would have an opportunity to vote against him.

A very sad and an unfortunate thing happened in Galveston while the city was under martial law. A soldier was on guard duty at night, with instructions not to permit anyone to pass inside the position he was guarding without first giving the password. A junior officer on duty with the troops approached the sentinel in his automobile. Apparently this officer did not see the guardsman or hear his command to halt. The officer had passed the guardsman when the soldier fired, according to his statement, at a rear tire of the automobile.

The shot killed the officer. General Wolters was shocked and grieved at this unfortunate occurrence, for he was very fond of this young officer who had been killed. This fact, however, did not affect General Wolters' attitude toward the soldier who had killed the officer. The newest private always received the same fair and impartial treatment from General Wolters as did the highest officer in his command. General Wolters asked me to give him a written opinion as to whether it was his duty to have the soldier tried by general court martial or to deliver him to the civil authorities.

I advised General Wolters that he could follow either course with safety to himself, and with assurance that in either event, the right of the soldier to a trial before a proper tribunal would be protected. If, I advised, the soldier was tried by general court martial and convicted, the soldier could then apply to a district court for a writ of *habeas corpus*, on the ground that the court martial had no jurisdiction to try him, and that he was, therefore, being illegally restrained of his liberty. If, I further advised, the soldier was acquitted by the court martial and was afterwards arrested and tried by the civil authorities, he could plead former jeopardy on the ground that he had been tried once for the same offense by general court martial, and if the civil court held that his trial by general court martial was a legal trial, his plea of *autro fois acquit* would be sustained and the case against him dismissed.

The soldier was tried by general court martial and acquitted. He was also indicted by a grand jury for manslaughter, and when the Governor's declaration of martial law had been lifted, General Wolters delivered the soldier to the civil authorities for trial. The venue of the case was changed from Galveston to Fort Bend County. The soldier filed in the district court of Fort Bend County a plea of *autro fois acquit*, wherein he asserted that he had theretofore been tried for the same offense by a legally constituted tribunal, namely, a general court martial, and acquitted. The soldier's plea was sustained and the manslaughter charge against him dismissed.

General Wolters asked me for an opinion as to whether or not the Governor could, while Galveston was under martial law, suspend the mayor, city commissioners, city attorney, corporation judge, the entire police and detective forces from office and govern the city with soldiers. I told General Wolters that I had never heard of such a thing being done except by General Butler in New Orleans, and I did not care to use General Butler's conduct as a precedent. General Wolters asked me to investigate the question carefully and to furnish Governor Hobby with a written opinion. I returned to Austin where I could use the Supreme Court library, and there I carefully read all the court decisions in martial law cases.

There was not a decision directly in point. The one nearest in point was the case of Grapeshot vs. Wallenstein, 9 Wall., 192, where the Supreme Court of the United States had upheld the action of General Butler, who, when in command at New Orleans, removed the civil authorities from office and appointed a provost marshal to try civil cases. The action of General Butler had been approved in a formal proclamation by President Lincoln.

I wrote an exhaustive opinion to Governor Hobby, reviewing all the authorities, and advised him, among other things, that:

> Where the local civil officers in a district declared to be under martial law make no attempt to enforce the law, suppress the insurrection and disorderly conduct and make no attempt to restore obedience to the law, or where the local civil officers aid and encourage the lawless element in their unlawful acts,

the Governor, as the Chief Civil Magistrate, has the power, if, in his judgment it is necessary in order 'to execute the laws of the State' and to 'cause the laws to be faithfully executed,' to suspend such officers from office during the period that martial law is in force in the district. When the local officers have been suspended, the militia, under instructions from the Governor, as the Chief Civil Magistrate of the State, may proceed to enforce the civil law in the district declared to be under martial law.

Anyone interested in the subject of martial law can find this opinion, which was approved by Attorney General Cureton, in the book on martial law, later written by General Wolters, and in the printed reports and opinions of the Attorney General of Texas, 1918-1920, Page 669.

Governor Hobby suspended most of the city officials, and General Wolters appointed a police and detective force from among the soldiers; also a provost officer to act as city judge and another soldier as prosecuting attorney for the city. The National Guard is a citizens' soldiery, and in its ranks can be found men of experience in all the professions and trades. General Wolters, for instance, was an excellent lawyer.

General Wolters was the anti-prohibitionist leader in Texas for many years. He barely missed being elected to the Senate of the United States. Honorable, able, and fearless, he was a great citizen. In 1920 statewide prohibition was in effect in Texas, as well as national prohibition. General Wolters, the anti-prohibition leader, and his soldier policemen enforced the prohibition law more effectively than it probably ever was enforced at any time in the City of Galveston. The town became as dry as the Sahara Desert. The bootleggers fled as before a pestilence, and foreign ships with liquor on board not properly manifested had their liquor seized and removed from the ship. This caused foreign entanglements. The Ambassador of a foreign nation protested to the Secretary of State at Washington, and that gentleman wrote a sharp note of protest to Governor Hobby. The latter referred the note to General Wolters. General Wolters furnished the Governor with the facts. Governor Hobby advised the Secretary of State that the liquor was on board ship contrary to law, within the jurisdiction of the State of Texas, and had been lawfully seized by General Wolters and would not be returned to the ship. That ended that episode.

A soldier policeman arrested a citizen and charged him with driving his automobile at an unlawful rate of speed. When the citizen was brought before the soldier acting as city judge, he demanded a trial by a jury. This was refused. The citizen was tried by the soldier judge, found guilty, and fined $50. The citizen refused to pay the fine and was remanded to jail. The prisoner applied to the United States District Court for a writ of *habeas corpus*, asserting that he was being illegally restrained of his liberty. In his petition the prisoner alleged that the Governor was without power to suspend from office the duly appointed and acting city judge of Galveston; that General Wolters was without power lawfully to appoint a soldier to act as city judge; that the soldier judge was without lawful power to remand him to jail; and that in any event, he had been denied his right of trial by a jury. This petition for a writ of *habeas corpus* afforded a test of the legal soundness of the opinion that I had given to Governor Hobby. Honorable Joseph C. Hutcheson, Jr., the United States District Judge for the Southern District of Texas, was out of the state, and Judge Rufus Foster of New Orleans, who was later to be promoted to the office of Circuit Judge for the Fifth Circuit, came to Galveston to try the case.

On the day before the case was to be tried, I was in my office in the Capitol at Austin making final preparation for the trial when Adjutant General Cope came to my office and told me the Governor wanted to send a Texas Ranger with me to Galveston as a personal bodyguard. Clifford Stone, an assistant attorney general, was going with me to Galveston. Mr. Stone was a powerful man physically, utterly fearless, had served as a Ranger when he was a boy, and had been elected sheriff of his home county when he was twenty-one. I knew that Mr. Stone would be armed and was entirely able, ready, and willing to afford me any protection that I might need, but I did not think I would need any. I thanked General Cope for the Governor's offer, and told him that I did not need a Ranger.

When Mr. Stone and I went to the depot at noon to get on the train to go to Galveston and were waiting on the station platform, a man approached me and asked if I was Mr. Smith of the Attorney General's office. When I answered in the affirmative, he told me that he was Ranger Rowe and had been ordered to report to me and stay with me until I returned to Austin. No good purpose could be served by my objecting to Mr. Rowe's going with me, for when a Texas Ranger is ordered to do something, he is going to obey his orders.

That afternoon while on the train from Austin to Galveston Mr. Rowe told Mr. Stone and me of an experience he had in the Big Thicket of East Texas. It was during the time of the World War, and Mr. Rowe and another Ranger had been sent to the big thicket to arrest some men who, it was charged, had evaded being drafted into the army. The Rangers penetrated the thicket and came in due time to the house where two of the three men they wanted were supposed to live. The Rangers arrived at the house at night and found no one at home. Mr. Rowe and his companion made camp and slept the remainder of the night in the yard.

The next morning while cooking breakfast they were fired on from the thicket. Mr. Rowe's companion was killed, and Mr. Rowe was shot through the body three times. He fell where he had been standing getting breakfast and was helpless to move his body. Mr. Rowe was some distance from his guns and was unable to reach them. He soon had a high fever from his wounds and suffered greatly from thirst. After a while two men and three women came into the yard. Mr. Rowe asked these people for a drink of water, and one of the women went to the well and drew a bucket of water, which she brought close to Rowe and where he could see her. She then used a gourd for a dipper and dipped the water out of the bucket, a gourd full at a time, and slowly poured the water on the ground. Mr. Rowe said that this was the nearest thing to torture that he had ever suffered, for he was famishing for a drink, and there was water being slowly poured on the ground within his sight. The next day, Mr. Rowe was rescued.

Apparently most of the people in Galveston wanted to be present and hear the *habeas corpus* trial in the United States District Court, for on the day of the trial, every seat was taken. Men and women were standing in the aisles and in the doors and windows, and a great many people were outside the courtroom. When our party arrived, we had to push our way through the people in the aisles to reach our position in the courtroom. Necessarily I had to sit with my back to the crowd, and also, when standing and addressing the court, my back was to the crowd. Ranger Rowe, who had come into the courtroom with me, took his seat between me and the rostrum upon which the judge would sit, so that he at all times faced me and faced the crowd.

In the argument of the case before Judge Foster, counsel for relator, that is, the prisoner, contended:

1. That while the Governor had the right to declare martial law, he had no right to remove or suspend any civil officer from his office, because there was no law authorizing him to do so.

2. That the Governor had no authority to suspend any law of the State; only the Legislature could do that.

3. Every citizen had the right, when accused of crime, to be tried by a jury.

4. That the soldier judge was not even a *de facto* judge, because he had no color of authority to the office, and his action in committing the prisoner to jail was an unlawful and an illegal act.

In reply to these contentions by counsel for relator, I replied:

1. The Governor, having declared martial law, had the power, in the absence of a law expressly authorizing him to do so, to suspend the city officials from office, if, in his opinion, such action was necessary to make his proclamation of martial law effective.

2. The Governor had not suspended any law; to the contrary, he was enforcing the law.

3. The Constitution of the United States does not contain any guarantee of a trial by jury in a state court.

4. That the provost officer, the soldier judge, was a *de facto* officer, because he was acting as the agent of the Chief Civil Magistrate of the State, the Governor, and indirectly was the appointee of the Governor during the emergency which had necessitated the declaration of martial law by the Governor.

Judge Foster took the case under advisement, and a few days later handed down a written opinion, wherein he upheld the action of Governor Hobby in suspending from office the city officials of Galveston, and denied the writ of *habeas corpus*.

In his opinion Judge Foster, among other things, wrote:

The only question before the court is the jurisdiction of the provost court...There is no doubt that under the Constitution and laws of Texas, the Governor is charged with the duty of enforcing the laws of the State, and has authority to call out the militia to enforce the laws, in case of riot or breach of the peace, or imminent danger there of...The question as to whether there is a riot or insurrection, or breach of the peace, or danger thereof is one solely for the determination of the Governor...Since he had the authority to institute martial law, notwithstanding there was no statute of the State of Texas authorizing him to do so, he could do anything necessary to make his proclamation effective. If the civil officers of Galveston were not performing their duties, and not aiding in the enforcement of the law, the Governor would be authorized to suspend them. He did that, and in my opinion the suspension was legal... The City Court of Galveston had been suspended and a military officer had been appointed to sit in place and stead of the judge, and to enforce the ordinance of the city; that is not without precedent in history. When General Butler was in command at New Orleans, he did this very thing. He appointed the provost marshal and gave him jurisdiction to try civil cases. Subsequently, President Lincoln created a provisional court, by proclamation, for the same district. The jurisdiction of this court was upheld. Grapeshot vs. Wallenstein, 9 Wall., 129.

The point is also made that only the Legislature can suspend a law...Suspending a judge is not suspending a law. On the contrary, in this case the military were directed to enforce existing laws, and the provost court was created for that very purpose.

In regard to the denial of a trial by jury, it is well settled the Federal Constitution does not guarantee a trial by jury in state courts.

(The opinion of Judge Foster in this case of the United States vs. Wolters is reported in 268 Federal, 69.)

This decision by Judge Foster fully sustained all that Governor Hobby and General Wolters had done. The decision in this case broke down all further resistance; commerce was opened and transportation of merchandise was no longer interfered with. The good people of Galveston, many of whom had remained on the sidelines, refraining from taking sides until it was apparent which side was going to win, came in ever increasing numbers to General Wolters and expressed their appreciation for what he had done. Soon martial law was lifted.

Before the troops left Galveston, the businessmen of the city tendered General Wolters and his officers a banquet, and gave to General Wolters a silver loving cup as an expression of their gratitude for the splendid service rendered by him and the soldiers to the City of Galveston. The finest and best thing of all was a banquet by the businessmen of Galveston to the enlisted men of the National Guard. At this banquet, General Wolters was toastmaster, and the businessmen, dressed as waiters, waited on the tables. To each enlisted man was given a medal upon which was engraved

"Galveston Defenders, June 7-October 8, 1920."

When martial law was lifted, General Wolters was kind enough to write me the following letter:

My Dear Mr. Smith:

Now that martial law has been lifted in Galveston and the mission of the National Guard Troops on duty there has been accomplished, I want to particularly thank you for the loyal and intelligent assistance you rendered as Assistant Attorney General. The military took care of the lawless efforts of lawless men to prevent the enforcement of the law, but you, Sir, took care to prevent, through the machinery of the court, the accomplishment by lawless men of lawless purposes. As legal adviser to the Commanding General, your assistance was invaluable.

I am taking the liberty to recommend you for appointment as Judge Advocate in the National Guard. I do not know whether just now a vacancy exists, nor do I know whether higher authorities will conform with my recommendation, nor do I know whether you wish such a commission, but I do know that I will, in the best interests of the service, continue the effort until I find a place, in which event I must insist that you accept whether you care to or not. As a result of your studies pertaining to the law relating to martial law, you owe it to your State as well as to the Federal Government to serve as Judge Advocate in this service.

With kindest personal regards, I remain,

Sincerely yours,

J. F. Wolters

Brigadier General, N. G. of T.

My work, however, in connection with martial law at Galveston was not yet ended. There was an aftermath that was peculiarly unpleasant to General Wolters and to me. We had tried to enforce the law and not to violate it. During the existence of martial law at Galveston, there was being published at Houston a newspaper that repeatedly criticized General Wolters and his actions as Commanding Officer at Galveston. This newspaper enjoyed a large circulation in Galveston.

Colonel Billy Mayfield, a trained, experienced and brilliant newspaperman, held the highest rank, next to General Wolters, of any army officer at Galveston. One night Colonel Mayfield, a captain and two lieutenants went to Houston in an automobile, and upon inquiry found that the editor of the newspaper to which I have referred was at one of the country clubs near Houston. Colonel Mayfield and his companions drove to this country club and there attempted to arrest the editor. They were prevented from doing so by a number of men at the club.

After martial law had been lifted at Galveston, the editor of the newspaper sued Colonel Mayfield and his associates in one of the District Courts of Harris County, alleging an unlawful assault on his person and asking for damages, I think, in the sum of $65,000. Attorney General Cureton, while frowning at the conduct of Colonel Mayfield, thought it was the duty of the State to defend the subordinate officers who had participated in the attempt to arrest the editor and who had acted, ostensibly at least, under the orders of their superior officer, Colonel Mayfield. Accordingly, Mr. Cureton directed Mr. Clifford Stone and me to participate in the defense of this damage suit.

Chief counsel for the editor was that truly great trial lawyer, Francis Marion Etheridge, of the law firm of Etheridge, McCormick and Bromberg, of Dallas.

Mr. Stone and I based our defense for the subordinate officers on three grounds: first, that the officers, in view of all the facts and circumstances of the case, were justified in their effort to arrest the editor; second, that the subordinate officers had no choice in the matter, but must act in obedience to the orders given them by their superior officer, Colonel Mayfield; and third, that if we were wrong about our first two contentions, the plaintiff had not suffered any real damages and was only entitled to recover nominal damages, if any. We lost on our first and second contentions, and certainly we should have lost on our first contention, and perhaps on the second as well. The officers of the National Guard at Galveston had no authority to make any arrest outside of the territory embraced in the Governor's proclamation of martial law.

A subordinate officer, who obeys an unlawful command of his superior officer, does so at his peril. This is in some respects a harsh doctrine of the law. A subordinate army officer must obey the commands of his superior officer or be subject to court martial, and if the order he disobeyed was a lawful order, he will be punished for such disobedience. On the other hand, no officer has a right to do an unlawful act, even though commanded to do so by a superior officer. The subordinate is between the devil and the deep blue sea. If he disobeys a lawful order, he is punished for his disobedience. If he obeys an unlawful order, he is punished for his unlawful act. The editor recovered a nominal judgment for his damages. Fifty dollars, I believe, was the amount he recovered.

The opinion of Judge Foster in the case of the United States vs. Wolters had, it was believed, clarified the law in regard to the power of a governor of a state to declare martial law and had established the right of the governor to suspend local officers when, in the governor's opinion, it was necessary to do so in order to make martial law effective. All power is dangerous. The arbitrary power of martial law, when exercised by a despot, or even by a man of good intentions but of unsound judgment, is extremely dangerous. It is a power that should never be exercised except in a case of absolute and undoubted emergency, and then great care should be taken to prevent any abuse of this extraordinary power.

Chapter XII:
Million Dollar Oil Suit

My acquaintance with the late Lud Williams, famous criminal lawyer of Waco, had its beginning in the trial of a land suit. The suit was one that Mr. Cureton had directed me to bring in an effort to recover for the State the title to, and possession of, a quarter section of land located in Stephens County, and for the value of the oil that had been produced from the land. The Gulf Production Company and others were the defendants. A mineral permit on the land had been issued by the Land Commissioner to a man by the name of P. K. Shuler, and he was co-plaintiff with the State in the suit.

The Land Commissioner had classified the land as dry grazing and non-mineral and had appraised it at $2.00 per acre. The Land Commissioner, as he was required by law to do, notified the County Clerk of Stephens County, the county in which the land was situated, of his action in so classifying and appraising the land. Anyone desiring to purchase the land must file his application to purchase with the county clerk. The county clerk would then send the purchase application to the General Land Office at Austin where the application would be accepted or rejected.

On January 22, 1900, the land, both the surface and the mineral estates, were sold to J. M. Kidd for $1.50 an acre. Kidd made the required cash payment and executed his obligation to the State for the deferred payments in the manner and form required by law. The principal of this obligation was payable forty years after the date of its execution, but the interest thereon was payable annually. On December 30, 1915, the sale to Kidd was forfeited by the Land Commissioner for non-payment of the annual interest due the State on Kidd's unpaid purchase money obligation.

After the sale to Kidd had been forfeited, the Land Commissioner reclassified the land as dry grazing and mineral,

and re-appraised it at $6.00 an acre. The land was then sold
to V. Griffin for $6.00 an acre and the State retained the
mineral estate.

Under the law, Griffin, in order to perfect his title to the
land, had to actually live on the land. On February 7, 1917,
the sale to Griffin was forfeited because of his failure to file
the required affidavit that he had occupied the land.

In the meantime, a man by the name of J. F. Lewis had acquired whatever title, or right to obtain the title, to this land
that Kidd had acquired from the State. The law provided
that whenever a sale was forfeited for non-payment of interest, the original sale could be reinstated upon payment of all
unpaid interest, provided that in the meantime no right of a
third person had intervened.

When the sale to Griffin was forfeited, Lewis applied to
have the original sale to Kidd reinstated and paid all the
unpaid interest on the Kidd purchase money obligation.
The Land Commissioner granted Lewis' application and
reinstated the original sale to Kidd in the name of Lewis as
assignee of Kidd.

After the reinstatement to Lewis of the original sale to
Kidd, Mr. Shuler applied to the Land Commissioner for
a mineral permit on the land. Mr. Shuler and his attorneys convinced the Land Commissioner that the original sale to Kidd was void because the sale had been made
at $1.50 an acre when the land was appraised at $2.00 an
acre.

In the suit for the recovery of the land and for damages
for the oil that had been taken therefrom, the defendants
were represented by D. Edward Greer, of Houston; Judge
Victor Brooks, of Austin; John G. Gregg, of Fort Worth;
Kay, Aiken and Kennerly, of Wichita Falls; White, Cartledge
and Wilcox, and G. B. Smedley, of Austin. Mr. Shuler was
represented by Mr. Lud Williams and his brother, Newton
Williams, Tom Conroy and John Maxwell, all of Waco, and
by E. R. Pedigo, of Austin.

The State and Mr. Shuler relied on three propositions:

1. That at the time the original sale was made to J. M. Kidd at $1.50 per acre, the land had been appraised at $2.00 per acre, and therefore, the Land Commissioner had no right to sell the land to J. M. Kidd for $1.50 per acre, and that the sale to J. M. Kidd was void.

2. That when the Land Commissioner forfeited the original sale made to Kidd for non-payment of interest and reclassified the land as dry grazing and mineral land, these acts on the part of the Land Commissioner gave to the public school fund of the State certain rights in the land which amounted, under the law, to an intervening right by a third person.

3. That when the Land Commissioner sold the land to V. Griffin, Griffin's rights thereto constituted an intervening right of a third person within the meaning of the law, and the fact that Griffin's sale was later forfeited did not alter the situation, because once the right of a third person intervened, even though that right was later lost, the original sale could not thereafter be reinstated.

The Gulf Production Company and the other defendants contended that the land had been appraised at $1.50 per acre at the time it was sold to Kidd at that price, and further contended that the reinstatement of the original Kidd sale was valid, because, so they contended, the reclassification of the land by the Land Commissioner and the resale to V. Griffin did not in either instance constitute such an intervening right of a third person as would prevent a reinstatement of the original sale to Kidd.

If either the original sale to Kidd or the attempted reinstatement of the sale to Kidd was void, then the land was mineral land under the law, and Shuler was entitled by reason of his mineral permit thereon to seven-eighths of the value of the oil already produced from the land by the Gulf Production Company, less whatever it had cost the company to produce the oil, and would be entitled to seven-eighths of the oil thereafter produced from this land. The State, in the event either the sale or the reinstatement of the sale to Kidd was void, would be entitled to one-eighth of the oil theretofore produced by the Gulf Production Company and to one-eighth of the oil thereafter produced by Shuler.

The case was tried in the 53rd District Court of Travis County, Texas, before Judge Calhoun and a jury. The evidence showed that the value of oil taken from the land up to some thirty days before the commencement of the trial was $737,429.24. The Gulf Company proved expenditures made in good faith in drilling and equipping the wells and in producing the oil to the amount of $417,068.56.

Judge Calhoun held that the rights accruing to the public school fund, if any, by reason of the reclassification of the land from dry grazing land to dry grazing and mineral land, did not constitute an intervening right within the meaning of the law such as would prevent the reinstatement of the original Kidd sale, provided the original sale to Kidd was a valid sale.

Judge Calhoun also held that while the sale to V. Griffin was an intervening right of a third person, the intervening right of Griffin ceased to exist when the sale to Griffin had been forfeited because of Griffin's failure to file the required affidavit showing that he had occupied the land.

This left, as the only issue to be tried, the question of whether the land had been appraised at $1.50 or $2.00 an acre at the time it was originally sold to Kidd at $1.50 per acre. The evidence on this question was voluminous.

I proved, from the records of the General Land Office, that the land had been appraised at $2.00 an acre on the 11th day of June, 1895; that the original sale to Kidd was made on the 22nd day of January, 1900, at $1.50 an acre. I then proved by the Land Commissioner that he had carefully examined the books, records and files of the General Land Office, and that he had not found where any change had been made in the appraised value of this land from the time it was appraised at

$2.00 an acre on the 11th day of June, 1895, until it was sold to J. M. Kidd on the 22nd day of January, 1900, at $1.50 an acre. I proved by the County Clerk of Stephens County, the county in which the land was situated, that his records showed that a notice had been received by his office from the Land Commissioner appraising the land at $2.00 an acre on June 11, 1895, and that he had made a careful examination of the records in his office, and that he could not find where his office had ever received any notice from the Land Commissioner of any change in the appraised valuation of this land from $2.00 an acre to $1.50 an acre up to the time the land was sold on January 22, 1900, to J. M. Kidd for $1.50 per acre.

The defendants introduced in evidence the "classification records" of Stephens County, and on this record and opposite the description of this land the figures "$1.50" appeared. J. M. Kidd testified that when he was preparing his application to purchase the land, he went to the office of the County Clerk of Stephens County and asked the County Clerk to fill in on his application the valuation of the land. The County Clerk, according to Kidd's testimony, examined some books and then wrote in the valuation of the land on his application to purchase the same at $1.50 per acre. There was other testimony which showed that the County Clerk forwarded Kidd's application to the General Land Office, where it was received and filed on October 30, 1899. This application, after it had been in the General Land Office for some time, was referred to the head sales clerk, who in turn referred it to the examining clerk. The application of Kidd to purchase this land bore on its back the endorsement, among other endorsements, "Appraisement, $1.50." The examining clerk in the Land Office entered his "O. K." on the back of the purchase application opposite the appraisement endorsement. The head sales clerk endorsed the application with the word "Accept."

The case was submitted to the jury on special issues. The jury was directed by Judge Calhoun to answer the following questions:

1. Was the valuation of the land reduced from $2.00 an acre to $1.50 an acre prior to the time J. M. Kidd applied to purchase the land?

2. If such reduction in valuation was made, did the Land Commissioner notify the County Clerk of Stephens County of such reduction?

3. If the Land Commissioner did notify the County Clerk of a reduction in the appraisement from $2.00 an acre to $1.50 an acre, did the County Clerk receive such notification before J. M. Kidd made application to purchase the land?

For the original sale to Kidd to be valid, three facts had to be established by the defendants; namely, (1) that the Land Commissioner had appraised the land at $1.50 an acre prior to the time that Kidd applied to purchase the land, (2) that the Land Commissioner had notified the County Clerk of Stephens County that the land had been appraised at $1.50 an acre, and (3) that such notification from the Land Commissioner of the $1.50 appraisement had been received by the County Clerk prior to the time Kidd filed his application with the County Clerk to purchase the land.

Judge Calhoun allowed the attorneys on each side five hours to present their arguments to the jury. The attorneys on each side were permitted to divide the five hours' time among themselves as they desired. One of Mr. Shuler's attorneys, John Maxwell, of Waco, an able and experienced lawyer and a former Assistant Attorney General of Texas, told me that Lud Williams, of Waco, should close the case for our side. Maxwell had known Williams for years. I knew him by reputation as one of the ablest criminal lawyers in the State, but in my judgment he did not know the facts in this case as well as his brother, Newton Williams. I knew that the other side would save Judge Brooks and G. B. Smedley to make the closing arguments for the defendants. I knew that Brooks and Smedley had mastered the facts in the case and would, in their arguments to the jury, analyze the facts in a way that was likely to convince the jury that the Land Commissioner had reduced the valuation of the land from \$2.00 to \$1.50 an acre prior to the time Kidd applied to purchase the land, and had notified the County Clerk of the new appraisement prior to the time Kidd had filed his application to purchase the land.

At Mr. Maxwell's insistence, I reluctantly agreed that Lud Williams could make the closing argument in the case. The order of the arguments and the amount of time used by each lawyer on our side were as follows: Newton Williams, one hour; E. R. Pedigo, one hour; one and one-half hours for me, and Lud Williams, one and one-half hours. The attorneys for the other side arranged their time as I anticipated they would, so that Judge Brooks and G. B. Smedley both spoke after I did, and before Lud Williams made his argument. Brooks spoke for an hour and Smedley for an hour and a half. Brooks and Smedley both made powerful arguments, as I knew they would. My reluctance in agreeing that Lud Williams should make the closing argument for our side was based on the fact that I knew that he had not given any time to a study of the voluminous and detailed documentary evidence in the case prior to the time we went to trial. Newton Williams and I spent weeks in our investigation of this documentary evidence, and it was much more voluminous than I have indicated in my brief summary of the evidence introduced. Any information that Lud Williams had obtained in regard to this documentary evidence had been obtained by him during the course of the trial which had lasted for several days.

Lud Williams was a man with a great personality. His personal magnetism was enough in itself to dominate an ordinary jury. In addition to this fine personality, he had a keen, analytical mind. Without any detailed knowledge of the voluminous documentary evidence that had been introduced in the trial, obtained prior to its introduction in evidence, the splendid mind of Lud Williams had grasped all the essential and material facts disclosed by this documentary evidence at the time it was introduced in evidence. He made one of the finest arguments that I ever listened to, where a lawyer had to discuss documentary evidence. He answered, I thought, completely the fine arguments that had been made by Judge Brooks and G. B. Smedley. His analysis of the documentary evidence disclosed that his fine penetrating mind thoroughly understood the vital and essential points of the evidence that had been helpful to our side and hurtful to the other side.

Toward the close of his argument, one juror persisted in appearing indifferent to what was being said and looked out of the window, apparently bored by the argument that was being made. Williams stopped talking and was still for a moment. The indifferent juror looked at Williams to see what had caused him to stop speaking. The moment Williams caught the juror's eye, he began to address him directly, using substantially the following language:

> Young man, you have a duty to perform in this case. An important duty. You, with eleven other men, must answer certain questions submitted to you by His Honor, Judge Calhoun. I am talking to this jury for the purpose of assisting you and the other eleven men on the jury to answer these questions correctly, according to the testimony that has been introduced in your presence. It is your duty to listen to what I have to say. You can agree or disagree with my conclusions, but you cannot answer or assist the other men on this jury in answering the questions submitted to you by Judge Calhoun, unless you have listened to the attorneys who have analyzed the evidence.

I was amazed at the boldness of Mr. Williams in thus addressing one of the jurors. I was convinced that at least one juror would be against us, and that the best we could hope to obtain from this jury would be a disagreement. I was wrong.

The jury was out only a few minutes, and then returned with a verdict that the appraisement or valuation of the land had never been reduced from $2.00 an acre to $1.50 an acre. Judgment was entered by Judge Calhoun giving the State title and possession of the land, subject to the mineral permit of P. K. Shuler, and for a cash judgment against the Gulf Production Company for $92,184.88, being the value of one-eighth of the oil already produced from the land and confirming the validity of the mineral permit of P. K. Shuler. The judgment also provided that Mr. Shuler should recover, after proper deductions were made for improvements made in good faith, $225,225.80 in cash and other property of the value of $114,199.80. This other property consisted of derricks, tanks, pipelines, etc.

The defendants appealed to the Austin Court of Civil Appeals. On appeal, the State of Texas and Shuler filed cross assignments of error, and in this way carried to the Court of Civil Appeals the two questions of law which had been decided against them by Judge Calhoun. The law requires the Supreme Court to equalize the dockets of the Courts of Civil Appeals each year. After this case had been appealed to the Austin Court of Civil Appeals, the Supreme Court, in equalizing the dockets of the Courts of Civil Appeals, transferred this case from the Austin to the San Antonio Court of Appeals.

Mr. Newton Williams and I briefed the case for Mr. Shuler and the State in the Court of Civil Appeals. We also made the oral arguments in that court. A few days before the case was to be argued in the Court of Civil Appeals, Mr. Williams and I were discussing the personnel of the court. One of the judges had been, before becoming a judge, for many years the land lawyer for a certain railroad that owned an enormous amount of land in Texas. Mr. Williams and I were afraid that this judge would be against us. We thought that his natural inclination would be to hold against the State in any attempt made by the State to recover land from anyone to whom the State had purportedly sold the land.

A few months before the case was argued in the Court of Civil Appeals at San Antonio, a vacancy had occurred on that court. A lawyer friend of mine had come to me and urged me to see Governor Hobby in an effort to get the Governor to appoint a certain gentleman to the vacancy on the court. I did not know this gentleman personally. At the request of my friend, I did see Governor Hobby. I told Governor Hobby that I did not know this particular applicant, but that a man whom I did know, and in whom I had confidence, had told me that the gentleman was in every way qualified to make an excellent judge. Governor Hobby said that he had heard some very unkind things said about this gentleman. I told the Governor that I had never known of any man who was an applicant for an official position and who had opposition, who had not had unkind things said about him. I had no interest in the matter, and I assumed that the Governor was not going to appoint this gentleman.

The next morning I discovered on the front page of the *Austin American*, the morning paper published in Austin, that Governor Hobby had appointed this gentleman as a judge on the San Antonio Court of Civil Appeals. A few days later I received a very nice letter from this gentleman thanking me for what I had done in obtaining the appointment for him. My friend had, of course, in the meantime acquainted the new judge with the effort that I had made in his behalf. I do not think that anything that I said to Governor Hobby had anything to do with his making the appointment. I did recount these facts to Mr. Williams and told him that I had a right to think that I had one friend at least on the San Antonio Court. Each Court of Civil Appeals has three judges.

The case was submitted to the Court of Civil Appeals on oral argument, with Mr. G. B. Smedley and Mr. John Gregg arguing the case for the appellants, who were, of course, the defendants in the trial court. Mr. Williams and I argued the case for Mr. Shuler and the State.

Under the rule of the court, the side making the opening argument had a right to make an opening argument lasting one hour; then the other side could be heard for one hour, and then the party making the opening argument had a right to conclude with an argument lasting fifteen minutes. The court could, upon request or by its own motion, extend the time for oral argument. Frequently an extension of time is granted when the case is an important one. The attorneys on both sides in this case thought the case an important one, because the land was supposed to have a value of three or four million dollars and had already produced oil having a value of approximately $800,000. The attorneys for both sides accordingly filed a joint motion requesting an extension of time for oral argument so that each side would have two hours.

When our case was called, the Chief Justice announced that the motion for additional time for oral argument had been considered by the Court and had been overruled. He said it was his own personal opinion that there was no case that would justify more than one hour's argument to each side. The Court permitted a division of time, so that Mr. Gregg, in opening for the Gulf Production Company, could use half of the seventy-five minutes that he and Mr. Smedley had between them, and Mr. Williams, who would make the opening argument for our side, would use thirty minutes, and I would use the remaining thirty minutes.

Mr. Gregg made the opening argument for his side and made a splendid presentation of his case. John Gregg was a young lawyer, but he had a keen legal mind and was in every respect an able lawyer and a fine gentleman. He was a son of former Congressman Gregg of East Texas. Mr. Gregg died, I believe, within a short time after the argument of this case.

Mr. Williams followed Mr. Gregg and made a sound legal argument. I followed Mr. Williams, and as there was much that I wanted to say that needed to be said, I spoke, contrary to my usual habit, very rapidly in order to get everything said that I could within the limited time which the court had given me. After I had almost finished my argument, the Chief Justice realized that there were important questions involved in the case which should be discussed, that could not be discussed in the limited time that the lawyers had been given. He conferred with his associates, and then interrupted me to announce that the court had concluded to extend the time for argument by granting an additional forty-five minutes to each side. By this time I had used up practically all of my original time and had summarized in a brief and in an unsatisfactory way the points I desired to present to the court. The granting of the additional time, after I had practically completed my argument, was highly confusing. I used a portion of the additional time, and then asked that Mr. Williams be permitted to use the remainder. Williams was in the same position that I had been in. He had already made a brief summary of the points he desired to present, and to be called on for an additional argument meant that he could only elaborate on what he had already said. The whole thing was highly unsatisfactory to Mr. Williams and me. Mr. Smedley was sitting there with an additional forty-five minutes added to his original time in which to answer both Mr. Williams and me.

Mr. Smedley had the closing argument, and with the additional time that had been granted, had almost an hour and a half in which to answer the arguments made by Mr. Williams and me. Mr. Smedley is one of the best land lawyers in the State of Texas. He never fails to make a clear and concise argument. With an hour and a half at his command, he reviewed the history of land legislation in the State of Texas, and pointed out that from the days of the Republic up to the present time it had always been the intent and purpose of the Legislature, both of the Republic and of the State, to protect the rights of those who purchased land from the State for the purpose of settling and making their homes thereon. He then reviewed the evidence of the case and repeatedly directed the attention of the court to the fact that Mr. Shuler had received, under the judgment of the district court, more than $225,000 in cash, and personal property of the value of $114,000, and the title to seven-eighths of the oil that remained in the land, probably worth millions of dollars, all for the consideration of ten cents an acre, for the mineral permit and certain filing fees, amounting in all to less than twenty dollars.

The continued repetition by Mr. Smedley of the great amount to be realized by Shuler from the mineral permit which he had obtained for twenty dollars may not have been a strong legal argument, but judges are human, and some of them are very much so. This argument of Mr. Smedley apparently convinced the Chief Justice that a great injustice had been perpetrated, because the Chief Justice was declaring from the bench before Smedley concluded his argument, that any law that authorized the State of Texas to take a proved oil field away from those who had, at great risk and expense, discovered the oil and developed the field, and give seven-eighths of it away for a twenty-dollar bill, was an outrageous law.

I do not mean to say that Mr. Smedley dwelt entirely on Shuler's permit and the amount of money that he had paid the State. He did not do this. He made a masterly legal argument and referred to the ten cents per acre permit just often enough to keep that fact continually in the minds of the judges of the court. Mr. Smedley based his legal argument on the proposition that when Kidd went to the office of the County Clerk and asked the County Clerk to fill in the appraised value of the land on his purchase application, and the Clerk went to his books and then filled in the appraised value at $1.50 per acre, that there must necessarily at that time have been on record in the office of the County Clerk a notice from the Land Commissioner advising that the land had been appraised at $1.50 per acre.

Then he stressed the fact that the endorsements on Kidd's application to purchase showed on their face that the proper clerks in the land office had examined the records of that office in connection with Kidd's application to purchase, and had approved the application to purchase the land at $1.50 per acre, and that, therefore, there must have been at that time an appraisement of this land on record in the General Land Office at $1.50 per acre. These facts, so Mr. Smedley contended, raised a conclusive legal presumption that the land had been appraised at $1.50 per acre at the time of the sale at that price, and a notice of such appraisement had been sent by the Land Commissioner to the County Clerk of Stephens County.

A few weeks later the Court decided the case. The opinion appears in 231 S. W. 124. The judge who wrote the opinion of the Court was the gentleman that I had asked Governor Hobby to appoint. He held that the evidence conclusively established the fact that the land had been appraised at $1.50 per acre at the time it was sold to J. M. Kidd. He overruled the cross assignments of error presented by the State of Texas and Shuler, reversed the judgment of the District Court, and entered judgment in favor of the defendants. Mr. Shuler and the State in due time filed a motion for rehearing. This motion was overruled by the Court. On this motion for rehearing, the judge who had, prior to becoming a judge, been for many years the land lawyer for a railroad company, wrote a strong dissenting opinion in which he agreed with every contention that had been made by the State and Mr. Shuler. In his dissenting opinion this judge declared that the State had introduced evidence to show that the land had, by the proper authority at the time of the alleged purchase, been valued at $2.00 an acre, and that it was sold to Kidd at $1.50 per acre. He then wrote:

> This issue of fact was fairly presented to the jury, who found against Kidd's contention, that is, the land was not valued at $1.50 per acre, but at $2.00 per acre. Accepting their finding, as we must, then Kidd acquired no right against the State. This Court, in its majority opinion, for the facts and reasons stated, decided to set aside the finding of the jury and substitute therefor the Court's findings and conclusions in lieu thereof, which cannot be done. I understand that it is well settled, it is true, that there is always a presumption of law that officials do their duty, but I do not understand that there

is any rule of law that will justify this presumption or inference to overcome the findings of the jury, where there is some evidence to sustain the jury's findings, however slight the evidence may be. The State will not be, in such case, estopped or bound by illegal acts of her officers.

The Mineral Permit Law was, in my opinion, a very unwise law. The fact remains, however, that there was a question of fact as to whether this land had been appraised at $2.00 an acre or $1.50 an acre at the time it was sold to Kidd. The jury found, as a fact, that the land was appraised at $2.00 an acre when it was sold to Kidd at $1.50 per acre. There was ample evidence to support this finding of the jury. The Court of Civil Appeals had no rightful authority to set aside this finding of fact by the jury and substitute in lieu thereof its own finding of fact. I will always believe that we lost the case because of the extension of time that was granted for oral arguments, and under which extension of time Mr. Smedley was permitted, as I have related, to have an hour and a half in which to make his concluding argument. In due course, Mr. Shuler and the State of Texas filed in the Supreme Court of Texas an application for writ of error. This the Supreme Court refused to grant.

Mr. Lud Williams, who made the great argument to the jury in the Gulf Production Company case, while a great criminal lawyer, could not free all the men he defended. He once told me the following story. (I have substituted fictitious names for the people mentioned by Mr. Williams.)

I defended a man by the name of Frank Brown on a murder charge. Brown was charged with killing a very prominent citizen. The deceased had a brother, Robert Jones, who was one of the most influential men in Texas. Brown was convicted and sentenced to life imprisonment. On appeal, the judgment of conviction was affirmed, and he went to prison.

For years I tried to obtain a pardon for Brown. Jones, however, made it his business to acquaint every new governor with the facts of the case, and I could not get a pardon for Brown. Finally both the Governor and the Lieutenant Governor were out of the state, and Senator Wise, President pro tern of the Senate, was the acting Governor. Wise and I were good friends. This was, I thought, my opportunity to get a pardon for Frank Brown.

The morning that Senator Wise assumed his duties as acting Governor, I was in Austin to see him. When I was ushered into the Governor's office, Senator Wise said: " 'Hello, Lud. What in the hell do you want?' I told him I wanted a pardon for Frank Brown.

"Nothing doing. Robert Jones saw me about that yesterday, and I promised him I would not pardon Brown. I will pardon anyone else you want me to."

I thought for a moment and remembered a young man by the name of Jim Hill that I had defended, and who had been convicted and was then in prison. I told Senator Wise that I wanted a pardon for this young man.

"What did he do?" Wise asked.

"Oh, he burned two or three cotton gins," I replied.

"All right," the Senator said. "I will pardon him for you. We have too many damn gins anyway."

The father of Jim Hill lived a long ways from Waco, and when I got back home, in Waco, I called the old man over long distance to tell him the good news. When the connection had been made, I said to him: "This is Lud Williams. I called to tell you that I was in Austin this morning, and Senator Wise, who is acting Governor, has pardoned Jim."

"How's that?" the old man asked.

I repeated what I had said, and added, "Jim will be home in two or three days."

"The hell he will!" the old man answered. "Jim is here now. The Governor pardoned him a month ago."

CHAPTER XIII:
THE RED RIVER BOUNDARY CASE

It is sometimes said that the great trial lawyer is born and not made. The statement is not entirely accurate. That there are men with a genius for trying lawsuits is a fact that no trial lawyer of experience will deny. There is, however, in the legal profession no substitute for careful, painstaking work. Lawsuits are not always won in the courtroom. The days, weeks and sometimes months of careful preparation for the trial are what often earns the victory.

The successful trial lawyer must know how to plead his case so as to present to the court and to the jury every issue in the case that is favorable to his client. He must be a master of the law of evidence. When a question is asked a witness by opposing counsel, there is no time to go to a law library and ascertain whether the answer called for by the question is or is not admissible. The lawyer must act instantly. If he fails to object to the question, or if he objects but fails to make the proper objection, the witness will be permitted to answer.

From the facts of the case the law governing that case arises. The facts of a case are proved by written documents and the evidence of witnesses. Important lawsuits have been lost because evidence was permitted to go to the jury that would have been excluded by the judge, if proper objection to its admissibility had been made. It is sometimes error even to ask a witness a certain question. The error, however, is lost unless an exception is taken and preserved for the record so that it may be reviewed on appeal by the higher court. Exception to every adverse action and ruling of the trial judge must be taken at the right time and in the right manner. The trial court may commit a gross error, one for which the final judgment of the trial court would be reversed by a higher court; but the error is waived if timely and proper objection is not made.

In the Texas courts, civil cases are submitted to the jury on special issues. The statute authorizing the submission of a case to the jury on special issues is simple, but the courts in construing the statute have made it a most difficult and complex subject. Perhaps fifty per cent of the cases that are reversed by the higher courts in Texas are reversed because the trial judge did the wrong thing, or failed to do the right thing in the form in which he submitted the case to the jury on special issues.

For many years I was a defense lawyer for railroads and insurance companies. I do not recall a single case which I lost in the trial court for a railroad or for an insurance company that I did not reverse in the higher courts, and generally the reversal by the higher court was because of some error committed by the trial court in submitting the case to the jury on special issues. It may be said that such reversals were on technicalities. I deny this. I reiterate that there is no such thing as a technicality of the law. A thing is either the law or it is not the law. In Texas, the trial lawyer must know the law of special issues.

Then there is that indefinable thing called the technique of trying a lawsuit. Some lawyers can and do create an atmosphere beneficial to their client in the trial of a lawsuit. This is something that cannot be accurately described. The natural talent of the lawyer, his personality, the manner in which he conducts himself, all form a part of his technique in the trial of a lawsuit. Some of the better trial lawyers are actors of great ability. I have seen lawyers simulate anger for the purpose of making it appear to the jury that they felt that something which had occurred and which was detrimental to their client was an outrage and should never have been permitted to occur. I have also seen lawyers smile at the testimony of a witness that hurt, and badly hurt, their cause, in an effort to make the jury believe that the testimony was of no consequence.

All these things are important, vitally important; in fact, they are the essentials of the trial lawyer's equipment, but the trial lawyer should know something more than the mechanics of the law. He should have a sound knowledge of substantive law. In every case the facts are different, and different rules of law are applicable. If the trial lawyer has learned the fundamentals of the substantive law, any competent law clerk can find, under his direction, the authorities, including the latest court decisions, which support the legal propositions relied on. This is not all the trial lawyer should know. The law is the product of the government. Therefore, the trial lawyer should be learned in history and in government. The government is, within the confines of the Constitution, at any given time, what a small group of men who happen to be in power want it to be. These men, who are for a time the government, are influenced in their acts by their environment, heredity, and the existing economic situation. The trial lawyer should be a student of the history of men and how they be have when invested with great power, and he should know the law of economics.

The trial lawyer is called upon to examine and cross-examine witnesses who are experts in many different professions. He cannot examine or cross-examine an expert witness or even understand his testimony, unless he has some knowledge of the subject the witness is being interrogated about, whether that subject is engineering, geology, medicine, botany, physics, chemistry, auditing, or the operation of a railroad train. There is not much that a lawyer can learn that will not at sometime or other be a real help to him in his professional work. Early in my career I began to buy books, and with the passing years, I accumulated thousands of books, on many subjects, and these I read and studied.

The value of real scholarship to a lawyer was well illustrated in Texas' most famous lawsuit, the Red River Boundary Case. The official style of this case is State of Oklahoma vs. State of Texas, the United States intervenor. When one state sues another state, the suit must be brought directly in the Supreme Court of the United States, for that court is the only court that has original jurisdiction to try a lawsuit between two states.

In the Red River boundary suit, the State of Oklahoma sued the State of Texas, and the United States intervened in the suit on the side of Oklahoma, for the purpose of protecting the rights, if any, of the Indian wards of the United States Government.

The suit was brought for the purpose of having the court ascertain and cause to be marked on the ground the boundary line between the State of Oklahoma and the State of Texas along the Red River for a distance of about six hundred miles.

The United States had acquired what is now the State of Oklahoma as a part of Louisiana by purchase from Napoleon. At the time of this purchase no one knew the boundary lines of Louisiana. The story is told that when the treaty between France and the United States was being drawn, whereby France was selling Louisiana to the United States, one of Napoleon's ministers advised him that it was impossible accurately to fix the boundary lines of the territory being sold and that necessarily the terms of the treaty in regard to the description of the territory would be ambiguous.

To this Napoleon is reported to have said: "That is all right. I prefer it that way. If, in fact, the treaty is not ambiguous, make it so. I may need an excuse some day for declaring war against the United States."

It was the contention of Oklahoma and of the United States that the boundary line between Oklahoma and Texas along the Red River was the south bank of said river, as said bank existed in 1819 at the time the treaty was made between the King of Spain and the United States, fixing the boundary line between Texas and the United States; that the south bank of Red River in 1819 was at the bluffs which are from one to eight miles south of the present location of the bed of Red River.

If Oklahoma and the United States won the suit, Texas would lose about one million acres of its territory, and the individuals who owned the land under titles emanating from the State of Texas would lose their lands. Much of this land is rich river-bottom farming land, and near Wichita Falls there was a great oil field north of the bluffs and extending to the center of the sand bar of the present bed of Red River that would be lost, if Oklahoma and the United States prevailed in the litigation. The value of the oil field alone was conservatively estimated at $300,000,000. The value of the other lands, which included many fine cotton plantations, was estimated at not less than $40,000,000.

Texas filed a cross-action seeking to establish and to fix on the ground the true boundary line between the eastern line of the Panhandle of Texas and the western line of Oklahoma. As to this part of the boundary line between Texas and Oklahoma, Texas claimed that the true boundary line was far enough east of the boundary line claimed by Oklahoma and the United States to include within the boundaries of Texas about forty thousand acres of land that had theretofore been a part of Oklahoma.

It was the contention of Texas that the true boundary line between the State of Texas and the State of Oklahoma along the Red River was the center of the bed of said river, and that the present bed of Red River was approximately where it had been in 1819.

It will be observed from the foregoing that there were two issues in the lawsuit, one of law and one of fact, in regard to the location of the boundary line along Red River. The issue of law was whether the south bank or the center of the river was the boundary line. The issue of fact was the location of the river bed in 1819, at the time the treaty was made between the United States and Spain.

In order to determine the issue of fact, it was necessary for all parties to the litigation to employ experts in geology, botany, ecology and soil, as well as engineers familiar with the history and behavior of rivers and watercourses. It was necessary to make innumerable soil tests along the course of the river. Trees had to be examined as to their age and condition. Plants had to be studied. The river's course had to be surveyed. Expert engineers had to trace and retrace on the ground the boundary line between the Panhandle of Texas and the west line of Oklahoma.

Voluminous testimony, forming four large volumes, was taken under the supervision of a Master appointed for the purpose by the Supreme Court of the United States. As chief counsel for Texas, Mr. Cureton had to examine the witnesses for Texas and cross-examine the witnesses for Oklahoma and the United States. He could not examine his own many expert witnesses, experts on many different subjects, and intelligently cross-examine the opposing expert witnesses until he himself was familiar with each subject on which they were to testify.

Mr. Cureton had been a student all his life, and he was not unfamiliar with the subjects that the expert witnesses were called to testify about. However, he was not satisfied to rely on the knowledge that he already possessed on these subjects. He bought book after book on geology, botany, soils, and the history and behavior of rivers, and on engineering. These books Mr. Cureton studied, and studied so well and with such painstaking care that he was able to successfully examine his own witnesses, and to confuse by his cross-examination some of the greatest experts in this country on geology, botany, soils and rivers. No expert witness introduced by Oklahoma or the United States was able to make any loose or general statement under the cross-examination of Mr. Cureton, nor did Mr. Cureton permit any opposing witness to state a conclusion until he had first stated in minutest detail the facts upon which he predicated his conclusion.

By the time Mr. Cureton had cross-examined the opposing witnesses on the minute details of their investigation of the physical facts, the conclusion of the witnesses (that the Red River in 1819 ran against the bluffs far south of where the river now flows) was weakened or destroyed. This examination of many experts in different fields of science by Mr. Cureton was a masterly piece of work. I doubt if in the history of jurisprudence, in this or any other country, it was ever surpassed.

This scientific work was not all that had to be done. A painstaking search of history had to be made, and the records of the Secretary of State at Washington had to be examined carefully in order to get the facts, and all the facts, pertaining to the correspondence leading up to and resulting in the treaty of 1819 between the United States and the King of Spain. Much correspondence had passed between the diplomatic representatives of the United States and Spain before the boundary treaty was finally signed between the contracting parties and ratified by the Senate of the United States. This correspondence was of great importance. By the terms of the treaty, the boundary line was fixed as follows:

> The boundary line between the two countries, west of the Mississippi, shall begin on the Gulf of Mexico, at the mouth of the River Sabine in the sea, continuing north along the west bank of the river, to the 32nd degree of latitude; thence by a line due north to the 33rd degree of latitude, where it strikes the Rio Roxo of Natchitoches, or Red River; then following the course of the Rio Roxo westward to the degree of longitude 100 west from London and 23 from Washington, then crossing the said river, and running thence due north to the River Arkansas...

A casual reading of the treaty provisions set out above would indicate a certain ambiguity in its terms, but this apparent ambiguity disappears when one understands the law that is applicable to river surveys, whether forming boundary lines between nations or boundary lines between private landowners.

When in a survey, or in fixing a boundary line, a river is called for as a line, the center of the river is always meant unless the contrary is indicated, but if the river is the boundary between private owners of land, then, if it is a navigable stream, the boundary line always stops at the edge of the water.

That the high contracting parties to the treaty were well aware of this international as well as domestic law, is in-

dicated by the fact that in fixing the boundary line of the
Sabine River, it was declared that the boundary should be
"along the west bank of the River." Without the use of this
specific language, the center of the Sabine would have been
the boundary line. When the boundary line left the Sabine,
the call was north to "where it strikes the Rio Roxo of
Natchitoches, or Red River," and the next call is "then following the course of the Red River westward" to where the
boundary line turns north, "then crossing said river."

The call to follow the course of the Red River westward was
clearly a call for the center of the river. The fact that when the
boundary turned and went north it called to cross the river,
does not change the rule, for the boundary line running up
the center of the river could not get to the north side without
crossing half the river. Therefore, the call to cross the river
was a correct use of language and did not, in the absence of
a specific call for the south bank of the river as a boundary
line, indicate an intent on the part of the high contracting
parties to fix the south bank as the boundary line. That this
is correct is established by the fact that exact language was
used when calling for the Sabine River, specifically fixing the
boundary line at the west bank of that river. If it had been the
intent of the parties to fix the boundary line on Red River at
the south bank of the river, it is self-evident that definite language to that effect would have been used. To the contrary,
language was used in calling for the Red River boundary
that, by a common usage recognized alike by courts of the
United States and Spain, called for the center of the river.

At the time the treaty was made, rivers were the high-
ways for transportation. A nation did not have the right
to navigate a stream wholly within another nation, unless
authorized by treaty to do so. Mr. Cureton, in his reading
and in his study of the subject, had become convinced that
the Red River in 1819 had been a navigable stream. If it
was a navigable stream at the time the treaty was made, that
would be an important reason why Spain had insisted that
the center of the river be the boundary line. If the center of

the river was the boundary line, then Spain and the United States had equal rights of navigation. Mr. Cureton caused a painstaking search to be made of many ancient records and documents, and from these he established the fact that the Red River in 1819 was a navigable stream.

John Quincy Adams was Secretary of State at the time the treaty was made. Like all members of the Adams family, John Quincy was a patriot, a voluminous writer, and not without personal egotism largely justified by his splendid abilities. He kept a diary. In this diary he recorded in detail many of the things that he did, and many of the things he observed others doing. In this diary he recorded that he had won a great diplomatic victory in the treaty of 1819 over Spain, in that the latter had finally agreed that the south bank of Red River should be the boundary line between the United States and the Spanish possessions. It may be that Spain did so agree, but, if so, both parties neglected to record that fact in the treaty itself.

There was another obstacle in the way of Mr. Cureton's establishing the center of Red River as the boundary line. By Act of Congress of May 2, 1890, the Attorney General of the United States was directed to institute suit in the Supreme Court of the United States against the State of Texas, "for the tract of land lying between the north and south forks of Red River where the State of Texas and the Indian Territory adjoin, east of the 100th meridian of longitude, and claimed by the State of Texas as within its land, and designated on its map as Greer County." The suit was instituted as directed.

The north and south forks of Red River unite at a point a few miles north of Vernon, Texas. The question in the case of the United States vs. Texas was whether the south or north fork of Red River was the boundary line. The answer to this question depended upon which fork of the river was the Red River referred to in the treaty of 1819. The United States claimed that the south fork was the Red River of the treaty. Texas claimed it was the north fork. The United States did not allege that the south bank of the south fork of the river was the boundary line. It simply alleged that the south fork of the river was the Red River of the treaty and was therefore the boundary line.

The court, however, in its decree in the case of United States vs. Texas declared that the true boundary line prescribed by the treaty of 1819 between the United States and Spain was "along the south bank both of Red River and of the river known as Prairie Dog Town fork or south fork of Red River until such line meets the 100th meridian of longitude." By this decree the State of Texas lost the territory that had been Greer County, Texas, and which is now Greer, Harmon, Jackson, and a part of Beckham counties, Oklahoma. The court declared without the question ever being before it, that "the south bank" of the south fork was the boundary prescribed by the treaty of 1819 between the United States and Spain. (United States vs. Texas, 162 U. S., 1.)

The case of the United States vs. Texas is generally referred to as the Greer County case and was decided in 1896. The very able lawyer who was then Attorney General of Texas had been assisted in the trial of the Greer County case by some of the greatest lawyers in Texas. Apparently it never occurred to these eminent lawyers to file a motion with the Supreme Court requesting that the form of the decree be corrected, wherein the court had declared "the south bank both of Red River and the river known as Prairie Dog Town Fork or south fork of Red River" was the boundary line prescribed by the treaty of 1819. It is believed that such a motion would have been granted, for there was no issue before the court as to whether the boundary line was the center or the south bank of the south fork of Red River. If it occurred to the eminent lawyers representing the State of Texas in the Greer County case that the decree of the Supreme Court was incorrect in attempting to fix the boundary line along the south bank both of Red River and the south fork of Red River, they probably considered it of no importance. They probably thought it did not make any difference whether the boundary line was in the center or on the south bank of Red

River. The judgment of the Supreme Court fixing the south bank both of Red River and of the south fork of Red River as the boundary line became a final judgment.

If the location of the boundary line on the south bank of the river had been properly raised by the pleadings of the United States and supported by any proof thereof, the judgment of the court had become *res judicata* and could not thereafter be questioned. Mr. Cureton was fearful that this decree of the court, even though not supported by any pleadings, became *stare decisis*, that is, a precedent, because it represented the deliberate opinion of the Supreme Court that the south bank and not the center of the river was the boundary line.

When Oklahoma and the United States sued Texas to establish the boundary line as the south bank of Red River from the 100th meridian to the eastern line of Texas, and contended that the bluffs far south of the present bed of the river were the south bank in 1819 when the treaty was made, Mr. Cureton was confronted with the proposition that the Supreme Court had already decided that the south bank was the boundary line. He therefore made a deliberate attack upon that part of the court's judgment in the Greer County case that fixed the boundary as the south bank of the river.

In the trial of this famous case, Mr. Cureton was assisted by Honorable Thomas Watt Gregory, former Attorney General of the United States under the administration of Woodrow Wilson; C. Carroll Todd, of Washington, D. C; Judge R. H. Ward, of San Antonio; Walter A. Keeling, First Assistant Attorney General; and by his assistants, C. W. Taylor, Thomas Beauchamp, Walace Hawkins, and me.

The judgment of the court in the Greer County case, fixing the south bank of the river as the boundary, and the assertions of John Quincy Adams recorded in his diary were too great to be overcome. The court decided that its judgment in the Greer County case was *res judicata*, and that even if it were not, the true boundary was the south bank of the river.

This decision of the court cleared the way for the next question to be determined; namely, where was the south bank of Red River in 1819? The court decided this question largely in favor of the State of Texas, and caused what it held to be the south bank of Red River to be permanently marked on the ground. The State of Texas lost but little of its lands south of Red River and saved practically all of its Wichita County oil field. The court decided in favor of Mr. Cureton's contentions as to the location of the boundary line between the western boundary of Oklahoma and the Panhandle of Texas. The value of these lands recovered from Oklahoma was probably equal in value to that of the small area of territory lost by Texas south of the present bed of Red River. As usual in such cases, innocent people suffered great loss.

Those who had acquired lands from the State of Texas south of the present bed of the Red River, and whose lands were by the decree of the court made a part of Oklahoma, lost their lands. The citizens of Oklahoma who had acquired title to their lands from the United States, and whose lands were decreed to be a part of the State of Texas, lost their lands.

CHAPTER XIV:
CONTEMPT OF COURT - TEXAS VS OKLAHOMA

While the main battle in the Red River boundary suit was fought in the Supreme Court of the United States, there were innumerable legal skirmishes fought in other and inferior courts.

In the Wichita Falls district, the land north of the bluffs and between the bluffs and the center of the river is not good land for agricultural or grazing purposes. Early settlers in this section of the State located their land with the bluffs, lying at this point several miles south of the Red River, as the north boundary lines of their farms and ranches. Later settlers and oil speculators bought the lands between the bluffs and the river. When oil was discovered between the bluffs and the river, the land lying between the bluffs and the river, which at one time had been considered worthless, became of fabulous value. Some of the owners of the lands whose north boundary was the bluffs contended that their land went to the river, wherever the river was, on the theory that the river was at one time at the bluffs, and that as the bed of the river had moved northward, the land between the bluffs and the river was added to their land by accretion. The State had many lawsuits with these people. Mr. Cureton assigned to me the task of representing the State in these lawsuits, all of which were won by the State.

Another cause of even greater annoyance, and one that appeared at one time likely to result in civil war, was that people of Oklahoma filed on the oil land between the bluffs and the river with the proper officials of the United States and Oklahoma, and moved on the land with armed men. In some instances these men from Oklahoma drove the Texas owners and their oil field workers away from the oil wells and took possession of the land. Governor Hobby had the Texas Rangers establish a camp on the land in order to protect the rights of the Texas claimants. In order to afford legal protection to the Rangers, in the event they were compelled to use force to protect the land from the Oklahoma invaders, I secured injunctions against some of the men from Oklahoma in the 53rd District Court of Travis County, Texas, restraining them from coming upon this land and interfering with the possession thereof by the Texas claimants. One gentleman from Oklahoma disobeyed the injunction issued against him. I cited this gentleman for contempt, and to my surprise, he actually came to Texas and submitted himself to the jurisdiction of the 53rd District Court of Travis County. He was tried before Judge Calhoun, found guilty of contempt, and fined $100 and sent to jail until such time as he purged himself of contempt by promising that he would in the future obey the injunction of the court. He immediately made such a promise and was promptly released from custody.

In the meantime, the District Court of Cottle County, Oklahoma, was issuing, at the instance of Oklahoma claimants, a number of injunctions against the Texas landowners. The Texas landowners disobeyed these injunctions, and when cited for contempt, refused to appear in the Oklahoma court, and as the Oklahoma officers had no desire to come across the river and attempt to arrest them with Texas Rangers present on the ground, none of the Texans were ever tried for contempt in the Oklahoma District Court.

Some of the Oklahoma claimants applied to the United States Court for the Western District of Oklahoma for injunctive relief, and secured a mandatory injunction commanding the Texas Rangers, who were on this land under orders from Governor Hobby, and the Texas men claiming title under the State of Texas to get off this land and to surrender it to the Oklahoma claimants. It was one thing to ignore the orders of an Oklahoma State Court and a very different thing to disobey the orders of the United States Court.

A copy of the injunction from the United States Court was delivered to Governor Hobby and he immediately requested an opinion from Mr. Cureton as to the legality of the mandatory injunction, and as to whether or not, as Governor of Texas, he should order the Texas Rangers to remain on the land or to retire from the land as directed by the United States Court. Mr. Cureton assigned to Assistant Attorney General C. W. Taylor and me the task of ascertaining whether, as a matter of law, the mandatory injunction issued by the United State Court was a valid injunction.

When I was directed to assist Mr. Taylor in this matter, I was a younger and much less experienced lawyer than I am now. I respected but did not fear the power of a United State District Judge.

Mr. Taylor and I concluded that the injunction decree issued by the United States District Judge was void, and of no force and effect, for the following reasons:

1. A judge does not have the power or the authority to issue a mandatory injunction dispossessing people of land until the question of who has the title to the land has been adjudicated and determined by a court of competent jurisdiction in a suit brought for that purpose.

2. That the jurisdiction of the United States District Court for the Western District of Oklahoma over persons and property was limited to persons residing within and to property located in the territory embraced within the Western District of Oklahoma.

3. That the injunction decree was an attempt on the part of the United States District Judge for the Western District of Oklahoma to exercise jurisdiction over land located south of the present bed of Red River, land over which the Republic of Texas and the State of Texas had, since 1836, claimed to be within the boundaries of the Republic, or the State, and over which these governments had continuously exercised governmental powers and jurisdiction.

4. The United States District Judge for the Western District of Oklahoma by his injunction decree was attempting to exercise jurisdiction over the persons of citizens and officers of Texas by commanding them to get off land over which the Republic of Texas, or the State of Texas, had continuously exercised civil and criminal jurisdiction since 1836.

5. A United States District Judge in Oklahoma could not decide the question as to whether this land was in Texas or Oklahoma; the Supreme Court of the United States was the court, and the only court, that could decide that question, and a suit was even then pending in the Supreme Court for the purpose of having that court determine the question.

We had no difficulty in finding plenty of respectable legal authority to support our conclusions. We drafted an opinion addressed to the Governor in which he was advised that in the opinion of the Attorney General, the injunction issued by the United States District Court for the Western District of Oklahoma was void.

To violate or to advise others to violate an injunction of a United States court constitutes contempt of court, provided the court had jurisdiction to issue the injunction. Punishment for such contempt is a heavy fine and usually the guilty person is confined in prison until he promises to obey the injunction. It seems to be the law that a person who wilfully violates a lawful order of a United States District Court, or who advises others to disobey such order, may be confined in prison for such length of time as the court may, in its discretion, believe to be proper punishment for the contempt.

Governor Hobby advised the Texas Rangers to stay on the land, which, in fact, they had never left, and for this disobedience of the court's order, the Rangers were cited to appear before the United States Court in Oklahoma City and show cause why they were not in contempt of court. The hearing on the contempt proceedings had been set down for a certain day, but the actual physical presence of the Texas Rangers was waived, and it was only necessary for the Texas lawyers to appear and present the Rangers' defense to the contempt proceedings.

The night before we were to leave Austin for Oklahoma City, there was a final and lengthy conference held in the office of the Attorney General. Mr. Cureton was in Washington in connection with matters pertaining to the boundary suit in the Supreme Court of the United States. Present at the conference were Judge Victor Brooks, of Austin; Thomas Watt Gregory, former Attorney General of the United States; Walter Keeling, then First Assistant Attorney General of Texas and later Attorney General of Texas; Mr. C. W. Taylor; Mr. C. L. Black, of Austin; others whose names I do not recall, and I. Former Attorney General Gregory was very much disturbed about the situation. As a former Attorney General of the United States, he was well aware of the power of a United States District Judge, and he may have known how some United States District Judges abuse the power that is vested in them. Mr. Gregory made it very clear to all of us that it was entirely possible that all the Rangers would be found guilty of contempt, and that citation for contempt might be issued by the court against Governor Hobby for instructing the Rangers to disobey the mandatory injunction, and against Attorney General Cureton, Mr. Taylor and me for writing an opinion advising the Governor that the mandatory injunction of the United States District Court was void. Mr. C. W. Taylor and I, who had formulated the opinion which had been sent to the Governor, were sitting together during the time that Mr. Gregory was making his alarming talk. At the conclusion of Mr. Gregory's remarks, Mr. Taylor turned to me and said, "By God, Smith, you and I need a lawyer."

The morning our party arrived in Oklahoma City, the *Daily Oklahoman*, a daily newspaper published in Oklahoma City, declared in its issue of that morning, in red ink on the front page, that "Texas lawyers will not be permitted to appear in court." It developed that the statement in the paper was incorrect. The judge who had issued the injunction did not preside at the hearing on the contempt proceedings. Judge Williams, of the Eastern District of Oklahoma, had come to Oklahoma City for the purpose of hearing the contempt proceedings. He was, so he said, outraged at the story appearing in the *Daily Oklahoman.*

During the course of the hearing before Judge Williams, a short recess was taken for some reason, and during this recess the United States Marshal called Mr. Taylor and me into his office and told us, in effect, that he was very much disturbed by the contempt proceedings, because if the court found that the Texas Rangers were guilty of contempt, warrants would be issued for their arrest, and it would be the duty of the marshal to cross the Red River and arrest the Texas Rangers. The marshal made it clear to Mr. Taylor and me that he did not look forward with any anticipation of pleasure to attempting to arrest the Texas Rangers south of the Red River. Mr. Taylor and I advised the marshal that he, too, needed a lawyer.

The contempt proceedings lasted for an entire day. Mr. Gregory, who, as Attorney General, had recommended to President Wilson the appointment of Judge Williams as United States District Judge for the Eastern District of Oklahoma, argued the case for the Texas Rangers, and made a magnificent argument in support of the proposition that the Rangers could not possibly be guilty of any contempt of the United States District Court for the Western District of Oklahoma. It became apparent by the questions asked and the remarks made by Judge Williams that he did not think the Rangers were in contempt. The attorneys for the private individuals who had secured the injunction realized this, and at the end of the day it was suggested that the court hold in abeyance until some future time the question as to whether or not the Rangers were in contempt. So far as I know, the matter is still being held in abeyance by the court.

Because of the friction that I have mentioned between the courts of Oklahoma and the courts of Texas, and because of this attempt on the part of the United States District Court to settle by injunction the issue as to the location of the boundary line between Oklahoma and Texas, the Supreme Court of the United States, within a few days after the hearing at Oklahoma City, took possession of the territory in dispute and appointed a receiver for the property involved. This receiver took over the operation of all the oil wells located on the territory in dispute and operated them for the benefit of whomever they might belong to, until the final disposition of the boundary suit was made by the Supreme Court of the United States.

In December, 1921, Mr. Cureton was in Washington concluding some of the matters in connection with the Red River boundary suit when Honorable Nelson Phillips, Chief Justice of the Supreme Court of Texas, resigned. The first information Mr. Cureton had that Judge Phillips had resigned was the receipt by him of a telegram from Governor Pat Neff tendering to him the office of Chief Justice of the Supreme Court of Texas. It was a promotion that Mr. Cureton had earned by his long, faithful, and efficient service to the State of Texas, as a member of the Legislature, as First Assistant Attorney General for six years, and as Attorney General for nearly three years. Mr. Cureton served as Chief Justice of the Supreme Court until his death in April, 1940. His term of service as Chief Justice was longer than any man had ever served in that office during the first one hundred years of Texas history.

The career of Judge Cureton should be an inspiration to all the sons of Texas. As a boy he worked on a ranch, and for a year was a student at the University of Virginia. When war came with Spain he enlisted as a private soldier. His record of public service is unusual. In time of peace he served his State in all three of its departments. In time of war he was a soldier. As a boy he was a student, and he never ceased to study. During his last illness he had books brought from his library to his sick room and from these he read to within a few hours of his death. Judge Cureton was a great scholar, as great as I have ever known. As a judge he was a judicial statesman.

By his appointment of Mr. Cureton as Chief Justice of the Supreme Court, Governor Neff created a vacancy in the office of Attorney General. This vacancy he filled by promoting to the office of Attorney General Honorable Walter A. Keeling, who had served so long and with such distinction in the office as an assistant during Mr. Looney's administration, and as First Assistant Attorney General during the administration of Mr. Cureton. To fill the vacancy thus created by his promotion to Attorney General, Mr. Keeling promoted me from assistant to First Assistant Attorney General.

CHAPTER XV:
TAXING OIL & GAS

Oil is a magic word in Texas. Oil was first discovered in Texas in 1889, but there was very little production until the discovery of the Spindle Top Field near Beaumont in 1901. Thereafter, other coastal fields were discovered: in Sour Lake in 1902; Batson in 1903; Saratoga and Matagorda in 1904; Humble and Dayton in 1905; and Blue Ridge in 1908. These discoveries were on privately owned land, in which the State owned no mineral interest. This new wealth was, however, a source of revenue to the State, for it could be, and was, taxed.

The real boom in Texas had its beginning with the discovery of the Ranger Field in 1917. This discovery was followed by other discoveries in West Texas, where the State owned in fee millions of acres of land, and where there were other millions of acres that had been sold by the State with an attempted reservation of the minerals. The interest of the State government in the oil industry was that of a government and a great landed proprietor.

The Attorney General had placed me in charge of the land desk, and to my desk came all the legal problems affecting the two-fold interest of the State in the oil industry. Many questions of law in regard to oil and gas had not yet been settled by the courts of Texas. In the judicial settlement of some of these questions I was to have an interesting part.

One of the legal questions that was agitating the oil industry was the legal status of the ordinary oil and gas lease. Did the owner of an oil and gas lease own an interest in the land described in the lease, or did he own a mere privilege to go upon the land and seek for oil, and, if found, to reduce it to possession? If the oil and gas lease represented an interest in the land, then that interest was taxable against the owner of the lease.

There came to my desk a letter of inquiry from the Comptroller of Public Accounts, asking for an opinion from the Attorney General as to whether oil and gas leases were taxable as an interest in land. The oil companies doing business in Texas were vitally interested in this question. The attorneys for a number of the companies requested and were given an opportunity to be heard on the question before First Assistant Attorney General Keeling, Assistant Attorney General Taylor, and me. The oil company attorneys, after discussing the legal questions involved, submitted to us written briefs in support of their contention that the oil and gas lease, in the form then in general use in Texas, did not vest in the lessee any interest in the land described in the lease. The work of writing a tentative opinion for the consideration of the Attorney General and the other lawyers in the Department was turned over to me. The question was a difficult one.

The Texas Supreme Court in the case of Texas Company vs. Daugherty, 176 S. W. 717, had held that the "so-called oil leases" before the court in that case did convey an interest in land, and that the interest so conveyed was taxable as real property. In the "so-called oil leases" before the court in the Daugherty case, the owner of the land, by the terms of the leases, "granted, bargained, sold and conveyed" to the Texas Company as grantee "all the oil, gas, coal and other minerals in and under" the land described in the leases, and further declared that the lease was "not intended as a mere franchise, but is intended as a conveyance of the property and privileges above described."

The court in its opinion in the Daugherty case said that if the "so-called oil leases" before it did no more than create a right to prospect for oil and gas, and when found, to remove it from the ground, such right, privilege or franchise would not be taxable as an interest in land.

After the Supreme Court decided the Daugherty case, the oil company lawyers changed the form of their respective oil and gas leases. In this new lease form no absolute words of conveyance were used, and instead of providing, as did the "so-called oil leases" before the court in the Daugherty case, that the lease was "not" intended as a mere franchise, the new lease form expressly declared that the lease did grant to the lessee the franchise and privilege of going upon the land to prospect for oil, and, if oil was found, to remove it from the ground.

I concluded that the new form of lease had precisely the same legal effect as did the "so-called oil leases" that were before the court in the Daugherty case. I wrote an opinion that was approved by the Attorney General, holding that the new form of lease conveyed an interest in the land described in the lease, and that this interest in the land was taxable as real property. Upon receipt of this opinion, the Comptroller of Public Accounts notified the county tax assessors and collectors of the state to levy and collect a tax on oil leases as an interest in land.

A test suit was brought by the Mid-Kansas Oil and Gas Company against the officials of Stephens County to restrain them from levying and collecting any tax on the company's oil and gas leases on land situated in Stephens County. The district court held that the leases were not taxable. Stephens County appealed the case to the Court of Civil Appeals at Fort Worth, and that court certified the question to the Supreme Court. When the case reached the Supreme Court, the officials of Stephens County suggested to the Attorney General that they would appreciate his defending in the Supreme Court the opinion of his department, holding that oil and gas leases were taxable as an interest in land. In response to this suggestion, the Attorney General instructed me to assist the attorneys representing Stephens County.

The Mid-Kansas Oil and Gas Company in this suit was represented by the law firm of Dean, Miller, Perkins and Dean. To the assistance of these lawyers came Messrs. H. G. Hendricks, R. F. Hardwick, George C. Greer, F. C. Procter and D. Edward Greer. These last named attorneys represented other oil companies that were interested in the outcome of the test suit that had been brought by the Mid-Kansas Oil and Gas Company.

The able attorneys who represented the oil companies in this suit contended with much force and logic that the Supreme Court, by the language used in its opinion in the Daugherty case, had, in effect, held that an oil and gas lease that did no more than vest in the lessee a franchise or privilege to go upon the land with the right to search for oil and gas, and, if oil and gas were discovered, to remove the same from the land, did not amount to a conveyance of any interest in the land itself. To this argument I replied:

1. That it was not necessary for the court in deciding the Daugherty case to use the language that it did use in its opinion, and upon which counsel for the oil companies relied; that this part of the court's opinion was argumentative and amounted to no more than a mere dictum of the court;

2. That while there was a difference in the language used in the "so-called oil leases" before the court in the Daugherty case and in the leases before the court in our case, the legal effect of the two forms of leases was the same;

3. That under both forms of leases, the lessee acquired the right to remove the oil from the ground, and when this had been done, the oil belonged to the lessee without any further deed of conveyance from the owner of the land. Therefore, it was the lease that conveyed the title to the oil, and as this conveyance was made when the oil was in the ground and a part of the land, the legal effect of the lease was to vest in the lessee an interest in the land;

4. That the consideration to the landowners for making and executing the leases before the court in the Daugherty case and the leases before the court in our case, was the same; that is, the right of the landowners

to receive as royalty a portion of the oil and gas produced from the land;

5. That the only right that ownership of property vests
in the owner is the right to use the property, and that
by the express terms of the leases in our case, the lessee was vested with the exclusive use of all the mineral
estate for a consideration of a portion of the oil and gas
produced from the land;

6. That there could be more than one estate in land;
that timber growing out of the surface of the land
constituted a timber estate that could be conveyed
separately and apart from the surface estate, and the
mineral estate lying below the surface estate could
likewise be conveyed separately and apart from the
surface of the land.

The court held that the oil and gas leases vested in the lessee an interest in land that was taxable as real property, and
that this interest so vested in the lessee was an estate in the
land separate and apart from the surface estate. (Mid-Kansas Oil and Gas Company vs. Stephens County, 113 Texas,
160.)

CHAPTER XVI:
OIL & INTERSTATE COMMERCE

The Government of the United States under its Constitution is a government of limited power. I am not referring to any actual government we may have had in the past, the one we have now, or that we may have in the future. My statement that the Government of the United States is a government of limited power is qualified by the phrase "under its Constitution."

In establishing our National Government, the people granted to the creature they had created the power to do certain things. In the same instrument which created the National Government, the people expressly prohibited the states from doing certain things. To remove any possibility of doubt then existing in the mind of anyone or that might thereafter at any future time exist in the mind of anyone as to their intention, the people, in 1791, adopted an amendment to the Constitution known as the Tenth Amendment, in which the people declared that: "The powers not delegated to the United States by the Constitution, nor prohibited by it to the states, are reserved to the states, respectively, or to the people."

The true test of the right of the United States under the Constitution to do a thing is: Did the people grant in the Constitution the power to the United States to do it? The true test of the right of a state to do a thing under the Constitution of the United States and its own Constitution is whether the Constitution of the United States or the Constitution of the state prohibits the state from doing it.

In other words, the United States may not under the Constitution do anything except those things which the Constitution of the United States expressly authorizes it to do or which may be necessary to carry into execution the powers expressly granted. A state may do anything that it is not prohibited from doing by the Constitution of the United States or by its own Constitution.

The public officials of the United States take a solemn oath to uphold and defend the Constitution of the United States. The public officials of a state take a solemn oath to uphold and defend the constitutions of the state and the United States. The government that we actually have depends on the good faith of our public officials. The President and a majority of the members of Congress, with a majority of the members of the Supreme Court, can, by working together, make of our National Government the kind of government that they want it to be, anything to the contrary in the Constitution notwithstanding. This small group of men can deprive a citizen of life, liberty, and property without due process of law. They can deny to the citizen freedom of speech, a free press, the right of public assembly, and the right of religious liberty.

In an effort to protect themselves from the despotism of their own government, and there is danger of despotism in any and all governments, the people provided in the Constitution that the powers of government should be divided. Certain powers were to be exercised by the Executive Department, other powers by the Legislative Department, and still other powers by the Judicial Department. It was believed and hoped that the men in each of these departments of government would be so jealous of the rights and prerogatives appertaining to themselves as members of their respective departments of the government that they would not permit any encroachment thereon by the officials of any other department.

The power of the sword is vested in the President as the Chief of the Executive Department. The power of the purse, that is, the right to appropriate money to hire men to wield the sword, is vested in the Legislative Department. The Judicial Department alone has no power within itself. It cannot even enforce its own decrees against the will of the President.

While John Marshall was Chief Justice of the United States, the Supreme Court held that an Indian tried, convicted, and sentenced to death by a state court of Georgia should be released from custody, because the Georgia Court did not have any jurisdiction over the person of the Indian. President Jackson is reported to have said: "John Marshall has written his opinion; now let him enforce it if he can."

Whether President Jackson did or did not make the statement that he is reported to have made, it is a historical fact that the Indian was hanged by the State of Georgia, notwithstanding the solemn pronouncement of the Supreme Court that the Indian had been convicted and sentenced to death by a court that had no power or authority to try him.

It has been said that our dual form of government with its divided powers and its delicate checks and balances is so complex as to make it a "horse and buggy" form of government in an age of stream-lined Diesel-engine powered dictatorships. Is our liberty, the inherent dignity of our status as free men, worth the time and thought which must be given by the people to the affairs of our government, if it is to function as those who created it intended for it to function? The recent nomination of Mr. Willkie as the Republican candidate for President is a fine example of what the people can do when they become active in the affairs of the government.

The people provided in the Constitution for short terms of office for all our public officials, except members of the Federal Judiciary. Every two years we elect all the members of the House of Representatives. One-third of our Senators are elected every two years. The President holds his office for four years. Our public elections are considered by some people as being little short of public nuisances. Our elections do disturb the peace and tranquillity of the people. This is a part of the price we must pay if we are to have the kind of government that is provided for in our Constitution. The statement is often made that our government is a democracy. The statement is inaccurate, for the people do not directly govern themselves. Under the form of government provided for in our Constitution, the people delegate the power to make, construe, and enforce the law to their chosen representatives. While the importance of having and maintaining a written constitution cannot be overemphasized, the fact remains that the kind of government that we are to have depends as much upon the kind and character of men whom the people elect to govern them as it does upon a written constitution.

The men who wrote and the men who, by their votes, adopted our National Constitution thought the judges who would necessarily have to pass upon the constitutionality of the acts of the members of the Executive Department and of the Legislative Department should be appointed for life, in order that they might be entirely free from all political passion and prejudice. I am not sure that life tenure of office for our judges is a wise thing. A judicial appointment does not always make a sheep out of a goat. Men have been tyrants on the bench as often as they have on thrones. A bad or an unwise President, who is elected to two terms, will, during the eight years he is President, have an opportunity to appoint many unfit men to judicial offices, which offices the appointees are entitled to hold during the remainder of their lives, or during their good behavior. The only way that a bad Federal Judge can be removed from office is by impeachment by the Congress of the United States. Such a proceeding is very unsatisfactory, because it takes up much time which Congress should devote to legislative matters, and the Congress is not properly organized to act in a judicial capacity. The attempt has been made to impeach only a few judges. Let us hope there have not been many instances where a judge should be impeached and removed from office.

We Americans like to boast that the Supreme Court of the United States is the greatest court in the world. We are likely to forget that the court is never at any given time any better than the men who are the judges on the court. There have been some great lawyers on the court, a few judicial statesmen, and it has been a happy landing place for some astute and shrewd politicians. I am a member of the bar of the Supreme Court of the United States; and for the court and its functions, I have a profound respect. In my opinion, however, there are a number of state supreme courts that have a far better judicial record over a long period of years than has the Supreme Court of the United States. I will agree that in one thing the Supreme Court of the United States surpasses any other court in this country, and that is its capacity to contradict itself.

A business man desires to organize and carry on a business in a certain way, provided he can legally do so. He goes to his lawyer for advice. His lawyer finds a case decided by the Supreme Court of the United States which holds that the business proposed to be conducted by the business man is a legal and legitimate business. The business man, relying on the law as declared by the Supreme Court of the United States, proceeds to organize his business venture. Years later, the business man becomes involved in litigation, and his case in due course reaches the Supreme Court of the United States and that court reverses its former decision and holds that the man's business is an illegal and unlawful business. The decision of the court may result in a heavy loss, perhaps financial ruin, to the business man. The action of the court in overruling its own former opinion is one of those "glorious uncertainties of the law" that Honorable Joseph C. Hutcheson, Jr., a United States Circuit Court Judge for the Fifth Circuit, discussed in a speech at the 1939 annual banquet of the Texas Bar Association.

A judge with a life tenure of office, knowing that he will so long as he lives, in health and in sickness, in prosperous times and in hard times, receive a salary check each month from his government, is likely to forget that he is one of the fortunate few who have financial security for however long he may live. Some of our Federal judges seem to enjoy making a plaything of the law. The doctrine of *stare decisis*, which is the law as declared by the courts in the decided cases, apparently means nothing to some judges. Some of these judges seem to enjoy setting aside former decisions of the court, making new rules of law, creating what Judge

Hutcheson was pleased to call "the glorious uncertainties of the law." These judges ignore the fact that businessmen must, in their business ventures, make long-time plans and many future commitments. Businessmen cannot afford to do this unless they first know what the law is and can depend on the law being the same in the future. High priced lawyers are employed by the businessmen to advise them what the law is, and in giving his advice, the lawyer relies on the law as it has been declared by the courts in the decided cases. To the people of this country, there is nothing glorious about the uncertainties of the law. Judges can, by making the law uncertain, greatly impair the business structure of this country.

One of the powers expressly granted by the people to Congress is the power to regulate commerce among the several states. Under this grant of power, the United States has jurisdiction over all commerce that crosses state lines. This is "interstate" commerce. The United States has no jurisdiction under the Constitution over commerce carried on wholly within the boundaries of one state. Such commerce is "intrastate" commerce, over which, under the Constitution, the state has exclusive jurisdiction.

When I was working in the Attorney General's office, Mr. Cureton directed me to defend a suit brought against him and the Comptroller of Public Accounts by Sonneborn Brothers, a partnership composed of citizens of New York and New Jersey. The suit was brought in the United States District Court for the Western District of Texas. The purpose of this suit was to restrain the Attorney General and the Comptroller of Public Accounts from collecting or attempting to collect from Sonneborn Brothers an occupation tax levied by a Texas law upon wholesale dealers in oil. This law required such wholesale dealers to pay a tax equal to two per cent of all gross sales made in Texas. There was no dispute as to the facts. Sonneborn Brothers were wholesale dealers in oil. They shipped oil products from their factory in New Jersey to Dallas, Texas, for storage in their warehouse. These oil products were then sold in Texas and delivered to the purchaser in Texas from the plaintiff's warehouse in Dallas in the original unbroken packages in which the oil had been shipped to Dallas from the plaintiff's factory in New Jersey.

In this litigation, Sonneborn Brothers was represented by Etheridge, McCormick and Bromberg of Dallas, with Mr. J. M. McCormick in charge of the case for his law firm. It was Mr. McCormick's contention that the law levying the occupation tax was unconstitutional as to his client, because the tax levied by the law was a burden on interstate commerce.

It was my contention that, when the merchandise arrived in Dallas and was stored in the warehouse, it ceased to be interstate commerce, and that, therefore, when the goods were thereafter sold, Sonneborn Brothers was liable for the tax on the sales.

It was Mr. McCormick's contention that our case was governed by the decision of the Supreme Court of the United States in the case of Standard Oil Company vs. Graves, 249 U. S., 389. This was a case that had come to the Supreme Court from the State of Washington.

The State of Washington had enacted a law which required that certain merchandise brought into that state from another state must be inspected and labeled by Washington state officials before being offered for sale. This law required the payment of an inspection fee to the State of Washington. The inspection fee was far in excess of the cost of inspection. The Standard Oil Company shipped oil from the State of California to the State of Washington, and there sold the oil in the original unbroken packages in which it had been shipped from California to Washington.

The Standard Oil Company attacked the validity of the Washington law on the ground that the inspection fee, being in an amount far above the cost of inspection, amounted to and was a tax upon the merchandise, and that this tax was a burden upon interstate commerce. This contention was upheld by the Supreme Court.

In its opinion the court wrote: "The statute imposing these excessive inspection fees in the manner stated upon all sales of oil brought into the state in interstate commerce, necessarily imposes a direct burden upon such commerce and is, therefore, violative of the commerce clause of the Federal Constitution."

It was my contention that our case was governed by the decision of the Supreme Court in the case of Wagner vs. City of Covington, 251 U. S., 95, decided December 8, 1919. The Wagner case was a much later decision by the Supreme Court than the case of Standard Oil Company vs. Graves.

Wagner was a manufacturer of soft drinks. His factory was located in Cincinnati, Ohio. The City of Covington, Kentucky, lies directly across the Ohio River from Cincinnati. Wagner sold his drinks in the City of Covington. The sales were made from a wagon, and the drinks were delivered at the time the sale was made. No sale was made of less than an entire and unbroken package of soft drinks. The City of Covington levied an occupation or license tax upon those engaged as wholesale dealers of soft drinks. Wagner attacked this city ordinance in the courts on the ground that as to him the tax was a burden on interstate commerce. The Supreme Court held the city ordinance valid, and in its opinion wrote: "It is settled by repeated decisions of this court that a license, regulation or tax of this nature, imposed by a state with respect to the making of such sales of goods within its borders, is not to be deemed a regulation of or direct burden upon interstate commerce; always enforced impartially with respect to goods manufactured without as well as within the state, it does not conflict with the 'commerce clause.'"

The Sonneborn case was first tried in New Orleans, on the application for a temporary injunction, before a statutory three-judge court consisting of United States Circuit Judge Walker and two United States District Judges. This court followed the decision of the Supreme Court in the Wagner case and held the Texas law valid.

After the three-judge court had decided the Sonneborn case in favor of the State, Mr. McCormick amended his petition and asked for a permanent injunction against the Attorney General and the Comptroller of Public Accounts, restraining them from attempting to collect the tax. The suit for permanent injunction could be and was tried before the United States District Judge for the Western District of Texas. Honorable W. R. Smith was the judge for the Western District of Texas at this time.

In the meantime, and after the three-judge court at New Orleans had decided the Sonneborn case, the Supreme Court of the United States had, on April 19, 1920, decided the case of Askren vs. Continental Oil Company, 252 U. S., 444, which involved the validity of a so-called inspection law of the State of New Mexico, imposing a license tax upon those selling gasoline in New Mexico, and an excise tax of two cents per gallon on the sale or use of gasoline. The Continental Oil Company brought gasoline into New Mexico from another state in tank cars and in original packages.

The oil company attacked the validity of the New Mexico law. The Supreme Court of the United States held the New Mexico law invalid. In the opinion of the court, it is said:

> As to the gasoline brought into the state in the tank cars, or in the original packages and so sold, we are unable to discover any difference in plan of importation and sale between the instant case and that before us in the Standard Oil Company vs. Graves, 249 U. S., 389, in which we held that a tax, which was in effect a privilege tax, as is the one under consideration, providing for a levy of fees in excess of the cost of inspection, amounted to a direct burden on interstate commerce. In that case we reaffirmed, what had often been adjudicated heretofore in this court, that the direct and necessary effect of such legislation was to impose a burden upon interstate commerce; that under the Federal Constitution, the importer of such products from another state into his own state for sale in the original packages, had a right to sell

the same in such packages without being taxed for the privilege by taxation of the sort here involved.

At the hearing before Judge Smith in Waco, Mr. McCormick, of course, relied upon the decision in the Askren case as controlling our case, because it was later in point of time than the Wagner case upon which I had relied at the hearing before the special three-judge court at New Orleans.

Judge Smith followed the law as announced in the Wagner case, and refused to grant to Sonneborn Brothers a permanent injunction. Mr. McCormick appealed the case directly to the Supreme Court of the United States, where he and I argued it on March 24, 1922.

In his brief and in his oral argument Mr. McCormick relied on a number of cases decided by the Supreme Court of the United States, but primarily he relied, I think, on the Standard Oil and Askren cases.

It was my contention that when Sonneborn Brothers brought their goods into Texas and stored them in their warehouse the goods had come to rest and had acquired a situs in Texas, and when they were afterward sold to purchasers in the original unbroken packages that Sonneborn Brothers was liable for the tax imposed by the Texas law; that this was true even though the goods were delivered to the purchaser in the original unbroken packages that they were in when first brought to Texas.

In addition to the Wagner case I relied on the old case of Woodruff vs. Parham, 8 Wall., 123. The Woodruff case involved the constitutionality of a tax levied by the City of Mobile, Alabama, on sales made at auction. Woodruff was an auctioneer. He received as consignee, or as the agent for others, large amounts of merchandise "the product of states other than Alabama, and sold the same in Mobile to purchasers in the original and unbroken packages."

The Supreme Court held that the tax imposed upon such sales by the City of Mobile was a valid tax because it did not "discriminate injuriously against the products of other

states or the right of their citizens, and the case is not, therefore, an attempt to fetter commerce among the states, or to
deprive the citizens of other states of any privilege or immu-
nity possessed by citizens of Alabama."

I contended that the Texas law did not deny to Sonneborn
Brothers any privilege enjoyed by any other wholesale
dealer, and the fact that Sonneborn Brothers sold their merchandise in the original unbroken packages in which they
were shipped into Texas should not give them any advantage
over other Texas wholesale dealers.

The judges of the court indicated much interest in the arguments that Mr. McCormick and I made. Mr. McCormick
and I returned to Texas and waited for the decision of the Supreme Court. We waited in vain. Finally we received notice
from the Clerk of the court that the case had been restored to
the docket for re-argument, and that the re-argument of the
case had been set for October 5, 1922. I resigned from the
Attorney General's office in May, 1922, but at the request of
the Attorney General I went to Washington and re-argued
the case.

In the meantime, on April 17, 1922, the Supreme Court
decided the case of Texas Company vs. Brown. This case
came up to the Supreme Court from Georgia. In this case
the Texas Company attacked the constitutionality of a
Georgia law levying fees for inspecting petroleum and petroleum products on the ground that the inspection fee was
greater than the cost of inspection, and therefore, amounted to a tax upon interstate commerce, and that as a tax it was
invalid insofar as it attempted to levy a tax upon the sale of
petroleum products brought into the State of Georgia from
other states for the purpose of sale and delivery in the original unbroken packages.

In deciding the case of Texas Company vs. Brown, the Supreme Court in its opinion said:

> A state may not, without the consent of Congress,
> impose this or any other kind of taxation directly

upon interstate commerce, and inspection fees
made to apply to such commerce, exceeding so clearly and obviously the cost of inspection as to amount
in effect to a revenue tariff, or to the extent of the
excess a burden upon the commerce amounting to
a regulation of it, and hence invalid because inconsistent with the exclusive authority of Congress over
that subject. Standard Oil Company vs. Graves, 249
United States, 389.

The court held, however, that the tax law of Georgia was
valid because oil and petroleum brought into the state in
tank cars and distributed from the tank cars to the gasoline
stations of the company, and there sold and delivered to the
purchaser, was a sale in bulk or broken packages and not a
sale in the original unbroken package in which the goods
were brought into the state. In its opinion, however, the
court approved the rule of law as announced not only in the
Standard Oil Company case, but also in the Askren case.

Mr. McCormick and I went to Washington and re-argued
the Sonneborn case. Mr. McCormick, as the attorney for
the appealing party, had the right to open and close the oral
argument. At the conclusion of his opening argument, I began my argument. I had not been speaking very long when I
was interrupted by Mr. Justice Van Devanter, who asked me
what I was going to do with the case of Standard Oil Company vs. Graves. For several minutes I attempted to answer
the question asked by Mr. Justice Van Devanter. I argued
that the question of taxation on sales of goods brought into
a state and thereafter sold in the original unbroken package
was not directly before the court in the Standard Oil Company case, the Askren or the Texas Company cases; that all
those cases dealt with state laws levying an inspection tax.
This inspection tax had been in excess of the cost of inspecting the goods brought into the state for sale, and, therefore,
amounted to a tax upon interstate commerce; that the Texas
law being attacked by Sonneborn Brothers did not levy an

inspection fee, but was a sales tax, based upon sales made in Texas on goods that were sold in Texas after the goods had arrived in Texas. The fact, so I argued, that the goods were resold after arriving in Texas in the original unbroken packages in which the goods had been shipped from New Jersey was entirely immaterial.

I realized that I had not conclusively answered the inquiry made by Mr. Justice Van Devanter. The Supreme Court had emphatically held in the Standard Oil Company case, although the question was not directly presented, that a state could not levy a tax on sales of goods, where the goods were brought into the state from another state, and thereafter sold and delivered in the original unbroken package.

When I had concluded my effort to answer Mr. Justice Van Devanter's question, I stopped for a moment to take a drink of water.

When I started to continue my argument, I was interrupted by Mr. Justice Day, who said: "Mr. Smith, what are you going to do with the case of Standard Oil Company vs. Graves?" This was precisely the same question that Mr. Justice Van Devanter had asked me.

In the Supreme Court, prior to the beginning of the oral argument in any case, each judge of the court is furnished by the Pages of the court with a printed copy of the briefs filed in the case. I mention this so that what follows may be understood.

Most lawyers in the argument of an important case, and certainly in the argument of a case before the Supreme Court of the United States, are at high tension when making their arguments. I confess that I was frustrated and annoyed by the question asked by Mr. Justice Day because I had attempted for the past several minutes to answer exactly the same question which had been asked me by Mr. Justice Van Devanter.

I replied to Mr. Justice Day: "Your Honor, I am not going to do anything with the case of Standard Oil Company vs. Graves. If I could do anything with that case, I would overrule it, because it is wrong and should be overruled."

To these remarks of mine, Mr. Justice Day replied: "Mr. Smith, this is a very important case; one that has been once argued before. It is a case to which the judges of this court have given much consideration, and because of the importance of the questions involved, this court invited you gentlemen to return and re-argue the case. I asked you the question that I did because I wanted information and not a facetious reply."

The remarks of Mr. Justice Day were amply sufficient to annihilate me, but I replied: "I beg your Honor's pardon. I did not intend to make a facetious answer to your Honor's inquiry. I have spent the past several minutes in an effort to answer an inquiry from Mr. Justice Van Devanter, and his inquiry was exactly the same inquiry that you made."

To this Mr. Justice Day replied: "I beg your pardon, Sir. I was reading your brief when you were answering the inquiry of Mr. Justice Van Devanter, and therefore, did not follow what you were saying." Chief Justice Taft, during the colloquy between Mr. Justice Day and me, was having one of his hearty and wholesome laughs.

The Sonneborn case was finally decided on June 11, 1923. The opinion of the court was written by Mr. Chief Justice Taft, and in discussing the Standard Oil Company case and the Askren case, Mr. Taft wrote in his opinion:

"Upon full consideration and after a re-argument, we cannot think this extension of the excise referred to, if intended to apply to oil sold after arrival in the state, would be justified either in reason or in previous authority, and to this extent, the opinions in the cases cited are qualified."

The judgment for the State of Texas entered by Judge W. R. Smith of the Western District of Texas was affirmed. The contradictions of the court's own holdings in the Standard Oil Company case and the Askren case, and the holding of the court in the Wagner case, could not be reconciled. This fact was recognized by Chief Justice Taft by the use of the language in his opinion quoted above. The Sonneborn case is reported in 262 United States, 506.

CHAPTER XVII:
THE TRIAL LAWYER & HIS WITNESSES

The Attorney General of Texas has more power than any other one individual officer in Texas. It may be that this power has been sometimes used to further the political ambitions of the incumbent of the office. I am sure that this was not true during the administration of either Mr. Cureton or Mr. Keeling. For almost three years I worked as an assistant to Mr. Cureton, and for several months I was First Assistant to Mr. Keeling. I never at any time saw or heard anything that caused me to believe that either of these gentlemen was ever influenced in his official action by political considerations. Mr. Cureton and Mr. Keeling, without any publicity or self-advertising, made it clear to the lawyers and the other attaches of the office that the Attorney General was the lawyer for the State of Texas, and it was his duty to represent the interests of his client. He was not to be diverted from his duty for any reason, political or otherwise.

I wrote an opinion while I was in the Attorney General's office which was approved by Mr. Cureton that I understand has been often cited and quoted from in subsequent opinions by the Attorney General's Department. The Land Commissioner submitted an inquiry to the Attorney General as to whether the State owned the minerals in certain land. Under the facts as detailed by the Land Commissioner in his letter of inquiry, it was not clear whether the State did or did not own the mineral estate in the land. In my opinion to the Land Commissioner, in reply to his inquiry addressed to the Attorney General, I wrote:

> If the State owns the minerals in this land, such ownership may be of little or great value, but if we advise that this ownership be surrendered on the state of facts presented, and our advice should be wrong, our error can never be corrected; whereas, if our advice not to surrender the rights of the State is wrong, the vendees

of Mr. Gibson can have our error corrected by proper legal proceedings.

In all controversies involving the rights of the State, it is the duty and likewise the policy of the Attorney General's Department to decide all substantial doubts in favor of the State for the reasons just mentioned.

Good luck was with me in my work for the Attorney General. Of the forty-one cases that I tried while working in the Attorney General's office, I lost four in the trial court, and one of these I reversed on appeal. Three of the judgments I obtained for the State were reversed on appeal. When I had been working for Mr. Cureton for about two and one-half years, I received an offer to join a very substantial law firm in which I was assured that my earnings would be much more than I was earning as an assistant attorney general. The offer appealed to me.

When I told Mr. Cureton of the offer that I had received, he said: "Smith, when I was First Assistant to Mr. Looney, a Fort Worth law firm offered me a partnership with a guarantee that my earnings would be twice the salary that I was receiving from the State. I talked with Mr. Looney about this offer, and Mr. Looney told me that he was depending on me to stay with him as long as he was Attorney General. I never bothered Mr. Looney again about resigning. You stay here and finish out my term of office with me, and you will get a better offer than the one you have now."

I did not want to do anything contrary to the wishes of Mr. Cureton, and advised the gentlemen who had been kind enough to make me the offer that I could not accept it.

When Mr. Keeling was appointed Attorney General for the remainder of Mr. Cureton's second term of office, it was his intention not to be a candidate to succeed himself. When this fact became known, those interested in the office of Attorney General began to discuss possible candidates for the office. My name was mentioned in private discussions and in the newspapers of the state as a possible candidate.

I wanted to be Attorney General, but there were reasons which I thought prevented me from being a candidate for the office. It requires the expenditure of a very large sum of money to conduct a campaign properly for a state office in Texas. Texas is an empire in size. A campaign advertisement in a daily newspaper in only one Texas city, such as Houston, Dallas, Waco, San Antonio, El Paso, Amarillo, Fort Worth or Austin, will be read by only a fractional part of the voters. For a political campaign in Texas to be effective, a candidate should advertise his candidacy, simultaneously and continuously, in the daily papers published in all sections of the state, an item of considerable expense within itself. In order to make personal contacts, a candidate should visit the county seat of every county in the state. There are two hundred and fifty-four counties in Texas. I did not have the money to spend to make a campaign for the office of Attorney General. Moreover, I did not believe that I could be elected. I had no personal following. Economically, the wise thing for me to do was to retire from office and engage in the private practice of law.

During the discussion of possible candidates for the office of Attorney General, the Austin correspondent for the *Dallas News* and the best newspaper reporter I have ever known, Mr. William Thornton, asked me the direct question if I was going to be a candidate. I gave him the positive answer that I was not. Mr. Thornton then wrote a story for his paper in which he discussed the possible candidates for the office, and was kind enough to say that my name had been frequently mentioned as the most logical candidate, but "Mr. Smith is strictly a lawyer, in no sense a politician, and he will not be a candidate for Attorney General."

Mr. Keeling was finally persuaded to be a candidate to succeed himself. As evidence of Mr. Keeling's character, ability, and the affection in which he was held by the people, no one had the temerity to be a candidate against him. I know that Mr. Keeling held the office of Attorney General at great financial sacrifice to himself, for he could have joined one of the large law firms of the state, where his earnings would have been several times the amount of his salary as Attorney General.

As an assistant and as First Assistant Attorney General, I had been given the opportunity to grow in my profession. I took full advantage of this opportunity. I probably won some lawsuits for the State that the State should have lost. In my opinion I lost one case for the State that should have been won. At the time I was trying lawsuits for the State, I did not have any doubt as to the justice of the State's cause in any case I tried. It may be that I was then, and even later, too aggressive in the courthouse. Perhaps in my conduct of some lawsuits, I gave offense to some of the great lawyers and fine men who opposed me. If I did, I am sorry.

I realize now that it was not so terribly important that the State win all of the lawsuits that I tried, but I did not know this when I was trying the cases. I thought at the time that it was of supreme importance that the State win every case that I tried.

In one land suit I tried for the State, in which there was a jury, it took thirteen weeks to try the case. At the end of the twelfth week, I became ill with influenza. I did not think that I could afford to stop and go to bed. For a week I continued in the trial of this case. Every day my fever was higher than it was the day before, but I stuck it out to the end and made a three hour argument to the jury. I was exhausted when I finished. The jury was out several hours, and when they returned, they brought in a verdict for the State. The verdict of the jury was a tonic for me, but it was not sufficient to cure me of my illness, for I went home and had to stay in bed for two weeks.

There was a splendid young man in the Attorney General's office, a brilliant and an ambitious lawyer, W. W. Meachum, who I verily believe killed himself in his zeal for his work. He was engaged in trying a lawsuit that was taxing him to the limit physically and mentally when he became ill. He did not quit the trial of the case. A few days later he was dead. I have never known a young lawyer who showed greater promise than did Mr. Meachum, and there was never a finer gentleman or a more loyal friend.

The work of the trial lawyer is fearfully hard work. Weeks are sometimes spent in preparing a case for trial. It may be that days will be spent in arguments before the court over demurrers, special exceptions to the pleadings, and other dilatory pleas. Perhaps the pleadings have to be re-written. I always prepared an exhaustive trial brief prior to the time a case was to be tried, but it was sometimes necessary to look up additional authorities during the course of the trial. This work had to be done at night. When all the preliminary matters were out of the way, the jury had to be selected. This might take a day. Then would come the witnesses for and against me. I had to confer with all my witnesses before I called them to the witness stand. I was careful to warn my witnesses that they would be severely cross-examined, and in order that they could understand what their cross-examination would be like, I would myself cross-examine them.

I dislike to think of the many times that I have had one of my witnesses almost wreck a lawsuit for me. As painstaking as I had been in questioning the witness before I called him to the stand, he would be dumb on my direct examination. To the ordinary observer it would appear that I was having to drag the testimony that was favorable to my client out of the witness, and that every favorable answer that the witness gave was reluctantly given.

Then on cross-examination, the witness would become glib, and not only contradict much of the testimony that he had given on direct examination that was favorable to my client, but he would make voluntary statements that were detrimental to the interest of my client. Such a witness as I have described did not intend to deceive me. He wanted to tell the truth, and the truth was helpful to my client. What happened was that the witness became nervous and excited, and did not fully comprehend questions that were asked him nor understand the answers that he gave in response to the questions.

Some of the worst jolts I have ever received in a courtroom were given me by the testimony of my own clients. I suppose some men be come afflicted with stage fright when they are on the witness stand. While on the witness stand, a witness occupies the most prominent place in the courtroom. All eyes are upon him. Every ear is tuned to catch his words. The witness is frequently interrupted while giving his testimony by objections made to his testimony. Sometimes these objections result in the jury being excluded from the courtroom while the lawyers argue for hours over the objection made to the question asked the witness.

In one case that I tried, I was being assisted by one of my law partners. I had called our client as a witness. On my direct examination he had not made a good witness. On cross-examination he was terrible. While he was being cross-examined, my partner who was sitting by me at the counsel table jabbed me in the ribs and excitedly whispered: "E. R., stop that damn fool. He is ruining our lawsuit."

There is not much that a lawyer can do to stop a witness from giving hurtful testimony if his testimony is legally admissible. Sometimes a diversion can be created by objecting to some question and by trying to get the court to hear an argument in support of the objection. It is not often that the able and experienced judge will permit a lawyer who objects to a witness answering a question to do anything more than state the legal ground upon which he bases his objection.

Generally the judge promptly rules, "Objection overruled," or "Objection sustained." If the objecting lawyer becomes too insistent upon his objection, the judge may make him sit down. In the meantime, it is possible that the lawyer, by his conduct, has made a bad impression on the jury. I have sometimes thought that when the evidence for the plaintiff and the evidence for the defendant were in sharp conflict and no one could tell for certain from the testimony who was in the right, the jury decided the case on their like or dislike for the lawyers who were trying the case.

Men who serve on juries are not fools. Any lawyer who tries his case on the theory that they are will soon be undeceived. My experience and observation have convinced me that the best tactics for the lawyer in the courtroom is to be dignified, calm, and refuse to permit himself to become perturbed by any incident that may occur during the trial. If the judge is deserving of respect, the lawyer should treat him with respect. I do not believe it is good policy for a lawyer to fawn upon the jury. He should do no more than be polite, friendly, and courteous in his intercourse with the jury.

A lawyer is sometimes called upon to try a case before a judge who is determined, apparently, not to give him a fair trial, or at least is permitting opposing counsel to dominate the trial. When a lawyer finds himself in such a situation, it is permissible and good technique for the lawyer deliberately to antagonize and irritate the judge, being careful not to commit an act which will constitute a contempt of court. If the judge is sufficiently antagonized and irritated, there is a fair chance that in his anger he will do something during the course of the trial that will be reversible error.

When all the evidence has been introduced, the charge of the court to the jury must be prepared. The procedure of preparing the charge differs among judges. The able and industrious judge, who wants to be fair will, from the time the pleadings are being read until all the evidence has been introduced, listen carefully and be ready immediately after all the evidence has been introduced to write his charge, or he may ask the lawyers on both sides to submit to him the issues that they think should be submitted to the jury. If the judge is lazy or a poor lawyer, or both, he will permit the attorney for the plaintiff to write the charge of the court. After the charge is prepared, it is submitted to counsel for examination and an opportunity is given to counsel to object to any and all parts of the charge. As a result of these objections, the charge may be re-written. Some parts of the charge are frequently re-written many times.

After I had retired from the Attorney General's office, I represented the defense more often than I did the plaintiff. I was always glad for plaintiff's counsel to write the charge of the court, for in his zeal for his client, he was likely to write something in the charge that would constitute reversible error. I recall a case that I tried in Houston for an insurance company where the judge was an able lawyer but had a strong distaste for doing any work that he could avoid. He permitted plaintiff's counsel to write the charge of the court. To the charge as written by the plaintiff's counsel, I made many objections. When these objections were submitted to the judge, he told plaintiffs counsel that a certain objection was good, and that he had better re-write the charge so as to meet the objection. Plaintiff's counsel said he was willing to stand on the charge as written.

"All right," the judge answered. "It is your lawsuit."

The judge gave the charge as plaintiffs counsel had written it. The jury found against my client, and upon the jury's verdict a judgment was entered against my client for more than $20,000. I appealed the case, and the appellate court reversed the judgment of the trial court, because of the error in the court's charge that I had objected to, and which objection the judge had told plaintiff's counsel was a good objection.

Under the Texas Special Issue Law, there may be fifty, a hundred, or possibly two hundred questions asked the jury in the court's charge. It sometimes takes several days to prepare such a charge and for the lawyers to make their objections to it. The court's charge and the lawyers' objections thereto must all be in writing and prepared before the case is argued before the jury. The lawyer engaged in the trial of a lawsuit may work all day and a good part of the night during the time the court's charge is being prepared. When the charge is finally prepared and all objections to it settled, the judge reads the charge to the jury. Then the lawyers, no matter how tired and exhausted they may be, must make their arguments to the jury. The trial lawyer should have the physique of an athlete, and at all times keep himself in good physical condition.

One day I was in my office in the Attorney General's Department when my telephone rang. When I took down the receiver, I found that Judge Hiram M. Garwood of Houston was at the other end of the line. Judge Garwood invited me to come to Houston that night for the purpose of conferring with the partners in his law firm in regard to the possibility of my joining his organization. This was the first notice that I had that Judge Garwood's firm was even considering me for a position in their organization. Judge Garwood was one of the senior partners in the then law firm of Baker, Botts, Parker and Garwood. Judge Garwood's invitation made me very happy, for I believed his was the greatest law firm in Texas. I recalled what Mr. Cureton had said to me on a former occasion when I had considered resigning. I told Judge Garwood that I must first talk to Attorney General Keeling, and if Mr. Keeling made no objection, I would be in his office in Houston the next morning. When I talked to Mr. Keeling, I found his attitude different from that of Mr. Cureton, for he said to me: "Go to Houston and see what Judge Garwood's firm has to offer you. Someday our term of office here will expire, and when the clock strikes twelve, out we must go, whether we have any place to go or not."

That night on the train from Austin to Houston, I met former State Senator McDonald Meachum, an older brother of my late friend and colleague, W. W. Meachum. Senator Meachum and I sat in a drawing room on the train and visited until two o'clock in the morning. I am very fond of Senator Meachum and admire him very much. He is an excellent lawyer, and as a State Senator had rendered fine and patriotic service to his state. He has all the requisite qualities to make a great Senator from Texas in the Senate of the United States. I know Senator Meachum well, and I was not surprised to learn from him, on the occasion of our visit on the train, his fine attitude toward the public service. Notwithstanding the splendid success Senator Meachum was making in private life, he made statements to me that night on the train that led me to believe that he regretted his action in voluntarily retiring from the public service.

Senator Meachum was devoted in his friendship for Judge Garwood and other partners in the law firm of Baker, Botts, Parker and Garwood. He assured me that if I was going to retire from the Attorney General's office, I would make no mistake in joining Judge Garwood's organization. He urged me, however, not to resign my place in the Attorney General's office. He asked me my age, and I told him that I was thirty-two.

"Why, Smith," he said, "you have an amazing opportunity to serve the people of Texas. Stay where you are. Mr. Keeling is going to be elected and this will give you two and a half more years in your present office, then you can succeed Mr. Keeling as Attorney General. After that will come further opportunities. Resign now and join the greatest corporation law firm in the state, and you will never again have an opportunity to enter the public service."

I explained to Senator Meachum that I was a poor man, and that it was necessary for me to earn more money than I could ever hope to earn holding any public office. I also told him what the old lawyer had told me long ago about there being two times in a lawyer's life when he should hold public office—once when he was young and again after he had earned a competence in the private practice of law.

"It never works out that way," Senator Meachum replied. "The demagogues have convinced the people that a man who has made a success in private life cannot be trusted in public office. This is particularly true of the lawyer with a corporation clientele. When you are as old as I am now and have made a success in private practice, there will be no opportunity for you to return to the public service. The demagogues will see to that."

I appreciated the interest shown by Senator Meachum in my future, and the confidence that he had in me, but I believed that I should first earn, if I could, a competence, and when I had acquired a reasonable amount of financial security, I could perhaps again hold public office when I would be free to serve the state without any disturbing thoughts in regard to my own financial situation.

Since the night that Senator Meachum and I visited on the train, I have tried many lawsuits and done other legal work for several corporations. In doing this work I became acquainted with many fine and patriotic businessmen. The work of a lawyer for and with honorable and patriotic businessmen, charged with the responsibility of carefully and wisely managing great business enterprises, will not disqualify him from thereafter rendering a disinterested public service to the state. Such an experience will make the lawyer better qualified to render an intelligent and worthwhile service to the people.

My attitude toward public and private affairs and toward life in general has not materially changed from what it was when I was a boy in the Indian Territory. I believed then, and I believe now, that it is not morally wrong for a man to make a financial success. I believed then, and I believe now, that all normal men desire to succeed. I could not understand then, and I cannot understand now, why we cry out against the men who have succeeded in doing what we would all like to do. I may not have thought so then, but I think now, that individuals and governments should be economical, keeping their expenditures within their incomes; that opportunity should be made as equal as possible to all young men and women; that a poor boy, who has to make his own way, has perhaps a better chance to succeed than does the rich boy.

My reception in Judge Garwood's office by his partners was all that I could expect. Mr. Ralph B. Feagin, the assistant managing partner, and I had a long talk. In the course of this conversation Mr. Feagin told me something of the history of his law firm and of its ideals. He made me a satisfactory offer, one that I was glad to accept. It was necessary for me to remain in the Attorney General's office for a few more weeks to complete some work that was on my desk. On May 15, 1922, I reported for work at the offices of Baker, Botts, Parker and Garwood.

CHAPTER XVIII:
A GREAT LAW FIRM

The law firm that was Baker, Botts, Parker and Garwood when I joined the organization in 1922 and which is now Baker, Botts, Andrews and Wharton is, I believe, the oldest law firm in Texas. It had its beginning in 1866 as Gray and Botts. Of the original senior member of the firm, Peter W. Gray, it has been said: "He was acknowledged to be a great lawyer, among as great lawyers as ever graced the jurisprudence of any country."

Colonel Botts, the junior member of the original partnership, was of Virginia stock. A kinsman of his, Benjamin Botts, when a very young lawyer, participated in the defense of Aaron Burr when the latter was tried before Chief Justice Marshall at Richmond, Virginia. A brother defended John Brown of anti-slavery fame.

When Judge James A. Baker, who while absent in the Confederate Army, was elected district judge, came to the firm in 1872, the name of the firm was changed to Gray, Botts and Baker. Judge Baker was the father of the present senior member of the firm, Capt. James A. Baker. In 1874 Mr. Gray was appointed Associate Justice of the Supreme Court of Texas. When Capt. James A. Baker became a member of the firm, the firm name was changed to Baker, Botts and Baker.

R. S. Lovett, a sturdy and determined youth from East Texas, came to Houston and studied law with Colonel Charles Stuart. Subsequently he became general attorney for the Texas & Pacific Railroad Company with his offices in Dallas, resigned that position in 1893, and became a member of the firm under the firm name of Baker, Botts, Baker and Lovett. In 1904 Mr. Lovett was summoned to New York by Mr. Harriman to become the head of the legal department of the Union Pacific & Southern Pacific Railway companies. Eventually Mr. Lovett became Chairman of the Board of the Union Pacific Railway Company.

Judge Edwin B. Parker and Judge Hiram M. Garwood became partners in the firm in 1904, and the name of the firm was changed to Baker, Botts, Parker and Garwood. When I joined the organization, the partners were Captain James A. Baker, Thomas Botts, Edwin B. Parker, Hiram M. Garwood, Jesse Andrews, Clarence R. Wharton, Clarence L. Carter, Jules H. Tallichet, Walter H. Walne, Ralph B. Feagin and Palmer Hutcheson. There were, in addition to the partners, about twenty other lawyers in the organization.

Captain James A. Baker is, in addition to being the senior partner of his great law firm, a successful banker and business man. By his quiet strength and excellent judgment, Captain Baker reminds me of my great hero, General George Washington.

Judge Edwin B. Parker was in many ways the most remarkable man that I have ever known. His was a dynamic personality. He was a great executive and organizer who could do a prodigious amount of work, and cause others to work to the limit of their physical and mental strength.

When I joined the organization Judge Parker was the managing partner of the firm, but he spent most of his time in New York where he was General Counsel of the Texas Company. Later Judge Parker was to serve with great distinction as Umpire of the Mixed Claims Commission, United States and Germany, to which position he was appointed in 1923. There were more than twelve thousand claims filed with this Commission. In something over three thousand of these claims awards were made by Judge Parker. These awards aggregated more than $200,000,000.

In the midst of his activities as an international judge, Judge Parker was called upon in May, 1927, to become Chairman of the Board of the United States Chamber of Commerce. To this task Judge Parker brought his great ability as an executive, organizer, lawyer, jurist, and his high business ideals. At the close of this service, Judge Parker delivered an address on "Responsibilities of Business" which has since been much quoted as an expression of the high purposes of great organized business enterprises.

Judge Parker was born in Shelby County, Missouri, in 1868, and died in Washington, D. C, in 1929. When he was fifteen it became necessary for him to take over the management of his father's farm. He wanted to be a lawyer, and came to Texas where he attended and was graduated from the Law School of The University of Texas. While in law school, Judge Parker earned part of his support by working for the state government, and by writing for current journals.

Judge Parker believed in the gospels of integrity and hard work, and was well rewarded. In his will, after making ample provisions for his wife (he was survived by no children) he left his estate to be used in establishing or maintaining a graduate school of international affairs for teaching young men "of proven character and ability subjects calculated thoroughly to equip them to render practical service of a high order" to their government or private institutions in respect to foreign relations.

While I have known most of the men who during the past twenty-five years have been great lawyers in Texas, I have not known them all. I shall not, therefore, make the dogmatic statement that I know who was the greatest lawyer in Texas during the past quarter of a century. After all, this is a matter of individual opinion. I do unhesitatingly make the statement that in my opinion Judge Hiram M. Garwood was the greatest lawyer I have ever known.

Hiram Morgan Garwood was born in Bastrop, Texas, July 11, 1864. His father was Major Calvin B. Garwood, and his mother was Frances Walker Garwood. Judge Garwood was a graduate of the University of the South at Sewanee, Tennessee. In 1922 his Alma Mater conferred upon him the honorary degree of Doctor of Civil Law. Upon the completion of his course at Sewanee, young Garwood returned to his home in Bastrop and began the study of law. Few lawyers of Judge Garwood's generation were law school graduates. It is doubtful if this was any handicap to Judge Garwood.

The literature of the law could be found in books, and no one better knew how to use books than young Garwood.

Judge Garwood applied himself diligently to the study of the law, and in a comparatively short time was admitted to the bar. When he had barely attained his majority, the people of Bastrop County elected him to the Legislature. He retired from this office to serve one term as County Judge of his county. At the expiration of his term of office as County Judge, he was elected to the State Senate, where he made a notable record. Referring to this period of Judge Garwood's life, the late Honorable R. L. Batts, who himself served with distinction as a United States Circuit Court Judge for the Fifth Circuit, and who had been the boyhood friend of Judge Garwood, said in an address before the Texas Bar Association in 1930:

> The English System recognizes and rewards genius; the American System favors mediocrity. Except for this, Garwood might easily, remaining in public life, have had as brilliant a political career as either Pitt or Disraeli.

> He gave thought to the conditions in Texas and in the South, and the relations which this section had at that time to the United States, and deliberately concluded that he should place behind him the allurements of a life in which he saw little probability of such a success as would satisfy him and compensate for the necessary sacrifices. That he chose wisely I do not doubt; I also do not doubt that if he had been willing to accept them, the people of Texas would have conferred upon him their highest honors.

> He chose rather to take up the work of those who build effectively while retaining the freedom of private life. He was one of the many men in Texas of first class ability, unwilling to be shackled with the limitations of an official life; unwilling to bend to the narrow views of a capricious electorate; who realized that Texas must

become great and quickly great, and that the best work could be done by directing public opinion, rather than by holding office at the cost of having to follow that opinion in its erratic course.

Men of this class have, in the main, directed the destinies of the state. There are periods of public aberration—outbursts of foolish public sentiment, occasions when even criminals participate in public affairs; but ordinarily the men successful in business, the men high in their professions—animated by patriotism—have determined the course of the current of a State grown great because of their devotion.

While he had deliberately retired from public life, Judge Garwood always had a lively interest in the public affairs of his state and nation. His interest in public affairs was not selfish, but wholly patriotic. In this connection Judge Garwood taught me a valuable lesson, a lesson that I shall never forget.

There was a matter of importance to the railroads of Texas pending before the Legislature at Austin. All the railroads in the state were interested in this proposed legislation, and sent their representatives to Austin in an effort to protect their interests. Judge Garwood sent me as the representative of the Southern Pacific Lines. As was usual with me in those days, all the right in every controversy that I was in was on one side, the side that I represented.

A member of the State Senate was a division attorney for the Southern Pacific Lines. This gentleman surprised, shocked, and outraged me by voting against the interests of the railroads. When I returned to Houston, I reported this fact to Judge Garwood. I assumed that Judge Garwood would be as outraged by the conduct of this Senator as I was.

Imagine my surprise when Judge Garwood quietly said: "I am surprised at the action of the Senator in voting against us, for the cause of the railroads in this proposed legislation is a meritorious cause. The services of the Senator as division attorney have been long and in every way satisfactory. We pay him for his legal services. As a member of the State Senate, the only obligation he owes to the company is to work and vote for legislation that he believes will be beneficial to the entire state. It will be a sad day for Texas when the votes of the members of the Legislature are controlled by those for whom they work in private life, or by anything other than the merits of the proposed legislation."

Judge Garwood was a master of the English language. In debate he was an adversary greatly to be feared. Judge Garwood and I once argued a case before the Supreme Court of Texas which involved a fortune. Our opponent was one of the truly great lawyers of Texas. Twenty years before our case was argued in the Supreme Court, Judge Garwood and our opponent had been on opposite sides in a very famous lawsuit. Judge Garwood had won that suit. In our case, I made the opening argument before the Supreme Court. Our able adversary then made his argument to the court and concluded with this remarkable peroration:

> For more than forty years I have been a student of the jurisprudence of this state. I have read and studied all the opinions ever written by the great judges who have served on this court, and in no one of these opinions can be found any statement of the law that will sustain the position taken by my opponents before the court in this case.

Judge Garwood made the concluding argument for our side, and in reply to the above quoted statement made by our opponent, he said:

> I am amazed at the statement made by our opponent; for I well remember that twenty years ago, standing in this very courtroom, he said that for twenty years he had been a student of the jurisprudence of this state, had read every opinion written by the judges of this court, and that in no one of these opinions could

anything be found to sustain the propositions of law that I was relying on in that case. A few weeks later, this court decided that case in favor of my client, and in the court's opinion, many previous decisions of this court were cited as sustaining the law propositions that I had relied on in that case. By its decision of our case of twenty years ago, the court demonstrated that my friend had wasted the first twenty years of his life as a lawyer in a vain effort to understand the opinions of this court.

Today my learned friend stands before this court and asserts that for forty years he has been a student of the jurisprudence of this state and has read every opinion written by the judges of this court, not one of which will support the law propositions upon which Mr. Smith and I rely. In reply to that amazing statement, I am compelled to say that my friend, not content with wasting the first twenty years of his life in a vain effort to understand the opinions of this court, has, in my opinion, wasted the last twenty years of his professional life, for I predict that this court will in the present case find, as it found in the case of twenty years ago, many of its own decisions to sustain the propositions of law upon which Mr. Smith and I rely.

Our opponent and Judge Garwood were good friends. When the arguments were concluded and Judge Garwood and I were in the office of the clerk of the court, our opponent came up to Judge Garwood and said: "Hiram, damn you, I would give five hundred dollars for fifteen minutes in which to answer before the court what you said about me."

A few weeks later, the court sustained the statement made by Judge Garwood, deciding the case in favor of our client; the court, in its written opinion, cited many prior decisions of the court as supporting the propositions of law upon which Judge Garwood and I had relied.

Like all great lawyers, Judge Garwood had courage physically and morally. While he was cautious and conservative in the handling of the legal affairs of his clients, he could and would, when it was necessary to protect what he considered the legal rights of his clients, take risks that involved himself as well as his clients.

One of the famous cases that Judge Garwood tried was the case of the GH & SA Railway Company vs. State of Texas. The State of Texas had enacted a law which attempted to impose a tax upon railroad companies equal to one per cent of their gross receipts, if such line of railroad lies wholly within the state. The lines of the GH & SA Railway Company were wholly within the State of Texas. Its lines connected, however, with other lines of railroad which extended to points outside of Texas. The gross receipts of the GH & SA Railway Company came from two sources: revenue derived from hauling passengers and freight, the transportation of which began and ended in Texas, this being intrastate commerce; and revenue derived from hauling passengers and freight, the transportation of which either began or ended at some point outside of Texas, this being interstate commerce. A tax on this commerce would be a burden on interstate commerce.

The Supreme Court of the United States, in the case of Maine vs. Grand Trunk Railway Company, 142 U. S., 217, had upheld an excise tax levied by a law of the State of Maine upon the receipts of railroad companies. The Maine law was in its terms very similar to the Texas law.

The Texas law provided heavy penalties for failure to pay the tax in the time and manner required by its terms. The officials of the GH & SA Railway Company, which was a part of the Southern Pacific System, asked Judge Garwood whether the railroad should pay the tax. The tax would amount to probably $200,000 a year. If Judge Garwood advised the company officials to pay the tax, it would be paid and no one could criticize Judge Garwood, for the Supreme Court of the United States had upheld a similar tax levied by the State of Maine. If Judge Garwood advised against paying the tax and attacked the validity of the law, the case would be in the courts for several years. If the courts finally upheld the law, the railroad company would, by that time, probably owe in accrued taxes and penalties as much as $2,000,000.

In talking to me about the case, Judge Garwood said: "I knew that if I advised the officials not to pay the taxes and the company lost its suit and was called upon to pay all the accrued taxes, plus the penalties, at one time, the Board of Directors of the Company at New York would want to know what damn fool was representing them in Texas."

Judge Garwood decided the Texas law was invalid, notwithstanding what the Supreme Court had held in the Grand Trunk Railway Company case. He so advised his client. This took moral courage of the highest order. If the courts held the law valid, the advice given by Judge Garwood would be, so far as his client was concerned, bad advice. Clients do not often, or for long, retain lawyers that are wrong on important questions of law. Many lawyers, and in my opinion most lawyers, would have played safe under the circumstances and would have advised their client to pay the tax on the ground that the Supreme Court of the United States had upheld a similar law enacted by the State of Maine.

In a suit filed in a state district court at Austin, Judge Garwood attacked the validity of the law. The district court held the law valid. Judge Garwood appealed to the Court of Civil Appeals at Austin. The Court of Civil Appeals held the law invalid. In its opinion, the Court of Civil Appeals said: "No state has the right or power to levy a tax on interstate commerce in any form, whether by way of duties made on transportation of subjects of that commerce, or on the receipts derived from that transportation, or on the occupation or business of carrying it on; and the reason is that such taxation is a burden on commerce, and amounts to a regulation of it, which belongs solely to Congress."

The Supreme Court of Texas granted the State's application for writ of error, and held the law valid. (97 S. W., 72.)

The Supreme Court of Texas based its opinion on what the Supreme Court of the United States had held in the Grand Trunk Railway Company case. Up to this time one district judge and the three judges of the Texas Supreme Court had held the law valid, and the three judges of the Court of Civil Appeals had held the law invalid. The Supreme Court of the United States, because of the federal question involved, took jurisdiction of the case on writ of error, and in deciding the case, held the law invalid. There are nine judges on the Supreme Court of the United States. Mr. Justice Holmes wrote the opinion of the court, holding the law invalid. Four other judges agreed with Mr. Justice Holmes. Mr. Justice Harlan wrote a dissenting opinion to the effect that he thought the law valid. Chief Justice Fuller and Justices White and McKenna agreed with the opinion expressed by Mr. Justice Harlan. Sixteen judges in all had passed on the validity of the law. Eight held it valid and eight held it invalid. Judge Garwood won his lawsuit, because five judges of the Supreme Court of the United States agreed with him.

"When opportunity came to Hiram M. Garwood, it was as a member of the great law firm of Baker, Botts, Parker and Garwood, and he was equal to his opportunity. He is probably the greatest expert on technical railroad law in the South, and among the leaders in the Nation. In the maze of rates by both rail and ship, he is one of the few who may be termed as learned."

I do not know who wrote the foregoing. The language used limits the attainments of Judge Garwood to the law of transportation. His expert knowledge of railroad law was such as to be of itself sufficient to place him high in the ranks of the legal profession, but his leadership in the law was not limited to his great learning in the one subject of railroad law.

Judge Garwood was the best constitutional lawyer I have ever known. He was familiar with every provision in the Constitution of the United States and the Constitution of Texas. He was familiar with the decisions of the Supreme

Court of the United States and of the State of Texas construing the provisions of these two Constitutions. For years he read and studied every decision of the Supreme Court of the United States as soon as the opinions of the court were available.

In the old days when equity practice in the Federal Courts was a dark and unknown mystery to most lawyers, Judge Garwood knew the intricacies of the equity practice as but few lawyers ever knew them. The fact is almost forgotten now, but Texas has had but few, if any, greater criminal lawyers than Judge Garwood. He had a statewide reputation in that highly important branch of the law many years ago, and virtually retired from criminal practice while still a young man. Judge Garwood was no stranger to any branch of the law, unless it was maritime law, which is a highly specialized branch of the law in which few men attempt to become proficient. He could, however, with this one possible exception, try with the knowledge and skill of an expert any lawsuit in any court, State or Federal, either before the court or before a court and a jury.

How fortunate indeed for me that I was permitted to work for and with this wonderful lawyer. He had the kindness and the talent to inspire younger men with confidence in their own abilities. There are many lawyers in Texas today who are indebted to Judge Garwood, because the confidence he had in them as lawyers gave them confidence in themselves, so that they could and did develop their latent abilities and powers.

Judge Garwood and I participated in the trial of many important lawsuits. When victory came to us, Judge Garwood never failed to insist that much credit was due me for the happy results. This, of course, I recognized as a delightful fallacy. No young lawyer ever left a conference or meeting in which Judge Garwood participated without being made to feel that he had contributed something worthwhile to the meeting. The modesty of this great man was exceeded only by his courage and his great ability.

Judge Garwood died in May, 1930. When he died, something went out of my life that I can never regain. The memory of his friendship, his helpful aid, his wise counsel, his high ideals, his philosophy of our present life and the life to come, has been and will ever be a blessing to me. This kindly, courageous and thoughtfully considerate man lived a supremely useful and beautiful life.

CHAPTER XIX:
AN ALLEGED $65,000 FORGERY

I was a trial lawyer for Baker, Botts, Parker and Garwood. One of the first cases assigned me was an old anti-trust suit. The State of Texas had sued a corporation in an effort to recover a judgment for $1,500,000 for an alleged violation of the anti-trust laws of Texas. The corporation had been incorporated under the laws of another state and its factory and general offices were outside of Texas. It had obtained a permit to do business in Texas. The suit had been brought by Mr. B. F. Looney when he was Attorney General. Before service in the suit could be had on the corporation, it had removed its offices and agents from the State of Texas and placed itself outside the jurisdiction of the state courts. It seemed a little strange to me to be representing a client in opposition to my old client, the State of Texas.

The company manufactured a commodity for which there was a great demand in Texas. After the company ceased doing business in Texas, the Texas wholesale dealers handling the commodity manufactured by the company could not purchase the commodity from the company, except by the payment of cash at the company's factory in an eastern state. Payments had to be made before the commodity would be shipped to Texas, for the company did not propose to subject property owned by it, whether merchandise or money owing to it, to the process of the Texas courts. The company was not so much inconvenienced by the anti-trust suit pending against it in the district court at Austin as were its customers, the Texas wholesale dealers. The Texas wholesalers and the company wanted the suit disposed of so that the company could again do business in Texas. In order to dispose of the suit, the company was willing for a judgment for a small sum to be entered against it.

I went to Austin and proposed to Attorney General Keeling that the State and the company enter into an agreement, whereby the company would submit itself to the jurisdiction of the court on a plea of *nolo contendere*, and that upon this plea, a judgment be entered against the company for $25,000 and upon the payment of this $25,000 the company be permitted once again to do business in Texas. Mr. Keeling was agreeable to settling the case on the terms I suggested, but took the position that under the provisions of the anti-trust law, a corporation found guilty of violating that law could not again do business in Texas until the expiration of ten years' time. I tried to convince him that under my plan there would be no adjudication by the court that my client was guilty of violating the anti-trust law. A plea of *nolo contendere*, I argued, was not an admission of guilt, but simply a statement by the defendant to the court that the defendant would not contest the charges made against it.

Mr. Keeling was of the opinion that a plea of *nolo contendere* is a plea by a defendant in a criminal action meaning that "I will not contest" the charges, and upon which the defendant may be sentenced; that there could be no sentence in a criminal case unless the defendant was guilty. If, he argued, my client was guilty of violating the anti-trust law, it could not, under that law, be permitted again to do business in Texas until after the lapse of ten years; that this ten year prohibition against a company guilty of violating the anti-trust law was a penalty imposed by the law that neither he nor the court could waive.

The Texas wholesalers and my client did not want to wait ten years before my client could again do business in Texas. The Legislature was in session, and I was determined to try to get the anti-trust law amended. I wrote an amendment to the law, providing that with the consent and approval of the Attorney General, a corporation charged with violation of the anti-trust law could, immediately after the payment of any judgment rendered against it for such alleged violation, be again permitted to do business in Texas, by complying with certain requirements of the law.

The amendment that I wrote to the anti-trust law was passed by the Legislature with the emergency clause, and when it was approved by the Governor, went into immediate effect. When the amendment to the anti-trust law had become effective, the Assistant Attorney General in charge of corporation matters and I, after a conference lasting several days, agreed upon a tentative form of judgment to be entered by the court on a plea of *nolo contendere* to be filed by my client. By the terms of this judgment the State was to recover $25,000 from my client, and my client was required to do certain other things before it could again do business in Texas.

The tentative judgment that the Assistant Attorney General and I agreed upon, while not satisfactory to me, was the best I could get the Assistant Attorney General to agree to. It was understood between us that the tentative form of judgment had to be submitted by me to my client's General Counsel for his approval or disapproval.

Judge Garwood thought I should go to New York and submit the form of judgment to my client's General Counsel. This I did. At the conference with the General Counsel I had an unusual experience. He carefully read the form of the judgment, and said that he did not like it. I told him that I did not like it either. He called in his stenographer and dictated a new form of judgment. When this had been typed, the General Counsel handed me a copy of it, and he kept a copy. When we had both read the new form of judgment, General Counsel asked me if I did not think it was an improvement over the form of judgment that I had brought with me. I told him it was a decidedly better form of judgment.

The General Counsel then said: "Can you get the Attorney General to agree to this form of judgment?"

"I do not think so," I replied. "The Attorney General, in my opinion, will never agree to a judgment more favorable to our client than the one he has agreed to."

The General Counsel asked me to hand him the copy of his judgment that I had in my hand. When I had done this, he said: "This is my judgment, is it not?"

I did not know what he meant, but I agreed that it was his judgment. He then took the several copies of the judgment that had been typed by his stenographer, tore them to pieces, and put the pieces in his wastebasket. Then he said: "Mr. Smith, the judgment that you and the Attorney General have agreed to, while unnecessarily onerous to our client, is satisfactory. You may file a plea of *nolo contendere* for our client, have the judgment entered, and then our client will comply with all the terms of the judgment."

When I returned to Texas, I filed a plea of *nolo contendere* and my client paid the judgment of $25,000 and met the other requirements, obtained a permit to do business in Texas, and is today doing business in Texas.

I consider the amendment to the anti-trust law of Texas that I wrote, and that was passed by the Legislature and approved by the Governor, one of the most constructive things I have ever done.

I am, as I suppose most people are, in favor of legislation that will prevent monopolies and the commission of acts in restraint of trade. Such legislation should, however, be helpful and not hurtful to the people. Anyone who violates the anti-trust law should be punished. The punishment should be inflicted against the person who has offended against the law, and not against innocent people. I do not know that my client had violated the anti-trust law. If it had, there was no reason why, once it had been punished for its offense, it should be thereafter, for ten years, denied the right to do business in Texas, thereby causing inconvenience and loss to many people of Texas.

A client of my firm lived in Illinois. He had entered into a written contract to sell a plantation in Brazoria County, Texas, to a Texas citizen for about $90,000. A deed from the seller to the purchaser, together with $5,000 advanced by the purchaser, was placed in a Houston bank under an escrow agreement. By the terms of the escrow agreement the seller was to furnish the purchaser with an abstract of title to the land, which the purchaser was to have examined by his lawyer. If the abstract showed a good, merchantable title to the land in the name of the seller, then the purchaser was to buy the land, and the $5,000 placed in the bank by the purchaser was to be applied to the payment of the purchase money for the land. After the attorney for the purchaser had examined the abstract of title, the purchaser refused to buy the land on the ground that the abstract did not show a good, merchantable title in the seller.

Mr. Barksdale Stevens, one of the lawyers in the Baker, Botts, Parker and Garwood organization, and I brought suit for our client in the United States District Court at Houston. In our petition we alleged that the abstract of title did show a good and merchantable title to the land in the name of our client, and we asked the court to compel the purchaser to buy the land for the price agreed upon, and in the alternative, we asked the court, in the event the court refused to compel the purchaser to buy the land, to give our client judgment for the $5,000 which the purchaser had deposited in the Houston bank as liquidated damages.

The case was tried before Judge Joseph C. Hutcheson, Jr., at that time the United States District Judge for the Southern District of Texas. Mr. Stevens and I satisfied Judge Hutcheson that the abstract showed that our client had good and merchantable title to the land. The real battle was fought over the question of whether our client should have judgment compelling the purchaser to buy the land, or for judgment for the $5,000 as liquidated damages. At the conclusion of the trial, Judge Hutcheson took the case under advisement. A few weeks later he decided the case, and held that our client was not entitled to specific performance of the contract by the purchaser, but was entitled to recover judgment for the $5,000 as liquidated damages. Mr. Stevens and I concluded that Judge Hutcheson's decision was probably correct, and advised our client not to appeal from the court's judgment.

Several days after Judge Hutcheson had decided the case, he called me over the telephone at my office and wanted to know if I was going to appeal the case. I told him that Mr. Stevens and I had advised our client not to appeal. He then wanted to know why Mr. Stevens and I had taken up the time of the court by contending that our client was entitled to specific performance of the contract, if we did not intend to appeal from an unfavorable judgment of the court.

I explained to Judge Hutcheson that Mr. Stevens and I were hired lawyers, and it was our duty to contend for everything that we believed our client could possibly be entitled to recover; that since the court had decided against our contention on the question of specific performance, we had concluded that the court was probably correct, and had so advised our client. This statement seemed to satisfy Judge Hutcheson. This was my first, last and only experience of this nature with a trial judge.

I tried a case before Judge Hutcheson in his court at Laredo in which my client was a private New York bank. For my client I had sued a Texas bank, and for cause of action I alleged that on October 5, 1921, a man representing himself to be Manuel J. Espinosa, presented to the defendant bank two drafts, one for $20,000 and one for $15,000, and on October 13, 1921, presented to the defendant bank another draft for $25,000; that the three drafts were purported to have been drawn by the Tampico Branch of the Banco Nacional de Mexico on the New York bank, and purported to be payable to Manuel J. Espinosa; that the person representing himself to be Manuel J. Espinosa was a stranger to the defendant bank, and the only identification he ever furnished that bank was a spurious passport; that the Texas bank accepted the drafts, and after endorsing on the back of each of the drafts "Pay to the order of any bank, banker or trust company, previous endorsements guaranteed," sent the drafts to New York for collection, where, in due course, they were received and paid by my client; that thereafter, the proceeds of the three drafts were paid by the Texas bank, less collection fees, to the pretended Manuel J. Espinosa; and that the pretended Manuel J. Espinosa had since absconded and fled to parts unknown.

I further alleged that Manuel J. Espinosa was a fictitious person; that the three drafts were forgeries, and that the Texas bank was guilty of gross negligence in paying over to the pretended Manuel J. Espinosa the money which the Texas bank had collected from my client on the three drafts; that the circumstances under which these drafts were presented to the Texas bank were such as to raise suspicion, and to have caused it to require the said Espinosa to give conclusive proof of his identity and the authenticity of the three drafts before the Texas bank undertook to represent him in collecting the proceeds thereof, by placing its endorsement thereon.

The Texas bank defended primarily on the proposition that it had relied, as it had a right to do, on the fact that my client was bound to know the signatures of its correspondents and depositors. The Mexican bank was a correspondent of my client and had large sums of money on deposit in New York with my client.

The Texas bank was represented by Mr. William Aubrey of San Antonio. Among the cases relied on by Mr. Aubrey was an English case decided by Lord Mansfield. The decision by Lord Mansfield was directly in point and fully sustained Mr. Aubrey's contention that my client was bound to know the signature of its correspondent, the Banco Nacional de Mexico. Mr. Aubrey presented to the court a motion to strike my petition, on the ground that it did not state a cause of action. It was in support of this motion that he cited the English case. The court overruled Mr. Aubrey's motion on the ground that I had alleged that the Texas bank was guilty of gross negligence, and if I offered any evidence in support of this allegation I would have the right to have the question of fact of the bank's negligence submitted to the jury.

One of the partners in the New York bank had come to Texas for the trial. When the court recessed at noon, he and I went to the hotel for lunch. He asked me who Lord Man-

sfield was. I told him he was a distinguished English jurist.
The New York banker then wanted to know when Lord
Mansfield lived. I told him that Lord Mansfield had lived
about two hundred years ago. He then asked me the pertinent question: "Well, what in the hell did he know about
modern banking?"

Before going into the trial of the case, I had told the New
York banker that, as it was a jury case, we should employ local counsel in Laredo. This was agreeable, and the banker
and I employed Mr. Marshall Hicks, a distinguished lawyer
and a splendid man, who maintained law offices at San Antonio and Laredo. I thought it likely that the court would
sustain the defendant's motion to strike my petition, and if
this occurred, there would be no trial before a jury, for the
court would enter judgment dismissing my suit. I explained
this situation to Mr. Hicks, and then employed him to assist me in the case with the understanding that if the court
sustained the motion to strike my petition, his services
would not be required, and that my client would not pay him
anything. If, however, the case went to the jury, and the jury
decided against us, Mr. Hicks was to receive a fee of $1,000,
and if the jury decided the case in our favor, Mr. Hicks was
to receive a fee of $2,500.

As I have stated, the court overruled the motion to strike
my petition. We then proceeded with the trial of the case,
which lasted some two or three days. When all the evidence
was in, Judge Hutcheson peremptorily instructed the jury
to return a verdict against my client and for the Laredo
bank. This raised an interesting question as to whether or
not, under the terms of Mr. Hicks' employment he was entitled to any fee, the case not having reached the jury at all.
I mentioned the matter to Mr. Hicks, and he said that he
was entirely agreeable to any decision concerning the matter that the New York banker might make. I submitted the
question to the banker, and he said: "I like that man, Marshall Hicks. He is a fine man, and, of course, my bank will
pay him his fee of $1,000."

I appealed the case to the United States Circuit Court at New Orleans, and that court affirmed the decision of Judge Hutcheson.

Chapter XX:
The Texas Schoolbook Case

Texas has a free textbook law. This law provides that the State shall buy the schoolbooks used by the children in the public schools and furnish them to the children free of charge. In 1922 this law provided for a Textbook Commission. It was the duty of the Commission to select and contract for the purchase of all free textbooks. When the contract for the books had been made, it was the duty of the State Superintendent to send to all the local school superintendents a form to be used by them in ordering the school books needed in their respective schools.

In December, 1922, the Textbook Commission selected and contracted to buy from The American Book Company certain school books. Under this contract, The American Book Company hoped to sell to the State more than $1,000,000 worth of books over the six year period covered by its contract. The written memoranda of this contract was prepared by the Attorney General, as required by the free textbook law. The State Superintendent of Public Instruction, Mr. S. M. N. Marrs, as Secretary of the Textbook Commission, checked the written memoranda of the contract prepared by the Attorney General with the minutes of the Textbook Commission and wrote "O. K." thereon. The American Book Company executed the bond required by law. Governor Pat Neff, as Chairman of the Textbook Commission, signed the contract for the State, as he had been directed to do by the Textbook Commission.

The State Board of Education was at that time composed of the Governor, the Secretary of State, and the Comptroller of Public Accounts. This Board had general jurisdiction over all the public school affairs of the State.

The State Superintendent refused to include the names of any of the books that The American Book Company had contracted to sell to the State on the forms which he sent to

the local school superintendents to be used in requisition-
ing school books needed by the school children. Unless the
names of The American Book Company books were on
these forms, the local school authorities could not requisition any of The American Book Company's books, and the
company could not sell any of its books to the State as it had
contracted to do.

The American Book Company retained Baker, Botts,
Parker and Garwood to represent it in this controversy.
Judge Garwood, Mr. Walne, Mr. Wharton, and I concluded
that we should get the Board of Education to enter an order
directing the State Superintendent to include the names of
the books that our client had contracted to sell to the State
on the requisition forms sent by him to the local school superintendents. If the State Superintendent refused to obey
this order, then we could apply to the State Supreme Court
for a writ of mandamus, commanding the State Superintendent to carry out the orders of the State Board of Education.
I went to Austin and saw Governor Neff, who was Chairman
of the State Board of Education. Governor Neff did not believe it was necessary for the State Board of Education to
make an order directing the State Superintendent to list the
names of the books of our client on the requisition forms,
because no such order had ever before been made by the
State Board of Education, and he declined to call a meeting
of the Board for that purpose.

There was a great deal of newspaper publicity about these
book contracts, for The American Book Company was only
one of several companies that had made contracts with the
State to supply the school children with schoolbooks. The
Legislature was in session in January, 1923, and the Lieutenant Governor requested an opinion from the Attorney
General as to the validity of these book contracts. The Attorney General advised that in his opinion the contracts
were valid. Notwithstanding this opinion of the Attorney
General, the Legislature passed a bill attempting to cancel
the book contracts. This bill was vetoed by Governor Neff in

a veto message which, I believe, is one of the greatest state papers ever written by any Governor of Texas. In his veto message Governor Neff, among other things, said:

> The school teachers who composed the recent Textbook Commission were not of my selection; they were named and vouched for, as provided by law, by the Superintendent of Public Instruction; the President of The University of Texas; the President of the College of Industrial Arts; the President of the Southwest Texas Normal, and the President of the Agricultural and Mechanical College, as the best qualified persons in all Texas to buy books for the children of the State, and I am unwilling without any facts tending even remotely to show any fraud, collusion, or bad faith in connection with the making of these contracts, to sacrifice the integrity and good name of the members of the Textbook Commission, or to say by the signing of this bill that the entire work of this legally constituted body and branch of the State Government should be set aside and held for naught. To do so would set a dangerous precedent.

> It is wrong in morals, as well as in law, for an individual, much less the State, to arbitrarily cancel a contract when neither fraud, collusion, nor improper influence are even alleged in connection with the making of the contract. None of these things has even been suggested as to the making of the contracts now under consideration.

> By this bill the State endeavors to break its own contracts without giving to the contract holders the right to go into the open court to establish the validity of their contracts. Texas, up to this hour, has never yet sought to impair the obligation of any contract she ever made.

The courts of the country are the proper forums in which the legality of contracts should be tested. This bill, contrary to this well-known principle, shifts the question as to the validity of contracts from the legal forum to Legislative halls. It is a dangerous innovation for the Legislature to usurp the functions of the courts.

Without question, the Texas State Textbook Commission that made the contracts sought to be cancelled by this bill, had the authority to enter into and make, as it did, contracts with certain publishing companies for the purchase of free textbooks for the children of the State. The contracts in question were legally and constitutionally made, prepared by the Attorney General's office, and approved by the State Department of Education.

In absence of fraud, corruption, or mistake, the Legislature has not the right in equity or in good conscience, to regard a contract made by the duly accredited agents of the State, as a 'scrap of paper.' Texas has not done so in the past. She should not begin it now.

I applied to the Supreme Court for leave to file a petition for our client for writ of mandamus, commanding the State Superintendent to include the names of the books our client had contracted to sell to the State on the requisition forms sent to the local school superintendents. The Supreme Court granted the application and permitted the petition to be filed.

I do not know why the State Superintendent refused to include the names of the books of our client on the requisition forms, unless it was because the Legislature, by a simple resolution, directed him not to do so. Neither do I know who employed the able lawyers who appeared as counsel for the State Superintendent. Representing the State Superintendent were Messrs. Francis Marion Etheridge of Dallas,

Charles L. Black of Austin, T. N. Jones of Tyler, and A. M. Frazier of Hillsboro, and a lawyer from the Attorney General's Department. I do not know why the Attorney General thought a lawyer from his department should represent the State Superintendent, for the Attorney General had held the contracts of our client valid.

It was the contention of counsel for the State Superintendent that our client had no contract at all. This contention rested on the proposition that the free textbook law provided that: "Each contract shall be duly signed by the publishing house or its authorized officers and agents; and if it is found to be in accordance with the award and all the provisions of this act, and if the bond herein required is duly presented and duly approved, the Commission shall approve said contract and order it to be signed on behalf of the State by the Governor in his capacity as Chairman."

The Textbook Commission itself had not "approved" the written memoranda of the contracts. The school teachers composing the Textbook Commission, after they had selected the books to be used in the schools, and had accepted written bids submitted by the several successful book companies, and after these facts had been made a matter of record in the minutes of the Textbook Commission, directed the Governor as Chairman of the Textbook Commission to approve the written memoranda of the contracts, which the law itself required the Attorney General to prepare. The State Superintendent had checked the memoranda of the written contracts with the minutes of the meeting of the Textbook Commission and found the provisions of the written memoranda of the contracts to be in accordance with the actual contracts as made by the Textbook Commission with the book companies and as shown by the minutes of the Textbook Commission.

Judge Garwood and I were afraid that our opponents would raise the question in the Supreme Court that we could not maintain our suit for mandamus, because the State Board of Education had not made any order directing the State Superintendent to include the names of the books of our client on the requisition forms sent by him to the local school superintendents. To our happy surprise our opponents did not raise this question. I assume that the able lawyers who were representing the State Superintendent were of the same opinion as Governor Neff, that no such order was necessary. It was true that no such order had ever before been made by the State Board of Education.

Judge Garwood and I argued the case in the Supreme Court for our client. Mr. Etheridge and Mr. John C. Wall of the Attorney General's office made the oral arguments for the State Superintendent. It was the contention of these gentlemen that our client had no contracts because the contracts had never been "approved" by the Textbook Commission as, they argued, the law required them to be. The provision of the law which these gentlemen said required the Textbook Commission to approve the contracts was, so they argued, mandatory, and had been deliberately written into the law for the protection of the public. This duty, so these gentlemen contended, to approve the contracts was a duty required by the textbook law to be performed by the Textbook Commission, a duty which the Commission could not delegate to its Chairman, the Governor. Judge Garwood and I, in our arguments, relied on the following propositions:

> 1. The Textbook Commission had, as appeared from the minutes of its meeting, made the contracts with our client. The State Superintendent, as Secretary of the Textbook Commission, had checked the provisions of the written memoranda of the contracts prepared by the Attorney General with the minutes of the Textbook Commission and found the same correct.

> 2. There was no variance between the terms of the contracts as actually made by the Textbook Commission, as disclosed by the minutes of its meeting, and the

written memoranda of the contracts prepared by the Attorney General.

3. The act of approving the written memoranda of the contracts did not require the exercise of any discretion but was a ministerial act, and being a ministerial act, the performance of that act could be delegated by the Textbook Commission to the Chairman of the Commission, the Governor.

4. The Textbook Commission could not have refused to approve the written memoranda of the contracts if they had been presented to the Commission itself, for the provisions of the free textbook law relied on by our opponents provided that when the written memoranda of the contracts had been signed by the book company and found to be in accordance with the award and the provisions of the free textbook law, and if the bond of the book company is presented and approved, "the Commission shall approve said contract."

5. That the duty of the State Superintendent to list the names of the books of our client on the requisition forms was a ministerial act which he could not lawfully refuse to perform.

6. By his refusal to list the names of our client's books on the requisition form, the State Superintendent was preventing the State of Texas and our client from carrying out the terms of the valid contracts that they had made and entered into.

The court, when it decided our case, held that Judge Garwood and I were right in all our contentions. (American Book Company vs. Marrs, 113 Texas, 291.) The court, however, pointed out in its opinion that we had not alleged in our petition that the State Board of Education had directed the State Superintendent to list the names of the books of our client on the requisition form.

The court then said: "The decision upon the matters involved in relator's petition lying with the State Board of Education, and not with Respondent, it is clear that Respondent could not by mandamus be required to do the thing prayed for here, unless and until the State Board of Education had ordered and directed him to do them, and he had failed or refused to do them. Therefore, Relator has not shown itself entitled to the relief sought."

The opinion of the court was handed down on the last day of the 1922-23 term of the Supreme Court. The court would be in vacation for three months. No relief could be obtained from the Supreme Court until it reconvened on the first day of October. In the meantime, the public schools of the State would open in September. I again went to Governor Neff and requested him to call a meeting of the State Board of Education and to get the Board to enter an order directing the State Superintendent of Public Instruction to list the names of the books that our client had contracted to sell to the State on the requisition forms to be sent to the local school superintendents by the State Superintendent. Governor Neff called a meeting of the State Board of Education, and the Board entered the order that I requested it to enter.

My experience in this case where relief was greatly needed and the Supreme Court was unable to grant any relief because of vacation, caused me to start a statewide agitation for an amendment to the State Constitution, providing that the Supreme Court should be in session twelve months in the year, instead of nine months. This agitation was successful, and in 1930, such an amendment was adopted by a vote of the people. The judges of the Supreme Court may take a vacation, but the court itself can function for the entire twelve months of the year.

Judge Garwood, Mr. Wharton, and I concluded that during the interim when the Supreme Court was not in session we had better protect the rights of our client by obtaining a court injunction, restraining the State Superintendent from ordering any school books to be used in lieu of the books which the State had contracted to purchase from our client. Our client was a New York corporation, and we filed our suit for injunction in the United States District Court for the Western District of Texas, which had jurisdiction because of the diversity of citizenship. The Judge of the United States District Court issued a temporary restraining order, restraining the State Superintendent from ordering school books in lieu of the school books which the State had contracted to purchase from our client, and set the case down for trial on our application for a temporary injunction.

The court was unable to try our case on the date which had been set for its trial at Waco. The judge of the court reset the case for trial in San Antonio, and requested counsel to file written briefs with him prior to the day of the trial. This was done.

Judge Victor Brooks of Austin was the attorney for another book company whose books the State had contracted to use, but which the State Superintendent refused to list on the requisition form. He had not filed any suit for his client, but was waiting for our suit to be determined on the assumption that if we won, the State Superintendent would comply with the law in regard to the books which his client had contracted to supply to the State. At my request, Judge Brooks came to San Antonio to assist us in the trial of our case.

On the morning of the trial, Judge Brooks was told by a friend of his, who was an attaché of the court, that Judge Duval West had written an opinion in the case based on the written briefs filed with him by counsel for both parties to the suit, and that he had decided the case in favor of our client. At nine o'clock, the lawyers were all in the courtroom when Judge West came in. The judge had some typewritten papers in his hand, and when he took his seat and the lawyers had again sat down, Judge West said: "In the case of The American Book Company vs. Marrs it appears that there is no dispute between the parties as to the facts. The only question before the court is one of law. Counsel for both parties have submitted to the court exhaustive briefs on the law questions. The court has carefully read these briefs which seem to cover the case fully, and the court sees no necessity for any oral arguments."

I will always believe that Mr. Etheridge had received the same information that Judge Brooks had received about the court having written its opinion and that the opinion decided the case in our client's favor, for Mr. Etheridge stood up and interrupted the judge with the statement that there were one or two matters not sufficiently covered in his brief that he would like to discuss orally. Judge West invited him to discuss these matters.

Mr. Etheridge began his argument a few minutes after nine o'clock and spoke for four hours. It was a masterful effort. His entire argument was made in support of his proposition that the Textbook Commission, and the Textbook Commission alone, could approve the written memoranda of our contract, and that the Textbook Commission had not done this, and that, therefore, we had no legal contract with the State. If we did not have any legal contract with the State, then, of course, we had no standing at all in the court and our suit for injunction should be dismissed.

Mr. Etheridge's argument lasted beyond the lunch hour, but the court did not interrupt him. At the conclusion of this argument, the court announced a recess of two hours. Judge Garwood, Judge Brooks, and I went over to the St. Anthony Hotel for lunch. We remained silent until we ordered our food. Then Judge Garwood said: "Etheridge made a great argument, but he cannot change the law. Judge West has written his opinion deciding the case for our client, and Etheridge's argument, great though it was, has not changed Judge West's mind. I know Judge West, and when he has once made up his mind as to what the law is, no one can change it. I am not going to answer Mr. Etheridge's argument."

This was the only time I ever knew Judge Garwood's judgment in regard to a lawsuit to be wrong. Judge Brooks and I believed that Mr. Etheridge's argument should be answered. Judge Garwood readily consented for us to reply to

Mr. Etheridge's argument, but declined to make any argument himself.

We returned to the courtroom, and later that afternoon when all the arguments were concluded, Judge West picked up the typewritten papers that had been brought into the courtroom by him that morning and began reading from them. He read two or three paragraphs and then he pushed the papers aside and began to talk. He concluded his observations by holding that our client had no contract to sell any books to the State, because the Textbook Commission itself had never approved in corporate meeting the written memoranda of the contracts that had been prepared by the Attorney General. It was the duty, Judge West held, of the Textbook Commission to approve the contracts, and this duty, he held, could not be delegated by the Commission to its Chairman, the Governor of the State.

Mr. Etheridge had won the greatest victory I had ever seen a lawyer win in a courtroom. The decision of Judge West was a blow to Judge Garwood, Judge Brooks, and me. Judge Garwood had reservations on a boat sailing from Quebec to Europe. To make this boat, he had to return to Houston that night. I told Judge Garwood I was going to stay in San Antonio, prepare an amended petition and present it to Judge West as soon as it was prepared, and try once more to get the court to issue a writ of injunction, restraining the State Superintendent from ordering books in lieu of those which the State had contracted to buy from our client. Judge Garwood declared he was going to stay with me and give up his European trip.

Judge Garwood had been working fearfully hard and was not well. He and Mrs. Garwood had all their plans made for the trip to Europe. Judge Garwood was my boss and I loved him, but I was determined that he should not stay with me in San Antonio and lose his trip to Europe and the rest he so much needed. I finally persuaded this gallant soldier of the law to return to Houston. I went to the depot with him and saw him on the train.

I returned to the hotel and worked all night on my amended petition. The next morning I employed two court reporters to whom I dictated my amended petition. I then went to see Judge West and advised him that on the next morning I would present to him an amended petition, asking for a temporary injunction against the State Superintendent. Mr. Etheridge and the other attorneys for the State Superintendent had all returned home. I sent telegrams to each of these gentlemen, advising them of what I was going to do. Judge Brooks had returned to Austin, and I called him over long distance and asked him if he could return to San Antonio that night.

Judge Brooks reached San Antonio about eight that night. He read my amended petition, suggested some changes that he thought should be made, and at about three o'clock the next morning the final draft of the amended petition was completed. The weather was hot, and when I finally went to bed, I could not sleep.

The next morning after being without sleep for two nights, I went with Judge Brooks to Judge West's courtroom. Mr. Etheridge and our other able opponents were all present. It was one of those hot mornings that we sometimes have in Texas. It took me about an hour to read my amended petition to the court.

When I had finished reading the petition, I began my argument. I had spoken for perhaps an hour, when everything in the courtroom began to go round and round in circles. I suppose I fainted, for the next thing I knew I was lying on a couch in the office of the clerk of the court. When the doctor who had been called arrived, I told him that I had not slept for the past two nights. He examined me and said that there was nothing the matter with me except a case of complete physical exhaustion and with a few day's rest I would be all right. I was soon able to go to the hotel in a taxicab.

Frank Adrien, State Manager in Texas for The American Book Company, was in San Antonio for the trial. I had not been in my hotel room long until Adrien came in and said:

"Mr. Smith, the court has decided the case for us. Why in the hell didn't you faint day before yesterday when the case was tried the first time?"

Adrien was wrong. The court had not decided the case for us. Judge West gave us a temporary restraining order and set the case down for trial on our application for a temporary injunction. This trial occurred some two or three weeks later in Austin. I was not physically able to participate in this last trial before Judge West. Mr. Walne of Baker, Botts, Parker and Garwood represented The American Book Company in this last trial. Judge West adhered to his San Antonio ruling that it was the duty of the Textbook Commission to approve the written memoranda of the contract of our client with the State, and that the Commission could not delegate this duty to its Chairman. From this decision we perfected an appeal to the United States Circuit Court of Appeals at New Orleans.

By means of the temporary restraining orders which the court granted us, we prevented the State Superintendent from ordering books in lieu of the ones the State had contracted to purchase from our client, until the vacation period of the Supreme Court was over. When the Supreme Court convened in October, 1923, we were again ready to ask that court for a writ of mandamus, commanding the State Superintendent to list the names of the books of our client on the requisition forms and to send these forms to the local school superintendents.

I again prepared a petition for a writ of mandamus, wherein, among other allegations, I made the direct allegation that the State Board of Education had made an order directing the State Superintendent to do those things which we, in our petition, were asking the court to compel him to do. I then prepared an application to the Supreme Court asking leave to file our petition for mandamus. When this had been done, the thought occurred to me that Judge West's adverse decision was *res judicata* of the real issue in the case, and that his decision was binding on the Supreme Court of Texas until reversed by the Circuit Court of Appeals. I investigated the subject and found that the courts were not in agreement on the question.

I believed then, and I believe now, that Judge West's decision was binding on the Supreme Court of Texas until reversed by a higher court. Judge West had held as a matter of law that our client did not have any legal contract with the State. If our client did not have a legal contract with the State, it was not entitled to a writ of mandamus to compel the State Superintendent to do anything. Judge West's court was a court of competent jurisdiction to determine the legal question that he had determined, and under the rule of comity between courts, his decision, I thought, should be respected by the Supreme Court of Texas. There are decisions by respectable courts that hold that the full faith and credit clause of the Constitution of the United States has application to judicial proceedings by the United States Courts as well as by state courts. On this question the Supreme Court of Texas has held to the contrary.

Judge Garwood by this time had returned from Europe, and we considered the question of whether the Supreme Court had any jurisdiction at all until Judge West's decision was reversed. We finally concluded to run the risk of again applying to the Supreme Court for a writ of mandamus.

The Supreme Court granted our application to file our petition for mandamus and set the case down for hearing on our petition. Our able opponents did not raise the question of Judge West's decision being binding on the Supreme Court until reversed. Again Mr. Etheridge, Judge Garwood and I argued the case before the Supreme Court. A few weeks after the case was argued, the court decided the case in our favor and granted to our client the writ of mandamus as prayed for. (115 Texas, 40.) As a result of this action by the court our client was able to sell to the State the books which the State had contracted to buy from it.

CHAPTER XXI:
TAXING PIPELINES

When this country entered the World War in 1917, it was necessary, in order to house our soldiers, for the government to build several great cantonments. An eastern client of Baker, Botts, Parker and Garwood built one of these cantonments in Texas. It had to be built hurriedly, and the cost of labor and material was a secondary consideration. Our client built the cantonment on a cost plus basis, its fee in no event to exceed $50,000. The work was done under the immediate supervision of an army officer.

After the war was over, the United States brought a suit in a United State District Court in Texas against our client for $3,000,000 damages alleged to have been suffered by the United States in the building of the cantonment by our client.

It was necessary for Judge Garwood and me to go to an eastern city to confer with the general attorneys of our client. Judge Edwin B. Parker was to be with Judge Garwood and me in this conference. It was winter time, and Judge Parker was in Washington. A snowstorm delayed his train so that he was late for the first conference. He sent Judge Garwood a telegram requesting that Judge Garwood and I proceed with the conference and he would join us as soon as he arrived in town.

The general attorneys for our client was one of the nation's great law firms. An elderly gentleman, one of the senior partners in the eastern law firm, and a younger member of the firm began the conference with Judge Garwood and me. Judge Garwood, with his usual modesty, was permitting the eastern lawyers to take charge of the conference. These gentlemen in a little while were attempting to tell Judge Garwood and me how we should manage a lawsuit in a United States District Court in Texas.

About two hours after our conference began, Judge Parker came in. He had on a great fur coat and fur gloves, and after he had divested himself of these garments, he took full and complete control of the conference. He did this in the most natural and courteous way possible. The born leader, the great executive, a man with a powerful personality had arrived. The atmosphere seemed to be different after the arrival of Mr. Parker. I observed this phenomenon in regard to Mr. Parker more than once.

After the arrival of Mr. Parker, it was accepted by common consent, and without anything being said directly to that effect, that Mr. Parker's law firm was to be in full command of the lawsuit in Texas, but suggestions from the eastern attorneys would be received with appreciation and given careful consideration. I sat in amazement and observed this remarkable man in action. Judge Parker was affable, courteous and kind, and nothing he said could give offense to the most sensitive, but he was in command by common consent.

Judge Garwood and I returned to Texas and were able to defeat the government's suit in the United States District Court on a question of law. From this decision the United States appealed to the Circuit Court of Appeals at New Orleans. Afterwards, its appeal was dismissed, and there was an end to the government's $3,000,000 lawsuit against our client.

By the provisions of Article 7374 of the 1911 Revised Civil Statutes of Texas, each and every individual, company, corporation or association, owning, managing, operating, leasing or letting any pipeline or pipelines within Texas was required to pay to the State of Texas an occupation tax equivalent to two per cent of its gross receipts "if such pipeline or pipelines lie wholly within this state; and if such pipeline or pipelines lie partly within and partly without the state, such individual, company, corporation or partnership, shall pay a tax equivalent to two per cent of such proportion of its gross receipts as the length of such line or lines within the state bears to the whole length of such line or lines."

The Texas Pipeline Company had refused for five years to pay this gross receipts tax on the ground that its pipelines, which were continuing pipelines, were partly within and partly without the State of Texas. Other companies with similar lines had also refused to pay the tax. During this period of time, the gross receipts of The Texas Pipeline Company had been almost $37,000,000, and if the law which attempted to levy the occupation tax was a valid law, then The Texas Pipeline Company owed the State of Texas, as a gross receipts tax, a little more than $740,000.

It became evident that the Attorney General of Texas was going to institute suit against The Texas Pipeline Company for the recovery of this gross receipts tax. The Texas Pipeline Company desired to anticipate the suit by the Attorney General by filing a suit of its own against the Attorney General attacking the constitutionality of the law and asking for an injunction against the Attorney General from prosecuting a suit against it.

Judge Garwood and I, representing The Texas Pipeline Company, prepared a petition in which all the facts were set out, and I went to San Antonio and obtained from Judge Duval West of the Western District of Texas a temporary restraining order, restraining the Attorney General from instituting suit for the collection of this tax, pending a determination of the constitutionality of the law.

A few days later, the Attorney General filed a suit in the 53rd District Court of Travis County, Texas, against the Humble Pipeline Company for the collection of the tax alleged to be due by that company to the State under the law attempting to levy the two per cent gross receipts tax upon pipeline companies. The facts in the two cases, except as to the amount of money involved, were precisely the same.

The Attorney General decided to have the questions involved determined by the State court rather than the United States Court, and he asked for an early trial of the case he had filed in the 53rd District Court. Accordingly, the Attorney General obtained an immediate setting of his case against the Humble Pipeline Company. Mr. T. J. Lawhon of the Legal Department of The Texas Company, later General Attorney in Texas for The Texas Company, and I went to

Austin to observe the proceedings in the trial of the Humble
Pipeline Company case.

Major John C. Townes, Jr., then of the Legal Department
of the Humble Oil Company, represented his company in
the trial of this case. Judge Calhoun of the 53rd District
Court decided that the law was unconstitutional. The
Attorney General proceeded immediately to perfect an
appeal from Judge Calhoun's court to the Third Court of
Civil Appeals at Austin. He completed his appeal and had
the case pending in the Third Court of Civil Appeals within two days after Judge Calhoun decided the case against
him.

The Attorney General, Major Townes, Mr. Lawhon, and
I were agreed that a decision by the Court of Civil Appeals
would not be final and conclusive, and that it would be ad-
vantageous to all parties if the Court of Civil Appeals would
certify the constitutional question involved to the Supreme
Court of Texas for its decision.

Mr. Lawhon and I assisted Major Townes in working out
this agreement with the Attorney General. The late Chief
Justice Key of the Court of Civil Appeals at Austin promptly
agreed to certify and did certify the constitutional question involved to the Supreme Court. This was done within
twenty-four hours after the appeal had been perfected in
the Third Court of Civil Appeals, and the case was in the
Supreme Court of Texas within three days after the trial of
the case had been concluded in the District Court of Travis
County. I believe this is a record.

With the case in the Supreme Court, Judge Garwood, Mr.
Lawhon and I, as well as the late Judge Robert A. Johns,
then General Attorney for The Texas Company in Texas,
believed it advisable that we obtain leave of the Supreme
Court to file a written brief and to make an oral argument
for our client, The Texas Pipeline Company, in the case as
amici curiae. We accordingly filed an application for leave to
file a written brief and to make an oral argument in the case.
Our application was granted, and we filed a written brief,

and upon the hearing of the case, I made an oral argument for The Texas Pipeline Company.

The principal case upon which I relied in my argument before the Supreme Court was the case of G. H. and S. A. Railway Company vs. Texas, 210 U. S., 217. This is the case in which Judge Garwood had won his famous victory for the railroad company, and of which I have already written.

The Supreme Court, in an able opinion by Mr. Justice Pierson, upheld our contention that the gross receipts tax attempted to be levied by the State on pipeline companies was unconstitutional. The case is reported in 112 Texas, 375.

My work with Baker, Botts, Parker and Garwood was very hard work, but it was in every respect agreeable. I have never known and never expect to know a finer group of gentlemen or better lawyers. I went to work for Baker, Botts, Parker and Garwood on May 15, 1922. At the end of that calendar year, the firm gave me a substantial bonus, and without any suggestion from me, gave me an increase in salary for 1923, and at the end of 1923, gave me a further increase in salary for the year 1924.

When I had sufficiently recuperated from my illness following my collapse in the courtroom in San Antonio in The American Book Company case, Mrs. Smith and I took a long vacation, and the firm paid all our expenses.

Houston is the great business town of Texas. It is the financial capital of the state, the center of the oil, lumber and shipping industries, I doubt if in all the world there is a city the size of Houston that has the wealth of Houston. Several hundred thousand people live in Houston, and I assume its climate is agreeable to most of these people. The climate was not agreeable to me. I had lived for years in the high semi-arid area of West Texas. Houston is less than one hundred feet above sea level. The rains and the humid summer heat were to me very disagreeable. My doctor advised that I had lived too long in the high altitude of West Texas, which was comparatively free from humidity, ever to become ac-

climated to the low altitude and the humidity of Houston.
I decided to leave Houston. Reluctantly, I told Judge Garwood of my decision. With his usual kindness, he wrote me
a letter, one that I prize very highly, wherein he told me how
pleasant our association together had been. In this letter,
Judge Garwood, among other things, wrote:

> While, of course, considerations of health must be
> controlling, I cannot refrain from expressing to you
> my very great regret at the severance of relations which
> have been so delightful. Every member of the firm, and
> I may say our entire organization, feels very keenly the
> loss, not only of a friend, but of a finished lawyer. Your
> association with the firm has been especially pleasant
> to me, because I have had the pleasure and benefit of
> that close association which comes from the trial of
> important and strenuously contested cases.

> I feel that a brilliant career as a lawyer is open to you.
> Your place in the profession has been won at an age
> when most of us are struggling for a foothold. That
> your future will fully carry out the promises of the past
> I have no doubt.

Judge Garwood gave me a steel engraved portrait of himself, and on the cover of this he wrote: "In memory of well
fought fields; to have lost without dejection; to have won
without elation; to have fought for love of truth that justice
might prevail, without thought of consequence to self—
what greater life can the world afford—Yours, Hiram M.
Garwood."

CHAPTER XXII:
1932 DEMOCRATIC NATIONAL CONVENTION

From Houston I returned to Austin. I did not have any clients, and no immediate prospects of obtaining any. I opened a law office in the Littlefield Building. Later I was to be at different times a member of two law partnerships in Austin. These were, with some changes in personnel, first; Smith, Caves and Gibson, and second, Smith, Brownlee, Goldsmith and Bagby. Austin is a beautiful little city, situated among low lying hills on the north and south banks of the Colorado River. It is not primarily a business town. It is a government town. The Capitol, the University and other government institutions are located in Austin.

When I returned to Austin from Houston in October, 1924, the United States, and Texas in particular, was in the midst of the great business boom that was to collapse with such disastrous consequences at the end of the decade. I soon found myself constantly employed in important litigation, litigation that was largely brought to me by lawyers who wanted my assistance in the trial of lawsuits, and in appellate court work, particularly in the Supreme Court of Texas, and in other legal work.

For the so-called Insull Interests, I obtained, under the laws of Texas, the water rights of the Colorado River from a point a few miles north of Austin to the headwaters of the river. It was the intention of the Insull organization to erect a series of great hydroelectric and flood control dams on this river above Austin. These plans were later carried out by the United States financed Colorado River Authority.

When modest prosperity came to us, Mrs. Smith and I built a small home. In this home, one room was set apart for our library. We had been buying books for years, and now we hoped we had adequate space for our books. Each year we went on a vacation trip. Many times we visited the Pacific Coast, New York, New England, Minnesota, Chi-

cago, Eastern and Western Canada, and once we went to
Florida and once to Mackinac Island. On many of these
trips we visited the bookstores of New York, Boston, and
Los Angeles, where we bought at different times hundreds
of books.

Within five years after we built our home, our library room
was full of books as was the otherwise unoccupied spaces in
the other rooms. We built a new home largely for the purpose of securing more library room. We thought we were
making adequate provision in our new home to take care of
the books we had and those we would acquire in the future.
In this we were mistaken. I suppose we shall have to sell
some of our old books in order to make room for new ones.
We dislike to do this. We have books that we will never open
again, but it is a satisfaction to know the books we once
enjoyed reading are in the library waiting to be read again.
Have I too often mentioned books? They have been my
friends since childhood and next to the pleasure of possess-
ing them is the pleasure of talking and writing about them.

Mrs. Smith always accompanied me on my business trips.
I suppose we have traveled a quarter of a million miles together on business and pleasure. On our pleasure trips I
was always restless, in a hurry to return home to my work.
Sometimes, at the urgent request of some client, we had to
return to Texas almost immediately after we had arrived at
the place where we expected to spend our vacation. In this
way Mrs. Smith and I have lived and are living our rather
uneventful lives.

For what purpose do we live? What do we accomplish?
What do we obtain from life? When we are growing old, we
ask ourselves these or similar questions. There is so much
we would like to do that we never can do. Most of us live rou-
tine lives. We work that we may eat and we eat that we may
work. I suppose love and work are the two most important
things in our lives and that from these we derive our greatest
happiness and contentment. In books we can read of others
who lived eventful and exciting lives.

Judge Cureton had a fine library in his home, and for years we visited each other once a month or oftener. On these occasions we would talk about the books we had been reading and the men and women who wrote them. As much as I read, it was not often that I read anything that was new to Judge Cureton. I remember that I bought and read with enjoyment the autobiography of John Hays Hammond, the famous American mining engineer. When I next saw Judge Cureton, I began telling him about this remarkable man and his adventures in the far-away places of the world. Soon Judge Cureton, who had not read the book, was telling me about Mr. Hammond. Finally I asked Judge Cureton if he knew who Mr. Hammond was named for. He replied that he did not. I had the satisfaction of telling Judge Cureton that Mr. Hammond had been named for his uncle, John Coffee Hays, the famous Texas Ranger Captain.

After we returned to Austin, Judge Garwood would come to see us when he was in Austin. One evening we had Judge and Mrs. Garwood and Judge and Mrs. Cureton in our home for dinner. Our dinner party ended at two o'clock the next morning. It was an intellectual treat to be present with these two great scholars and listen to their conversation. A few weeks later Judge and Mrs. Garwood were again in our home for dinner. About eleven o'clock that night, we left our home to drive Judge and Mrs. Garwood to their hotel. After we were in the automobile, I mentioned to Judge Garwood that Judge Cureton could, if locked up in a room without a reference book, write an authoritative textbook on geology.

"I wish I had known that the other night when we were together in your home!" Judge Garwood exclaimed. "I would have enjoyed discussing with him a number of interesting geology subjects, including the Balcones fault. You know, Smith, when I was a student at Sewanee, I majored in geology. My old geology teacher tried to persuade me to go to Harvard and obtain a master's degree in geology. He said if I would do this, he would procure a place for me on the faculty at Sewanee, and in a few years I could succeed him."

By the time we arrived at the hotel, Judge Garwood was in the midst of a learned geology discussion, and for an hour we sat in the automobile while Mrs. Garwood, Mrs. Smith and I listened to Judge Garwood discuss geology. We enjoyed the discussion, for Judge Garwood could make any subject that he discussed interesting. He would have made a great teacher. I had known Judge Garwood intimately for years, and I thought he had in his conversations with me discussed every subject with which his great mind was familiar, but never before this night had I ever heard him mention geology. I wonder how much this great man did know that even his intimate friends did not suspect he knew.

When I was a boy, I had read a book, *The Sunset Trail*, by Alfred Henry Lewis. In it were stories of Bat Masterson, the famous sheriff of Dodge City, Kansas. I wanted it for my collection of books about the gun-fighters of the West and Southwest. I searched for it in many book stores throughout the country. At my request a bookstore in Austin made inquiries for it, offering ten dollars for a fair copy. The book was out of print and the store was unable to locate a copy of it.

One summer, Judge Cureton, Mrs. Cureton, Mrs. Smith and I were together in California. One day Judge Cureton and I were, as usual, in a bookstore looking at books. We were back toward the rear of the store among the old secondhand books, when Judge Cureton handed me a book and said: "Smith, is this the Lewis book you have been looking for?"

It was. The book was in fair condition. I asked the clerk in the store the price and he told me fifty cents. The book is now in my collection of books about the gun-fighters.

My work often required me to visit our northern and eastern cities. On these visits I would buy one or more books, and on the flyleaves of these books I would write the date of purchase and the style of the lawsuit, or otherwise designate the nature of the legal work that had brought me to the city where I bought the book. These books constitute for me an interesting collection.

In 1929 the depression came, and by the spring of 1932, Mrs. Smith and I had lost a substantial part of our modest savings. I admired Mr. Hoover. I believed then that Mr. Hoover was a good man and I believe now that he is a good man, and that he is unselfish and patriotic. I did not believe then, and I do not believe now, that he was responsible for the financial depression that had its beginning in the fall of 1929, and that is still with us. By 1932 I was convinced that Mr. Hoover had lost the confidence of the people and that a change should be made in the administration at Washington. I read everything that I could find on the subjects of government and economics.

As a result of my reading, experience, and observations, I reached the definite conclusion that the American people for the next few years must work harder than they had ever worked before, and produce more goods, so that there would be a great abundance of everything needed by the people; that our governments, national, state and municipal, must greatly reduce their expenditures; that as individuals, we must live more economically, save more of our earnings, and that our public and private debts must be paid in full and as quickly as possible. I believed that if the policies I have suggested were adopted by the people, that idle men and idle money would be employed, and the cost of living reduced; that most creditors would be lenient and forbearing with their debtors, and in the few instances where the creditors were unwilling to voluntarily forego their pound of flesh, that public opinion would be such as to compel them to do so.

I knew that the policy that I had formulated would entail hardships, lasting over a period of several years. Sooner or later I thought these hardships had to be faced and endured, and the sooner we did our penance for our unwise extravagance as individuals and as governments, the better it would be. I decided to become active in national politics, not as a seeker of public office, but as one of many who might have some influence in shaping the political and financial policy of my country. Mrs. Smith and I attended our precinct convention. There the issue was not what the financial policy of our nation should be, or who should be the nominee of the Democratic Party for President. The issue at the precinct convention was whether we should or should not repeal the Eighteenth Amendment to the National Constitution. I was elected a delegate at the precinct convention to the county convention.

At the county convention the only issue discussed was whether the Eighteenth Amendment should or should not be repealed. The county convention elected me as a delegate to the state convention which met in Houston. I thought that at the state convention, the state leaders of the Party would give serious consideration to the real problems of the country—what general policy should the country adopt for a restoration of confidence and prosperity to the end that men might have work, clothes, food, and shelter. These matters were given but little attention. Repeal of the Eighteenth Amendment was the issue at Houston. Congressman Sam Rayburn of Bonham was elected temporary chairman. He made the keynote speech. He denounced the wickedness of the Republican Party, indulged in some Jeffersonian platitudes, but did not outline a constructive policy to be adopted by the Democratic Party.

A lawyer by the name of Brown, a former mayor of San Antonio, was elected permanent chairman. A motion was made that the convention go on record as favoring the repeal of the Eighteenth Amendment. With the making of this motion, the war was on. On a *viva voce* vote, Brown declared the repealists had won. This ruling brought on a battle that lasted for two hours. Brown apparently lost control of the convention, for Amon Carter, a newspaper publisher of Fort Worth, took charge. Finally the convention was polled, county by county, on a motion to instruct the Texas delegation to the national convention to vote to submit the question of repeal to the people. This motion was adopted. The Texas delegation to the national convention was also instructed to vote for John N. Garner as the Democratic

Nominee for President until released by Mr. Garner, and to vote as a unit on all questions. At the state convention I was elected as a delegate-at-large from Texas to the national convention.

The Texas delegation chartered a special train to take us to Chicago. We had a forty-piece uniformed band with us. Mr. Waggoner of Fort Worth paid the expenses of the band. Each delegate and each alternate paid, of course, his own expenses. We were met at the station in Chicago by William G. McAdoo and the California delegation. We immediately paraded down Michigan Avenue and another street to the Sherman Hotel, which was headquarters for the Texas delegation. Mrs. Smith and I stayed at the Stevens Hotel on Michigan Avenue where we had a fine view, from our hotel room window on the twelfth floor, of Lake Michigan and of the park between the hotel and the lake.

We were able to secure the badge and book of tickets of admission of an alternate, who did not come to Chicago, for Mrs. Smith. This gave her a reserved seat on the convention floor. Visitors could not gain admission to the galleries except by ticket. Tickets were in great demand and sold, so I was told, for as high as forty dollars for one session of the convention. I did not hear of any delegate or alternate selling his tickets of admission.

Politics! Hip hip, hurrah! Patriotism and greed. Prohibition and anti-prohibition. Preachers and turks, philosophers, lawyers, and clerks. Fanatics and fools. Courage, sincerity, cowardice, and a desire to be on the bandwagon at any cost. Men of fine ability with an honest desire to serve their country and their fellow man. Cheaters, grafters, and political racketeers. Huey Long and others of his ilk. Alfred Smith and Thomas Walsh. Governor Richie and Melvin Traylor, John W. Davis and Mrs. Woodrow Wilson. John Raskob and Jim Farley. The good, the great, the wise, the rich, the poor, the patriot, the gentleman, the gentlewoman, the ruffian, the boor, the mean, the miserable. We were all there, including Mr. and Mrs. F. D. Roosevelt toward the last.

"Happy days are here again," the organ thunders. Twenty thousand men and women shout and sing, "Hail, hail, the gang's all here." The Tammany delegation sits grim and silent across the aisle from the Texas delegation. Governor Murray with his band of fifty lovely girls dressed in kilts. "The eyes of Texas are upon you." The Texas delegation stands and cheers. "My Maryland, My Maryland." The handsome Richie and his delegation of fine looking men and women march by. The quiet cold voice of the permanent chairman, Thomas Walsh, "For what purpose does the gentleman address the chair?" A fight among the delegation from Texas.

Alfred Smith addresses the convention and pleads for a plank in the platform favoring the repeal of the Eighteenth Amendment. He receives a great reception from the delegates and an even greater one from the visitors in the gallery. For the fourteenth time there is a row among the delegates from the District of Columbia. The Texas delegation caucuses, curses and right nobly disagrees. Texas votes to throw Huey Long and his delegation out of the convention. The Roosevelt crowd save him.

The convention adopted a platform that was sane, sound, and courageous. It squarely faced the repeal of the Eighteenth Amendment issue by declaring that the Democratic Party favored the outright repeal of the amendment. It declared in definite terms that if the Democrats were placed in power, the expenditures of the national government would be reduced twenty-five per cent, and that this was a wise policy for the state and municipal governments to follow. In general, the platform conformed to my ideas of the policy the American people should follow. It is my opinion that no political party in American history has ever written a better political platform than the one adopted by the Democrats in Chicago in 1932.

After the platform had been adopted, the nominating speeches began. Former Governor Ely of Massachusetts nominated Alfred E. Smith. I thought it the best nominating speech of the convention. The convention remained in session all night. At four o'clock in the morning Mrs. Smith was asleep on three chairs. The next day her picture, taken while she was asleep, appeared in a Chicago newspaper under the caption: "Mrs. E. F. Smith of Austin, Texas, is holding out for Garner." Jimmy Walker, then Mayor of New York, came to the convention in the early hours of the morning wearing his pajamas and voted for Alfred E. Smith.

When the sun arose the next morning, the convention was still in session. The bands blared, the organ thundered, delegates paraded. Three ballots were taken without a nomination. There was a recess until nine o'clock at night. The Texas delegation held another and its last caucus. A trade was made. Texas and California changed their votes from Garner to Roosevelt. We piled into taxicabs and again rushed to the convention hall. Mr. McAdoo addressed the convention. Many of the twenty thousand in the galleries booed him. Mayor Cermak finally restored order. Another ballot was taken, and Roosevelt was nominated. There was a delay of another night and another day, and then Garner was nominated for Vice-President. Mr. Roosevelt made a sensational airplane flight to Chicago and addressed the convention. After six days and nights, the convention adjourned *sine die*. The next President and Vice-President of the United States had been nominated.

Chapter XXIII:
Election Trouble in Hidalgo County

In 1900 the population of Hidalgo County was 6,837. In 1920 it was 38,110, and in 1930 it was 77,004. The southern boundary of Hidalgo County is the Rio Grande. Fifty years ago the entire county was ranch country, except isolated instances of dry farming and irrigation near the river. All the land in the county was owned by people of the Spanish and Mexican races. This ownership was in large tracts, originally granted by the King of Spain or the Government of Mexico. As a Republic and as a State, Texas recognized and has always respected these grants.

Mr. A. Y. Baker, when he was a young man, was a Texas Ranger. He was sent to Hidalgo County, where, as a Ranger and later as sheriff, he brought protection to the Mexican ranchmen from the raids of Mexican bandits, who would, at frequent intervals, cross the river from Mexico, visit the ranches of Hidalgo County, sometimes murdering the men or abducting the women, and driving the cattle and horses of the ranch owners back across the river. It is said that in self-defense and in the enforcement of the law, Mr. A. Y. Baker pistoled many desperadoes and ruffians out of existence. In the language of the Southwest, Mr. Baker raised "the flag of law and order in Hidalgo."

Out of gratitude to Mr. Baker and in order to keep him in Hidalgo County so that he could continue to protect their interests from the outlaws, the ranchers of the county sold to him many thousands of acres of land. The land was of small value at that time and the consideration for the conveyance of the land from the Mexicans to Mr. Baker was not large.

Mr. Baker was elected sheriff of the county and held that office until his death in November, 1930. Sheriff A. Y. Baker was a man of vision and born to be a leader of his fellows. He foresaw the Magic Valley that was to be, when thousands of acres then covered with brush would be covered with the finest citrus fruit orchards in the world. Sheriff Baker, in addition to his duties as sheriff, devoted his time and talents to business enterprises of a financial nature, such as lands, banks and irrigation projects. He became the political boss of the county and for two decades or more ruled with an iron hand. He had his devoted followers and his bitter enemies.

In the later years of his life, the political enemies of Mr. Baker referred to him as the "multi-millionaire sheriff of Hidalgo County," and sought, by innuendo, to leave the impression that Mr. Baker acquired his wealth in some illegal way as the result of his being sheriff of the county for such a long period of time. Mr. Baker's wealth was doubtless exaggerated. The increase in the value of his lands could easily account for whatever wealth he may have acquired. Land in Hidalgo County had a value in 1925, if improved, of from $300 to $5,000 an acre, and if unimproved, from $25 to $50 an acre according to the accurate and conservative Texas Almanac of 1925, published by the publishers of the *Dallas News*.

Judge C. F. Gibson and I were law partners in 1928. Judge Gibson had, as an Assistant Attorney General, been in charge of the bond desk in the Attorney General's Department for several years. He was, when we were partners, and is now, one of the few experts in the law of municipal bonds in Texas. When we were partners, he devoted practically his entire time to bond matters. Printing companies would submit bids to municipalities for printing all supplies needed in holding bond elections, and if bonds were voted, would print the bonds. For some of these printing companies, Judge Gibson prepared the necessary legal papers.

In Hidalgo County irrigation, road and school districts voted immense bond issues. Judge Gibson prepared some of these bond records. I make this statement as a possible explanation of how I came to be employed by Sheriff A. Y. Baker in the election contests, and other litigation, civil and criminal, that followed the general election held in Hidalgo County in 1928. Prior to the November election of 1928, I did not know Sheriff Baker, or any other official of Hidalgo County.

On November 14, 1928, my law firm, Smith and Gibson, received a telegram from A. W. Cameron, County Judge of Hidalgo County, reading as follows: "When election returns are not made in accordance with law is it the duty of the Commissioners court to refuse to estimate the returns? Please reply immediately."

I made an investigation of the election laws of Texas and sent Judge Cameron the following telegram:

"Your telegram of inquiry received. Article 3026 prescribes how election returns shall be made. If election returns are not made as required by law, the commissioners court is forbidden to consider them in compiling its estimate by Article 3031, Revised Civil Statutes, which statute reads as follows: 'No election returns shall be opened or estimated unless the same have been returned in accordance with the provisions of this title.' Our Supreme Court in Fowler vs. George, 68 Texas, 30, said: 'It is true that our present statute says that election returns shall not be opened or estimated unless same have been returned in accordance with its provisions.' In Jackson vs. Houser, 298 S. W. 186, our Court of Civil Appeals held: 'That the commissioners court was acting within the province of its lawful duties in determining whether particular returns should be estimated.' Other cases in point are Wells vs. Commissioners Court, 195 S. W. 606, and Griffith vs. Ainsworth, 216 S. W. 469."

I later learned that the situation which caused Judge Cameron to send the telegram that he did send to Smith and Gibson was as follows:

In Hidalgo County there is a town by the name of Weslaco. Evidence later introduced before a Congressional Committee and in the State and Federal Courts was to the effect that in the general election in Hidalgo County in 1928, the Democratic candidates for all the county offices and for district judge were opposed by the nominees of the Citizen's Republican Organization of Hidalgo County. In a legal controversy between those claiming to be Republicans, the San Antonio Court of Civil Appeals held that the candidates of the Citizen's Republican Organization for the local offices in Hidalgo County were not the candidates of the Republican Party, but were the nominees of a faction that had bolted the regular Republican Convention of Hidalgo County.

Judge J. E. Leslie, a Democrat and one of the District Judges of Hidalgo County, had been appointed to his office by the Governor. Thinking that he had two more years of his current term to serve, he was not a candidate at the Democratic primary, and neither he nor anyone else was nominated by the Democrats for District Judge. The Secretary of State at Austin ruled that Hidalgo County must elect a District Judge in 1928. This meant that those favoring the re-election of Judge Leslie must write his name in on the ballot. It was in 1928 that Texas, for the first and probably the last time in its history, cast a majority of its votes for the Republican Presidential Electors. This meant that some 200,000 Texas voters voted the Democratic ticket for state and local officers, but scratched the Democratic nominees for presidential electors, and scratched the Republican nominees for state and local offices, and voted for the Republican nominees for presidential electors. This failure on the part of the voters to vote the Democratic ticket straight resulted in many ballots being mutilated, because the voters, in attempting to scratch a part of the Republican ticket and a part of the Democratic ticket, did not in every instance scratch the ticket correctly, with the result that their ballots showed a vote for a Democrat and a Republican for the same office.

The evidence further showed that there had been considerable controversy, bickering, disturbance and excitement at the polling place in the town of Weslaco. There was evidence that the envelope in which the election returns were returned by the election officials of Weslaco to the County Judge had never been sealed as required by law, and that the affidavits of persons who voted at Weslaco, by making affidavits that they had paid their poll taxes but had lost or misplaced the receipts, did not accompany the election returns, as required by the election laws.

The Commissioners Court, composed of all the County Commissioners and the County Judge, is required by law to make up the official election returns of the county from the election returns of all the election precincts. In this connection the law expressly provides that "no election returns shall be opened or estimated, unless the same have been returned in accordance with the provisions of this title."

The election law further provides that when all the ballots have been counted by the persons holding an election, triplicate returns of the election shall be made out showing the results of the election at that voting place, and these returns, together with poll lists and tally sheets, "shall be sealed up in an envelope" and delivered to the County Judge.

I did not know it at the time I sent my telegram to Judge Cameron, but he also obtained from the County Attorney of Hidalgo County and from James A. Graham, an attorney living at Brownsville who had been a District Judge, an opinion as to whether the Commissioners Court should estimate the election returns from Weslaco. These two gentlemen gave Judge Cameron the same advice that I had given him in my telegram.

It was claimed that if the Commissioners Court, in making up the election returns of Hidalgo County, had counted the returns from Weslaco, District Judge Leslie, the Democrat, would be defeated, and a gentleman by the name of Gordon Griffin would be elected. I thought it was the legal duty of the Commissioners Court to exclude the election returns from Weslaco, if the election returns had not been returned as required by law. The provision of the election law declaring that no election returns which have not been returned according to law shall be opened or estimated by the Commissioners Court is, I believe, mandatory.

During the Congressional investigation of the Hidalgo County election and the civil and criminal court proceedings that resulted from the action of the Commissioners Court in excluding the election returns from Weslaco from the official election returns of Hidalgo County, the statement was made over and over again that the Commissioners Court had, in excluding the election returns from Weslaco, taken advantage of a mere technicality of the law; that the fact that the envelope containing the election returns had not been sealed did not constitute any evidence that the election returns had been tampered with, and that it was an outrage for the Commissioners Court to disfranchise the several hundred qualified voters who had voted at the Weslaco voting place for no other reason than that the election officials of that precinct had failed to seal the envelope in which the election returns had been returned to the County Judge.

These reiterated statements by my opponents about a mere technicality of the law reminded me of the grief I had suffered in the school book case, where my opponents had relied on the proposition that my client had no contract, because the Textbook Commission had not itself approved the written memoranda of the contract prepared by the Attorney General. Once more I reiterate that there is no such thing as a technicality of the law. Either a thing is the law or it is not the law.

Honorable John N. Garner was a candidate for Congress in 1928. Hidalgo County was in his Congressional District. The Republicans had carried the nation by a large majority in the 1928 election, and even Texas had cast a majority vote for the Republican Presidential Electors. To Hidalgo County came the Select Committee on Campaign Expenditures of the House of Representatives of the United States to investigate the election that had been held in Hidalgo County. Representing the Democrats at the hearing held in McAllen by the Congressional Committee were Messrs. E. A. McDaniel of McAllen, B. D. Tarlton, Jr. of Corpus Christi, James R. Daugherty of Beeville, James A. Graham of Brownsville, D. W. Glasscock of Mercedes, and I.

The hearing was held in the Baptist Church in McAllen. The people were excited. From all parts of the county they came to McAllen, bringing their children and their lunches. Temporary seats were placed in the aisles of the church, and these seats and all other seats in the church were taken hours before the time arrived for the hearing to begin. Most of the people remained in their seats during the recess for luncheon, for once a person gave up his seat, he would not be able to get another. The members of the Committee and the attorneys could not even enter the church by the front door. We had to come in at the rear, walk across the raised platform upon which the pulpit was situated, then jump down in front of the pulpit, where a small place had been reserved for the members of the Committee and the attorneys. The hearing lasted two or three days.

A majority of the Committee were Republicans, but by unanimous vote the Committee held, even before it left McAllen, that Mr. Garner was innocent of any wrongdoing. I prepared and filed with the Committee a written brief for the Hidalgo County officers. It did no good. The Committee, after returning to Washington, filed a report with Congress in which it recommended that the Attorney General of the United States investigate the Hidalgo County election of 1928, with the end in view of bringing indictments against certain county officials.

Mr. Gordon Griffin, who had been a candidate for District Judge against Judge Leslie, filed an election contest against Judge Leslie in Hidalgo County and then brought suit in the 53rd District Court at Austin, of which court Honorable George C. Calhoun was the judge, wherein it was sought:

1. By mandatory injunction to compel the Commissioners Court to open and estimate the election returns from Weslaco.

2. By mandatory injunction to compel the County Judge to send to the Secretary of State the election returns from all the election precincts of Hidalgo County, including the election returns from Weslaco.

3. By prohibitory injunction to restrain the Secretary of State from counting the election returns for District Judge that had been sent to the Secretary of State by the County Judge of Hidalgo County.

4. To adjudicate that Mr. Griffin was entitled to the certificate of election as Judge of the 93rd District Court of Hidalgo County, Texas.

To Mr. Griffin's suit in Travis County, my associates and I filed a plea to the jurisdiction of the court. It was our contention that the court was without jurisdiction to try the case, because it involved a political matter, and that injunction did not lie to protect a person in a political right or to assist in acquiring such a right; that Mr. Griffin had an adequate remedy at law, namely, the right to contest the election of Judge Leslie, and that he had taken advantage of this law and had filed a statutory election contest against Judge Leslie.

Judge Calhoun overruled our plea to the jurisdiction of the court. We then filed an answer to the merits of the case, and demanded a jury. Upon the trial of the case and when all the evidence had been introduced, Judge Calhoun instructed the jury to return a verdict in favor of Mr. Griffin. The jury obeyed the court's instruction, and thereafter the court entered judgment in all respects as prayed for by Mr. Griffin.

I do not recall ever being so angry over losing a lawsuit as I was over losing the Leslie case in Judge Calhoun's court. Every court in the land that had ever passed on the question, including many decisions by the Supreme Court of Texas, had held that the right to hold office or to enjoin an election board could not be tried in a court of equity for injunction, because the remedy of injunction is not available to determine political questions. The courts were unanimous in holding that persons feeling themselves aggrieved by the action of election tribunals must seek relief at law by instituting election contests in the manner provided by law.

The trial before Judge Calhoun had lasted for about a week, and I was tired, as well as angry. Shortly after the court had instructed a verdict against Judge Leslie, I had to pass through Judge Calhoun's office in going to the office of the District Clerk. Judge Calhoun greeted me in his usual pleasant manner and wanted to know how I was feeling. To his inquiry, I replied: "Disgusted and outraged. But," I added, "just as sure as God made little green apples, I am going to reverse your judgment in this case, and the higher court will order the case dismissed, because your court had no more jurisdiction to try this case than has His Royal Highness, the King of Siam."

Judge Calhoun laughed and said: "Do you know, I will not be surprised if you do get the higher courts to reverse my judgment in this case."

This pleasant reply by Judge Calhoun took all the fight out of me. Judge George C. Calhoun was one of the great trial judges of Texas. For about a quarter of a century he was the judge of the 53rd District Court of Travis County. He resigned that office to become a member of the Commission of Appeals of the Court of Criminal Appeals of Texas.

It was foolish for me to make the statement that I made to Judge Calhoun. No lawyer can assert with absolute assurance that the higher courts will reverse any judgment of a lower court. This is true even though the appellate court may in the past have many times declared the law to be what the losing lawyer in the trial court claims it is.

My associates and I appealed the Griffin case. The Court of Civil Appeals at Austin affirmed the judgment of Judge Calhoun, 23 S.W. (2), 535. We applied to the State Supreme Court for writ of error, and our application was granted. Thereafter the Supreme Court held that Judge Calhoun's court had no jurisdiction to try the case and ordered that Mr. Griffin's suit be dismissed. 25 S.W. (2), 820.

In the meantime, the candidate for the Legislature, who had been defeated for Representative to the State Legislature by the Democratic nominee, had filed an election contest for that office in the House of Representatives. My associates and I were able to defeat this contest. During the hearing before the Legislature, large crowds of people drove the three hundred or more miles from Hidalgo County to Austin to be spectators at the election contest in the House of Representatives.

About the time the Supreme Court decided the Griffin vs. Leslie case in favor of Judge Leslie, the United States Government moved its "heavy artillery" into action. In response to the recommendation made by the Congressional Investigation Committee, the Attorney General sent his representatives into Hidalgo County. My information at that time was that an attempt was made to obtain an indictment against the Hidalgo County officials in the Brownsville division of the Western District of Texas. The grand jury refused to return an indictment. Then the effort was repeated in the Houston Division of the Southern District of Texas with success. The grand jury at Houston returned the following indictment:

The grand jurors for the United States of America empaneled and sworn in the District Court of the United States for the Houston Division of the Southern District of Texas at the February Term of said court in the year 1930, and inquiring for said district, upon their oath present, that theretofore, to wit, on November 6, 1928, a general election was held in Hidalgo County, in said State of Texas, and in the Brownsville Division of said Southern District of Texas, for State and County officials; for Presidential Electors of the United States; for a member of the Senate of the United States from Texas and for a member of the Congress of the United States for the Fifteenth Congressional District of said State of Texas, at which said election George W. Hackney, Earl Preston Savage, Dar Ratliff, Tina Phillips, Harry G. Solether, Harry Stebbins, William Ownes, Emma Blackwell, Lewis Annan, Alma B. Fort, Yancy P. Yarbrough, Eva Adams, Minnie E. Arbuckle, Sam Martin, Howard Wright, Walter Fawcett and John W. Bennett among others, citizens of the United States and of said State of Texas who had resided in said State of Texas for one year next preceding said General Election, and in said county and in Precinct No. 14 thereof for six months next preceding said General Election were respectively over the age of twenty-one years, and had paid poll taxes under the laws of said State of Texas for the year 1928, and therefore then and there being respectively qualified electors and voters in said precinct, having the qualifications requisite for electors of the most numerous branch of the Legislature of said State of Texas for such Presidential Electors, for such member of the Senate and for such member of Congress, whose rights and privileges to vote for the candidates for the office of such Presidential Electors, member of the Senate and member of Congress, and to have their votes counted, canvassed, estimated and certified in said election when cast were rights and privileges the free exercise of which were then and there secured to them respectively by the Constitution and laws of the United States, and did in fact each cast his vote in said precinct and at said elections for one of the candidates for members of Congress for said Congressional District.

And the grand jurors aforesaid, upon their oaths aforesaid, do further present, that _____, _____, _____ and ____, hereinafter called defendants, throughout the period of time extending from October 1, 1928, to December 1, 1928, and within said county, division and district, constituted a majority of the members of the County Commissioners' Court and the Election Board of said County each duly qualified and then and there acting as such member; and that said defendants, throughout said period of time there unlawfully and feloniously did conspire, combine, confederate and agree together, and with ____, ____, ____, and ____, hereinafter also called defendants, to injure and oppress said citizens, electors and voters in the free exercise and enjoyment of their said rights and privileges to vote for the candidates for said office of member of Congress for said Congressional District and for said Presidential Electors and for said members of the Senate, and to have their votes for such candidates counted when cast, by said defendants ____, ____, ____, and ____, as such members of said County Commissioners' Court and Election Board arbitrarily and without right neglecting and refusing to canvass or count any of the votes cast in said precinct at said election for any of said officials or candidates, including such candidates for said office of member of Congress for said Congressional District, and said Presidential Electors, and for said member of the Senate, and by their arbitrarily and without right neglecting and refusing to estimate, canvass, regard or consider such votes as affecting the results of said election to the State Election Board of said State of Texas, and by said defendants, ____, ____, ____ and ____ and aiding, assisting, counseling and advising said first named defendants in so doing: Against the peace and dignity of the United States, and contrary to the form of the statute in such case made and provided." [*I have omitted the names of the several defendants named in the indictment.*]

The defendants named in the indictment employed Messrs. E. A. McDaniel, B. D. Tarlton, James R. Daugherty, Jacob F. Wolters of Houston, and his partner, Walter Woodul, and me to defend them in the United States District Court. The indictment returned by the grand jury at Houston was returned to Brownsville. By agreement between the court and counsel for the government and counsel for defendants, the case was transferred to Houston, where it was tried.

To the indictment against our clients, I prepared a motion to quash. As grounds for this motion, I alleged:

1. That the indictment alleged that the persons named in the indictments as having been deprived of their

right to vote and to have their votes counted were qualified voters on November 6, 1928, because they had paid their poll tax for the year 1928. The law is that in order to vote on November 6, 1928, the voter, if subject to the payment of a poll tax, must have paid on or before February 1, 1928, his poll tax for the year 1927.

2. That the indictment alleged that the conspiracy consisted of an agreement on the part of the defendants that the Commissioners Court would not count the votes of the alleged voters named in the indictment. The law is that the votes are counted by the election officials and then the ballots are locked in ballot boxes and delivered to the County Clerk. All that the Commissioners Court does is to estimate the election returns, which is an entirely different thing from counting the votes.

3. That the indictment alleged that the defendants had agreed that the Commissioners Court would not certify the election returns to the State Election Board. The law does not authorize the Commissioners Court to certify the election returns to anyone. That is done by the County Judge, and there is no such thing as a State Election Board; but the County Judge certifies the returns to the Secretary of State of Texas, at Austin.

The case was tried before Judge Joseph C. Hutcheson, Jr., then United States District Judge for the Southern District of Texas. Judge Hutcheson overruled my motion to quash the indictment, and in this he was in error. Many years ago Judge Maxey, the United States District Judge for the Southern District of Texas, held that the Commissioners Court could not count the ballots of the voters. In this case, reported in the 42nd Federal Reporter, Judge Maxey construed the same election laws of Texas under which the 1928 election was held.

It is no violation of the law for men to agree not to count votes, if it is no part of their duty to count them. Such an agreement is a lawful agreement. It is no violation of the law for men to agree not to certify election returns, if it is not their duty to certify such returns. It is no violation of law for men to agree not to certify election returns to a State Election Board, when there is no such Board to which such election returns can be certified. According to the allegations in the indictment, the persons whom it was alleged the defendants had deprived of their election privileges were not qualified voters, because there was no allegation that they had paid a poll tax that entitled them to vote in the 1928 election.

After the motion to quash the indictment was overruled, the Special Assistant Attorney General, who had come down from Washington to prosecute the defendants, proceeded to introduce his testimony. He failed utterly to make out any case at all as against two of the defendants. This failure was conceded by the prosecutor, and he moved the court to dismiss the case as against them and his motion was by the court granted. When all the evidence had been introduced, my associates and I filed with the court a motion to instruct the jury to return a verdict of not guilty for all the defendants.

We argued the motion before the court, and when the arguments of counsel for the government and counsel for the defendants had been concluded, Judge Hutcheson discussed the matter from the bench for thirty minutes or more, and then announced that he would act on the motion after the noon recess.

Two of the lawyers associated with me in the trial of the case are devout Catholics. These two gentlemen and I went over to the Rice Hotel for lunch. After we had ordered our food, one of these lawyers said: "Do you men know what I was doing while Judge Hutcheson was discussing our motion?"

I told him that I did not know what he was doing, to which he replied: "I was praying that Almighty God would make Judge Hutcheson grant our motion and instruct the jury to return a verdict of not guilty."

The second lawyer then spoke up and said that he had been praying too, but said he: "I was praying that Almighty God would make Judge Hutcheson do what was right."

To this the first lawyer replied: "Hell, I know what's right, and if God makes Judge Hutcheson do what's right, the Judge will grant our motion."

At the time our case was being tried before Judge Hutcheson, there was a vacancy on the Circuit Court of Appeals for the Fifth Circuit, and it was believed that the President would appoint someone to fill the vacancy within the next few days. The friends of Judge Hutcheson were endeavoring to get the President to appoint him. Our case was one in which the government was apparently very much interested, for it had sent a Special Assistant Attorney General to prosecute the case. Judge Hutcheson had the courage to follow the law, for he granted our motion and instructed the jury to return a verdict of not guilty. In a few days, President Hoover appointed Judge Hutcheson to the United States Circuit Court of Appeals. This distinguished jurist has caused me more grief in the trial of cases before him than any other one judge, but candor compels me to make the statement that Judge Hutcheson is an excellent lawyer and a judge of unquestioned integrity.

Prior to the trial of the case in the Houston court, Sheriff A. Y. Baker had died. Sheriff Baker had many enemies; he also had many true and loyal friends. I never saw or heard Sheriff A. Y. Baker do or say anything that indicated to me that he was anything other than an outstanding, public-spirited citizen.

I have often wondered whether Mr. Griffin, or Judge Leslie, was elected District Judge. If Mr. Griffin received a majority of the legal votes he should have had the office.

If Mr. Griffin had pressed his election contest, instead of attempting to obtain the office by injunction, the Weslaco box could have been opened and the ballots counted. This would have determined whether he or Judge Leslie received the more votes.

The members of the Commissioners Court who voted to exclude the Weslaco election returns were bitterly criticized, and prosecuted in the United States Court for their action, notwithstanding the fact that the evidence showed the election returns were not returned as required by law. The law forbids estimating election returns not returned as required by law. The purpose of this law is to prevent any tampering with the election returns.

The lawyer in a case frequently does not know, and cannot know, whether his client's cause is just or unjust. The evidence in the Hidalgo cases was such as to convince me that my clients were not guilty of any crime. Apparently Judge Hutcheson was of the same opinion for he instructed the jury to return a verdict of not guilty.

CHAPTER XXIV:
MARTIAL LAW IN EAST TEXAS OIL FIELD

The East Texas Oil Field has enriched thousands, but it has brought grief on several occasions to many people. It was the direct cause of my losing a small fortune and indirectly it wrecked my reputation as an alleged expert on the subject of martial law.

Prior to the bringing in of the great gushers in the East Texas Field, I had been retained in a lawsuit that involved the title to a section of oil land in West Texas. For my services I had been paid a cash fee and if I won the case, I was to have an interest in the land. The Supreme Court of Texas held that my clients were entitled to the land. Our opponents had a right to file a motion for rehearing in the Supreme Court. Our opponents agreed not to file a motion for rehearing and to recognize our title and pay us for one-eighth of the oil that had been produced from the land, provided we would give them an oil and gas lease on the land, by the terms of which they would pay us the value of one-eighth of the oil thereafter produced from the land.

I wanted to accept the offer, for I knew the point of law upon which we had won the case was a close one, and I was afraid the Supreme Court would grant the motion for a rehearing. My clients refused the offer, and our opponents filed an able and vigorous motion for rehearing. Oil was selling at $1.50 a barrel at the time the motion for rehearing was filed. My interest in the section of land was worth at that time $100,000. The court did not act on the motion for rehearing for more than a year after the motion was filed. In the meantime, the East Texas Field had been brought in and the price of oil was 10 cents a barrel. The Supreme Court finally overruled the motion for rehearing, and I was glad to sell my interest in the land, at the then low price of oil, for a few thousand dollars.

The Legislature of Texas enacted conservation laws and vested in the Railroad Commission of Texas the power to make rules and regulations, including proration orders, to conserve the crude supply and to prevent waste thereof. In my opinion the Judges of the United States Courts in Texas, by reason of their inability to comprehend the legal questions involved in proration as a conservation measure, or by reason of their disinclination to accept as an actuality the power of the state government to conserve its natural resources, as represented by oil and gas, brought about by their decisions in the earlier conservation cases a deplorable situation in the East Texas Oil Field.

In the McMillan case, 51 Federal (2), 400, a three-judge court presided over by Circuit Judge Joseph C. Hutcheson, Jr., held the orders of the Railroad Commission as applicable to the wells of the McMillans in the East Texas Field invalid. In the Danciger case, 49 S. W. (2), 837, the Texas courts had held a similar order of the Railroad Commission valid.

The tragedy of the Federal Court's refusal in the McMillan case to uphold the orders of the Railroad Commission becomes apparent when it is recalled that thereafter, in 1932, the Supreme Court of the United States, in the case of Champlin Refining Company vs. Oklahoma Corporation Commission, 286 U. S., 210, sustained a statute of Oklahoma and orders made pursuant thereto by the Oklahoma Commission, not dissimilar from the Texas Conservation Laws and from the order of the Texas Railroad Commission, that was held invalid in the McMillan case.

After the decision of the court in the McMillan case, the situation in the East Texas Field became intolerable. Hundreds, probably thousands, of small operators were facing ruin, for oil was 10 cents a barrel. This meant that after proper deductions were made, the landowners and royalty holders were receiving less than 1 cent a barrel for the oil that was being produced from their land. In addition to this low price, it was the opinion of geologists and other experts that the unregulated production in the East Texas Field, if continued, would result in damages to the field such as would prevent the recovery of millions of barrels of oil that, under proper production regulations, could be recovered.

The Legislature was called in special session and new conservation laws were enacted. The Railroad Commission entered an order fixing the production of oil in East Texas at two hundred and twenty-five barrels per well per day. This order did little good, for it was disregarded by many operators and new wells were being drilled at a very rapid rate. The Commission made a new order, reducing the per-well allowable to one hundred and sixty-five barrels per day. The so-called "hot oil" producers disregarded this order. By petitions and resolutions passed at mass meetings in East Texas, the Honorable Ross S. Sterling, Governor of Texas, was urged to declare martial law in East Texas in order to enforce the law. The Governor received advice that unless this was done there would be riots and bloodshed in the East Texas Oil Field.

On August 16, 1931, Governor Sterling declared martial law in the East Texas Oil Field and directed General Jacob F. Wolters to take command of the troops and without delay to shut down "each and every producing crude oil well" in the territory embraced in the Governor's declaration of martial law. This order was later modified so as to allow the oil wells to produce in accordance with the orders of the Railroad Commission.

Mr. E. Constantin and other owners of oil wells in the military district brought a suit in the United States District Court for the Eastern District of Texas against the members of the Railroad Commission, and others, for a temporary injunction, restraining the enforcement of the allowable of the one hundred and sixty-five barrels per well per day. The Governor was not at first made a party to this suit. Honorable Randolph Bryant, the judge of the court, without any notice to or any opportunity for the defendants to be heard, granted a temporary restraining order. This paralyzed the Railroad Commission so that it could no longer participate in the enforcement of its proration orders.

According to the evidence later introduced upon the trial of this case, when it became known that Judge Bryant had enjoined the Railroad Commission, many persons, in their desperation implored the Governor to police the oil field or there would be great destruction of property and possible loss of life. The Governor directed General Wolters to enforce proration, and the Governor made his own proration orders, eventually reducing the daily allowable to one hundred barrels per well.

Mr. Constantin and the other plaintiffs amended their petition and made the Governor a party to the suit, and sought to enjoin the Governor and General Wolters from interfering with their production of oil. The principal legal points relied on by Mr. Constantin and the other plaintiffs were:

1. That the oil conservation law was unconstitutional.

2. That the action of the Governor in restraining them in the production of oil from their property located in the military district amounted to a taking of their property without due process of law.

3. The act of the Governor in declaring martial law was null and void and of no force and effect, because there was no authority given him by either the Constitution or laws of Texas to declare and enforce martial law.

Because of the allegation that the conservation law was unconstitutional, the hearing for a temporary injunction had to be heard by a three-judge Federal Court. The hearing was held in Houston before United States Circuit Judge Hutcheson, District Judge Bryant of the East Texas District, and District Judge Grubbs of Alabama.

The plaintiffs were represented by two able lawyers: the late Judge Luther Nickels and Honorable Joseph W. Bailey, Jr., both of Dallas. Honorable Dan Moody, former Attorney General and former Governor of Texas, Mr. Paul D. Page, Jr., and I represented Governor Sterling and General Wolters. It was our contention that the Governor had not declared martial law primarily for the purpose of enforcing the proration orders of the Railroad Commission; that the Governor had in his order declaring martial law found as a fact that "a state of insurrection, riot and breach of the peace does exist in the defined area," and that this necessitated a declaration of martial law in order that the laws of the state be faithfully executed.

In our defense of the suit, we relied on the proposition that had always been followed by the courts, that a declaration by the Governor of a state that a necessity exists for declaring martial law is conclusive, and "no court will review the evidence upon which the Executive acted, nor set up its opinion against him."

We filed a motion to dismiss the suit on the ground that the court was without jurisdiction to try the case, because the court had no power or authority to substitute its judgment for that of the Governor as to the necessity of declaring martial law in the East Texas Oil Field. In attempting to present the law to the court in support of our motion, I was constantly interrupted by Judge Hutcheson who made long dissertations on what he thought was the law of the case.

In the midst of one of these speeches from the bench, he said, referring to what Governor Sterling was doing in East Texas: "I think the real question in the case is what is he doing up there; whether he is up there to enforce the law, or to enforce anarchy, and if he is up there to enforce anarchy, I don't believe he has got a right to be there. That is my off-hand view." (Printed Record of the Case, page 155.)

In one of his interruptions, he used the terms "martial" law and "military" law as synonymous terms. To anyone who has given any study to the subject of martial law, it is known that "martial" law relates to domestic insurrection or invasion and that it is a part of our domestic or municipal law, while "military" law is the law that governs persons in the military service. When I suggested that there was a difference between "martial" and "military" law and that the use of these two terms as being synonymous might be confusing, Judge Hutcheson said: "Well, I think you should assume that the court has half as much intelligence as you have and is not any more likely to be confused on it than you are; we will go on that assumption." (Printed Record of the Case, page 156.)

Finally I was able to drive home one point I was trying to make, that the Constitution vests in the Governor the power to determine whether an emergency exists requiring a declaration of martial law. Having declared martial law, the Governor had the right to restrict the production of oil in order to suppress or prevent insurrection. To this observation, Judge Hutcheson replied: "That is a very shrewd and cunning statement of the case, I will say that." (Printed Record of the Case, page 166.)

When Judge Hutcheson made the statement just quoted, I saw it was useless to attempt to argue the case any farther and sat down.

My ideal judge is one who has a reasonable amount of patience, will listen to counsel who have prepared their case for trial in an effort to ascertain what the lawsuit is about, and to the respective contentions of counsel as to what is the law of the case. I have known men who developed into great judges by following this simple rule. I know of no reason why a judge should take advantage of his judicial position to heckle a lawyer who, in a respectful way, is trying to present his views of the law to the court. The judge who assumes that he knows more about a lawsuit than do the lawyers who have been retained to try the case is indulging in a very dangerous assumption.

Prior to the Constantin case, the law in this country was as declared by all the courts:

1. That the Governor is necessarily constituted the judge of the existence of the exigency in the first instance, and is bound to act according to his belief of the facts. If he does so act and decides to call forth the militia, his orders for this purpose are in strict confor-

mity with the provisions of the law; that the authority to decide whether the exigency has arisen belongs exclusively to the Governor and his decision is conclusive upon all persons.

2. It is no answer that such a power may be abused, for there is no power which is not susceptible of abuse. The remedy for this, as well as for all other official misconduct, if it should occur, is to be found in the constitution itself. In a free government the danger must be remote, since in addition to the high qualities which the Executive must be presumed to possess, of public virtue and honest devotion to the public interests, the frequency of elections, and the watchfulness of the representatives of the nation, carry with them all the checks which can be useful to guard against usurpation or wanton tyranny. Martin vs. Mott, 12 Wheat., 19.

3. When a Governor abuses the power vested in him to declare and enforce martial law, and as a result of such abuse a citizen suffers injury in his person or property, the injured person has his remedy in a civil action for damages against the Governor after the military operations have ceased. Mitchell vs. Harmony, 13 Howard, 115.

4. The measures to be taken in carrying on war and to suppress insurrection, are not defined. The decision of all such questions rests wholly in the discretion of those to whom the substantial powers involved are confided by the Constitution. Stewart vs. Kahn, 78 U. S., 176.

5. The Governor "shall make the ordinary use of the soldiers to that end, that he may kill persons who resist and, of course, that he may use the milder measure of seizing the bodies of those whom he considers stand in the way of restoring peace. Such arrests are not necessarily for punishment but are by way of precaution

to prevent the exercise of hostile power." Mr. Justice Holmes in Moyer vs. Peabody, 212 U. S., 78.

6. The Governor may make the ordinary use of soldiers to suppress insurrection and his declaration of the existence of a state of insurrection is conclusive. United States vs. Fischer, 280 Federal, 208.

7. Once martial law has been declared, the Governor can "do anything necessary to make his proclamation effective." United States vs. Wolters, 268 Federal, 69.

The three-judge court, in an opinion by Judge Hutcheson, held that the Governor should be enjoined from restricting the production of oil from plaintiff's property and a writ of injunction was issued. Governor Moody and I went to Washington in an effort to obtain an order from Mr. Justice Brandeis staying the injunction until we could perfect our appeal and the Supreme Court could pass upon the law questions involved. We saw Judge Brandeis at his home, but he refused to grant a stay order. From the judgment of the three-judge court, we appealed directly to the Supreme Court of the United States. That court, in an opinion by Chief Justice Hughes, affirmed the judgment of the three-judge court. Sterling vs. Constantin, 287 U. S., 138.

Once I knew the subject of martial law as well as it was possible for any man to know it. Today I do not know what the courts will hold on the subject. The contradictory holdings of the courts in the martial law cases is another illustration of the uncertainty of the law.

CHAPTER XXV:
JUSTINIAN, THEODORA AND THE CIVIL LAW

The complete story of the efforts made by the citizens of Texas to preserve inviolate their homes, farms, and ranches from the repeated attempts made by their state government to deprive them, in whole or in part, of their property, has never been told. For a period of about twenty years I was, as a lawyer, a participant in this struggle. This struggle in Texas had its beginning in the age-old conflict between the civil law of Rome and the common law of England. The battle between these two legal systems was continued in Texas, and the settlers and landowners were the unhappy victims of the conflict.

In Texas there is an intermingling of the common law and the civil law. This is particularly true in our land and mining laws. To understand the nature of this conflict, the differences between the two legal systems must be understood. These two great legal systems came to us from people who thought and acted differently, two races that had little in common, and who were actuated in their conduct and behavior by utterly different motives. The influences of these two different races of people met in Texas. The differences between the principles of the civil law and of the common law, as related to public lands and mining, cannot be reconciled. One must survive and the other must perish. This is a question of governmental policy. The policy of the government of Texas is found in its written Constitution and in its legislative enactments. "The fundamental rule for the government of courts in the interpretation or construction of a constitution is to give effect to the intent of the people who adopted it."

The intent and purpose of the men who drafted and those who by their votes adopted the pertinent provisions of the Constitutions of 1866, 1869 and 1876, cannot be determined unless there is an understanding of the historical influences which actuated these men.

Justinian, Emperor of Rome, was in many respects a most fortunate man. He had Theodora, the actress, for his wife; Procopius to write his history; Belisarius, one of the world's great commanders, and Narces, the eunuch, to do his fighting; Anthemius for his architect; and, most important of all, Tribunian to edit and revise the Roman law. The work of Tribunian is one of the greatest intellectual accomplishments of all time. He made a lucid restatement of the Roman laws and edicts, which were enacted, decreed and issued over a period of a thousand years. When completed, his work contained the essence of all the Roman laws. Afterwards it was designated the Corpus Juris Civilis, the body of the civil law.

The Nika riots occurred in 532. This was at first a fight between the rival factions known as the Blues and the Greens. Soon the two factions united and made war against Justinian. Against his will a nephew of a former emperor was named Emperor by the mob and because they had no crown a gold collar was placed around his neck. Justinian became frightened and decided on abdication and flight.

There was a final conference between Justinian and his advisers. Present at this conference were Belisarius and Theodora. Justinian and his advisers were agreed that safety could be found only in flight. According to Procopius, Theodora alone opposed such action. She made a bold and daring speech, in which she declared that she had rather be dead than be addressed by any title other than queen. "Death," she said, "must come to all, but when I am dead I prefer to be buried in the purple shroud of royalty."

Justinian was persuaded by Theodora's speech to remain in Constantinople. Belisarius won a great victory over the rebels. These events occurred while Tribunian and his assistants were busy with their great task, and prior to its completion. The Pandects or Digest and the Institutes were completed in 533. A year later Tribunian produced the revised version of the Code.

If Tribunian had not been able to complete his task there would have been no Corpus Juris Civilis and the civil law as we know it would never have existed. However, he was able to complete his work because Theodora preferred a purple shroud to a white one. Because of this preference on the part of a woman who lived fourteen hundred years ago the State of Texas attempted to sell its lands with a mineral reservation.

The civil law has many admirable features. The whole history of modern civilization would have been different had it not possessed the civil law to inspire and guide it. It was, however, the law of a conquering people. It was the summation of the edicts of a hundred kings exercising despotic power. As applied to conquered people and subjugated nations, it was often harsh and sometimes brutal. Necessarily, it had to be and was vitally concerned with royal revenues. Care was therefore exercised to protect and retain for the Emperor all mines and minerals. This was a natural consequence of the Roman system of government. To keep people and nations in a condition of subjugation, an immense army was necessary. The army had to be paid and cajoled, for it was, throughout the decline of the Roman Empire, the army that placed men on the throne and removed them therefrom at its pleasure.

The civil law of Rome recognized two estates in land; the surface or soil estate, and the mineral estate. The ownership of the surface and the mineral estate was vested in the State. This was the *dominium strictum*. The individual could acquire the possessory ownership of the surface estate. This was the *dominium utile*. The right of the Emperor, or the crown, in mines of gold and silver was exclusive. In these mines the *dominium strictum* and the *dominium utile* were united in the Emperor, or the crown. In mines other than gold or silver, the individual could acquire a contingent or conditional title, subject to the payment of a proportion of the metals produced, or the value thereof, to the State.

As disclosed by the foregoing, there was no private ownership of land under the civil law, as we understand and use the term "ownership." The individual acquired a possessory right in the surface estate. This right was subject to be terminated at the will of the State whenever it was necessary for the State to use the land for mining purposes.

Spain was the discoverer of America. To it as to no other nation was given the opportunity to colonize, expand, establish and maintain itself as the greatest of all nations. An effort was made to take advantage of this amazing opportunity. The effort resulted in miserable failure. Possibly to some extent the Latin temperament was to blame. This, however, is not a satisfactory answer. The correct answer is to be found in the fact that Spain employed its zeal for the exploitation of a continent in searching for mines and minerals and neglected to give first and primary attention to the settlement of the country by those who wanted land and a home.

The civil law was the result of the needs and necessities of a world-conquering people. It was adopted by the Kings of Spain with such changes and alterations as were necessary to meet their need and their greed. The provisions of the civil law, in regard to mines and minerals, were peculiarly suitable to Spain. America was to Spain a mere appendage. There was no thought of extending the boundaries of the Kingdom so as to include within such boundaries any part of America. The Spanish thought of America as a place to "get rich quick." Exploration was made for the primary purpose of obtaining mines and minerals.

It is impossible in this book to discuss in detail the many decrees, edicts and ordinances of Spain in regard to mines, mining, and minerals. It is sufficient for the purpose of this discussion to know that the Spanish ordinance of May 23, 1783, was adopted by the Republic of Mexico, with such modifications as were rendered necessary by the change from a monarchical to a purported republican form of government.

The Spanish ordinance of May 23, 1783, is too long to copy. It may be epitomized as follows:

1. Mines were the property of the royal crown.

2. The right to operate mines could be granted by the crown to individuals.

3. The grantee was obligated to pay to the crown a certain proportion of the metal, or the value thereof, that he obtained from the mine.

4. Failure of the grantee to comply with all the requirements of the ordinance subjected the grant to forfeiture.

5. Any person who informed the crown that a miner was operating his mine in violation of the terms of the ordinance was entitled to a grant to the mine.

6. Anyone could obtain a grant from the crown who discovered a mine on crown land or on the property of an individual.

7. If the mine was on private property, the miner was required to pay the owner of the soil for the damage caused by the mining operations.

8. The owner of a mine could sell, pass by will, or otherwise dispose of his rights in the mine. The person so acquiring the mine took it subject to all the rights of the crown therein.

There is a vast difference between the interest in the land acquired by the individual under the Roman law and that acquired under the Spanish-Mexican law. In the former, the individual acquired a possessory interest and was subject to eviction at the will of the State. Under the latter, he acquired an interest that amounted to a contingent ownership of the surface estate, as we use and understand that term.

All the while, however, Spain and later Mexico owned all the minerals. The law did, however, recognize that the individual could acquire an interest in the surface estate separate and apart from the retained or reserved mineral estate.

Mexico acquired its independence in 1821. The Americans who came to Texas prior to 1836 became acquainted with the Spanish-Mexican land and mining laws. This had its influence as will presently appear. In logical sequence, the principles of the common law should be considered before entering upon a detailed discussion of the land and mining laws of the Republic of Texas and the State of Texas.

CHAPTER XXVI:
THE COMMON LAW

The American influence on Texas, its ideals and laws, had its beginning in England. The review of the American influence on Texas must necessarily commence with England.

It is believed that it was in England that effect was first given in modern times, to the thought that men as such possess certain rights which by their nature are inviolate, even by the act of the King. There it was that expression was first given to the idea that must for centuries have lain dormant in the minds of men, that government was a creature of the governed; created for service to the people, and not for the benefit of the King and the royal family. The arbitrary power of the King over the life and the property of his subject was taken away. It is true that this power continued for a long time to be exercised, as witness the activities of the bloody Judge Jeffries, but such action was taken in form, at least, according to the law of the realm.

The barons wrested from the hands of King John the Great Charter. Men were made secure in their rights; the humblest home was as safe from kingly intrusion as was the greatest castle in the realm.

Among such people the civil law was not applicable, and would not work. A strong effort was made to introduce the civil law into England. This effort had the support of the King and the Church. The arbitrary powers of the civil law naturally appealed to those who desired to exercise such power.

Blackstone, Book 1, pages 17 et seq., says: "The ancient collection of unwritten maxims and customs, which is called the common law, however compounded or from whatever fountains derived, had subsisted immemorially in this kingdom; and though somewhat altered and impaired by the violence of the times, had in great measure weathered the rude shock of the Norman conquest. This had endeared it to the people in general, as well because its decisions were universally known, as because it was found to be excellently adapted to the genius of the English nation."

Blackstone then describes the effort made to force the civil law upon the people of England, and mentions the frequent conflicts arising from this effort between the clergy on the one side and the nobility and the laity on the other. He then says: "And we find the same jealousy prevailing above a century afterwards, when the nobility declared with a kind of prophetic spirit, 'that the realm of England hath ever been, unto this hour, neither by the consent of our Lord the king and the lords of parliament shall it ever be, ruled or governed by the civil law.'"

Legal authorities everywhere recognize that the civil law in matters of contract, commerce, and other relations between individuals, was in disputably founded in principles of justice and wisdom. But, as between the State and the individual, it was often arbitrary. This made it odious to the people of England.

Not alone were the arbitrary provisions of the civil law odious, but Englishmen would never tolerate that principle of the civil law whereby the individual could never acquire a permanent home; by which his title to land must ever be held subject to the superior right of the State and he be liable to eviction at any time the State desired to develop its mineral estate.

Under the common law, minerals were, with a few exceptions, the property of the owner of the land; title in the surface carrying with it title to everything beneath and above the surface.

"Land hath also, in its legal signification, an indefinite extent upwards as well as downwards . . . Therefore, no man may erect any building or the like to overhang another's land: And downwards whatever is in a direct line, between the surface of any land and the center of the earth, belongs to the owner of the surface; as is every day's experience in the mining countries. So that the word 'land' includes not only the face of the earth, but everything under it or over it. And therefore, if a man grants all his lands, he grants thereby all his mines of metal and other fossils, his woods, his waters, and his houses, as well as his fields and meadows." (Blackstone, Book 2, page 18.)

The exceptional instances in which ownership of the surface did not under the common law, carry with it ownership of the minerals, may be enumerated as follows:

1. Land that contained gold or silver, that is, royal mines;

2. Some particular custom, such as had existed from time immemorial—possibly from the time of the Roman occupation—in the tin mines of Cornwall and Devon, and the lead mines of Derbyshire;

3. Where, by conveyance or in some other way, the mineral estate in the land had been separated from and was owned by someone other than the owner of the surface estate.

In disposing the public domain, under the common law, the crown reserved the royal mines. By the term "royal mines" was meant mines of gold and silver. These mines belonged exclusively to the crown. This was true even if the mine was in land owned by an individual. In this respect, the rule under the common law was the same as under the civil law. The contention was at one time made that mines containing the baser metals in combination with either gold or silver were royal mines. This contention must have been given serious consideration for during the reign of William and Mary statutes were enacted which declared that no mine should be considered a royal mine by reason of its containing the baser metals of tin, iron, copper, or lead, in association with gold or silver. After the enactment of these statutes only the mines in which were found gold and silver alone were classed as royal mines.

This reservation by the crown of gold and silver amounted to exactly nothing, because there is no creditable record of any gold and silver ever being mined in England. There are certain traditions to the effect that these precious metals were mined in England during the Roman invasion.

There were certain local customs in Cornwall, Devonshire, the Forest of Dean and in Derbyshire, where the mines produced tin, coal and lead, of paying to the "lord of the soil" a proportion of the minerals mined. In some instances, under these local customs, the mineral estate was owned in fee simple, and descended to the heir at law in like manner as did the surface estate. In other instances the ownership of the mineral estate continued in, or reverted to, the crown.

These local customs in all probability originated during the Roman occupation. These rights, having been once acquired, were respected. Eventually they were recognized and established by acts of parliament. This action of parliament was based on the theory that the rights to these mineral estates existed by virtue of some antecedent grant or concession made by the crown.

These local customs were the customs of the miners, later recognized and established by statute. They were not an exception to the general rule of the common law. This is established by the fact that the crown sold public land without a mineral reservation.

Possessed with this immemorial habit of land ownership, carrying with it everything above the surface and all beneath the surface to the center of the earth, and accustomed to owning their own homes, which the King himself could not invade except by due process of law, men of England, Scotland, Wales and Ireland came to America.

Their purpose in coming to America was utterly different from that of the Spaniards. They came in order that they might acquire homes, and political and religious liberty. Naturally, the English scheme of colonization differed from that of the Spanish.

The men and women who settled New England were a great people. They did not come to America in search of gold and silver. What they sought in the New World was peace and freedom. They wanted an opportunity to make their own laws and demanded the right to worship God according to the dictates of their own consciences. They cleared the primeval forests, fought back the savages, and built homes, schools, and churches. Without complaint they cultivated a soil that yielded but slight return for the labor which they expended upon it. They intended to build, and did build, a permanent settlement. This they did in order that they might own land and have homes of their own.

The settlement in Virginia was by a type of men very different from the type of men who settled New England. In the first shipload of colonists to Virginia there were "four carpenters, twelve laborers and fifty-four gentlemen." The leader of that adventurous expedition complained in bitterness of spirit of the policy which sent such settlers into the American wilderness. It did not, however, take him long to learn that no one of the carpenters or laborers could fell more trees in a day than one of the "gentlemen adventurers."

If this leader had been endowed with the vision to see into the future for two or three centuries, he would have taken courage. In the permanence of the racial qualities which these men possessed and exhibited lay the foundation of the greatness which their successors of the same strain were to achieve and illustrate upon the continent of America.

During the Commonwealth period in England, there was a veritable exodus of the Cavaliers from England to Virginia. During his exile, Charles II granted the "Northern Neck" of Virginia to some half dozen of his courtiers, and when, with his restoration, he returned to power, he ratified the gift. The grantees were empowered to convey the land to settlers. George Washington surveyed these lands. One of the first employments that came to John Marshall, as an attorney, had to do with this grant of land. The State of Virginia protested vigorously and long against this grant.

The question was finally settled by the Supreme Court of the United States in favor of the grant and the settlers. The primary purpose of the grant was to establish a permanent settlement, and what a settlement it proved to be!

The original grant passed to Lord Culpepper, and from him to his daughter, Katherine, who married Lord Fairfax. Their son, Thomas, Sixth Lord Fairfax, became in due course the proprietor of the "Neck," and resided for many years in the colony. To this settlement came John Washington, Richard Lee, George Mason, Thomas Marshall, Robert Carter, the Walkers, the Byrds, the Balls, the Popes, the Tayloes, the Grymes, the Wormleys, the Fitzhughs, and many other families of great worth.

Here were no gold seekers. There was no mineral reservation on their plantations and lands. These people established a permanent settlement because there was assurance of permanence in their titles to their lands. The wilderness was reduced to possession, the savages driven away, and lovely homes erected, in which the visitor, friend and stranger alike, always found a cordial welcome.

In a comparatively short time these settlers, in what had been a primeval forest inhabited by savages, established a civilization which in its culture, gentleness, hospitality, and happy living was not inferior to any that preceded it.

The civilization that we enjoy, and which had its beginning in this country in New England and Virginia, was made possible by the fact that the individual could own land and a home in fee simple. Such ownership was impossible under the civil law of Rome. It was this Roman law that the court attempted in the Cowan case to make the law in Texas. Such ownership was possible under the common law, and no one, not even the government itself, may lawfully impair such ownership, except upon payment of adequate compensation to the person owning the land.

Chapter XXVII:
The Opinion of the Court Repudiated
by the People

The conflict between the civil and the common law in Texas was as unavoidable as was the physical conflict between the Latin and the Anglo-American peoples. The law, history, traditions, ideals and aspirations of the two races are different. The differences were irreconcilable.

During the past three hundred years, the English-speaking peoples have ventured to many new and unsettled countries. This has been one of the most striking ventures in the world's history and was, of all other events, most far-reaching in its effect and its importance. Bacon, the philosopher, refused to use the English language in his writings, because he feared that if he did, his writings would remain forever unknown to all but the inhabitants of a relatively unimportant insular kingdom. The English language is now the speech of two continents. The common law of England is now the law of the land throughout the vast region of Australasia and of America north of the Rio Grande.

The Anglo-American, wherever he goes in any considerable numbers, carries his cherished form of government and laws with him. It has not been so long since the Americans first crossed the Allegheny Mountains and penetrated the Mississippi Valley. This interfered with the plans of both the Spanish and the British. The United States Government with New England pulling back had to follow its people. The purchase of Louisiana and the War of 1812 were direct results of this western immigration.

The Americans in Texas won independence from Mexico. They established their own Republic. These men had become accustomed to the laws and customs of Mexico, but they were Anglo-Americans who had inherited the principles of the common law.

Among the early acts of the Texas Congress was that of June 3, 1837. In this law it was declared "that no land granted by this government shall be located on salt springs, gold or silver mines, copper or lead, or other minerals, or on any island of the Republic."

If the principles of the civil law are used as an aid to interpret the provisions of the Act of June 3, 1837, the language used means that an individual could locate on land containing "salt springs, gold or silver mines, copper or lead, or other minerals," but that his location carried with it no greater right than that of possession, and that he would hold his right subject to the pleasure of the government. In other words, at any time the government desired it could dispossess the individual and repossess itself of every estate in the land, in order to make use of the salt springs or to mine the minerals.

If the law of Spain and Mexico, as disclosed by the terms of the Spanish ordinance of May 23, 1783, is used as an aid to the interpretation of the language used in the Act, an individual could locate on such lands as are described in the Act, but the State retained the right to use the salt springs and to mine or permit to be mined the minerals, provided payment was made to the owner of the surface estate for the damage caused by the mining operations. The amount of such damage could be determined by arbitration in case of disagreement between the miner and the owner of the surface estate.

If the principles of the common law are used as an aid in interpreting the language used in the Act of June 3, 1837, it is apparent that it was intended to prohibit location by an individual on any land known to contain minerals or on any island of the Republic.

The same session of Congress that enacted the Act of June 3, 1837, also enacted a judiciary act wherein it was provided that the common law of England "as now practiced and understood, shall, in its application to juries and to evidence be followed and practiced by the courts of this republic, so far as the same may not be inconsistent with this Act, or any other law passed by Congress." The young republic did not, however, until the Act of January 20, 1840, adopt the common law in its entirety.

In State vs. Delesdenier, 7 Texas, 76, the Supreme Court of Texas interpreted the Act of June 3, 1837. The action was one in trespass, whereby the State sought to recover possession of about twenty-two acres of land located on Galveston Island. A patent to the land was introduced in evidence by the defendant. The judgment of the trial court was against the State, and the State appealed to the Supreme Court. The case was heard in the Supreme Court before Chief Justice Hemphill and Special Associate Justices John Sayles and Asa M. Lewis.

Sayles wrote the opinion of the court. He said: "By the acts and resolutions above cited the intention of the government is clearly shown to reserve all islands from location...We are therefore of the opinion that the court erred in permitting the patent to Jones and Hall to be read in evidence; the patent being for lands not subject to appropriation by individuals by location, is absolutely null and void."

The court, by its decision in the Delesdenier case as far back as 1851, interpreted the Act of June 3, 1837, according to the principles of the common law. This was correct. The people of Texas were Anglo-Americans. What would be more natural than for them, in the enactment of the Act of June 3, 1837, to intend by the language there used to give effect to the principles of the common law?

The decision in the Delesdenier case should have established for all time the proposition that in a suit by the State to recover land located on an island or land that contained a salt spring or that contained minerals it would only be necessary for the State, in order to recover, to prove that the land was in fact on an island or that there was a salt spring on the land or that at the time the land was located it was known to contain minerals. Proof of any one of these essential facts would make the location and the patent for the land void.

In 1862, eleven years after the decision in the Delesdenier case, was decided by the Supreme Court the case of Cowan vs. Hardeman, 26 Texas, 217. In the very beginning of its opinion the court said that "the main question for our decision in this case depends upon the construction that must be placed upon" the Act of June 3, 1837. The court then proceeded to interpret that act as follows:

"The object and purpose of the legislature was simply to reserve to the republic the islands and the salt springs, gold and silver mines, copper and lead and other minerals, as corporeal hereditaments out of the public domain; and thus, while the mineral resources of the country that were then known to exist or that might afterwards be developed were thereby secured to the government, no embarrassment was placed in the way of the citizen in acquiring the fee in the quantum of land to which his certificate or scrip entitled him."

The court then said that this was the common law. As we have seen, it was nothing of the kind. The court further said, "and this is also the civil law." In that statement, the court was eminently correct. It is the civil law of Justinian in all its purity. Chief Justice Wheeler, in a concurring opinion, made this very clear, indeed. He said: "...We hold that the patent is not absolutely and necessarily void because there is found to be a salt spring or minerals upon the land embraced within the grant...In so far as concerns the use, it may, however, be avoided in part or in whole by the state in the exercise of its reserved right in the salt spring and minerals embraced within it. The state must have the easement of going upon the land for this purpose; and if to the full enjoyment of the right of the state, it should become necessary to use the whole of the land, timber and water upon the tract, the right of the state to an easement to that extent cannot, I apprehend, be questioned..."

By the above language, Chief Justice Wheeler ignores the kindlier provisions of the Spanish ordinance of May 23, 1783, and goes back to the civil law of Justinian. The statement of the court that the law so announced is the common law is amazing. There is as great a difference between the principles of the civil law and those of the common law, in regard to the subject dealt with in Cowan vs. Hardeman, as there is between the principles, if any, of Soviet Russia and the principles upon which our government was founded.

The land involved in the Cowan case was alleged to contain "saline," and evidence was offered that the "saline" mentioned in the petition "was a salt spring."

At the time Cowan vs. Hardeman was decided, the men of Texas were away from home. They were in the Confederate Army. When they returned home, about the first thing they did was to give attention to the doctrine announced in the Cowan case. By its decision, the court held that the State owned all minerals, including salt, in all lands granted, sold and conveyed by it, and that the individual had only the right of possession, and that this right could be taken away at the will of the State, whenever the State desired to use the surface for mining operations. No such situation as this had ever been permitted to exist in any country governed by the English-speaking race. The men of Texas would not tolerate it.

The Constitution of 1866, adopted by the convention, called by proclamation of President Johnson, four years after the decision of Cowan vs. Hardeman, by Article 7, Section 39, provided: "...That the State of Texas hereby releases to the owner of the soil all mines and mineral substance that may be on the same, subject to such uniform rate of taxation as the Legislature may impose..."

Then again in the Constitution of 1869, Article 10, Section 9, it was provided: "The State of Texas hereby releases to the owner or owners of the soil all mines and mineral substances that may be on the same, subject to such uniform rate of taxation as the Legislature may impose..."

Then once more, and for the third time, in our present Constitution, the people in 1876 declared in the organic law of the State, Article 14, Section 7, that: "The State of Texas hereby releases to the owner or owners of the soil, all mines and minerals that may be on the same, subject to taxation as other property."

The Supreme Court, in 1884, in the case of State vs. Parker, 61 Texas, 265, had occasion to interpret the above quoted provision of the Constitution of 1866. It was there held: "Theretofore in making grants of land, the State had reserved the mines and mineral substances. But by this provision these were released to the owner of the soil whether the grant was made before or after that time."

This construction, given to the provisions in the Constitution of 1866, was equally applicable to the similar provisions in the Constitutions of 1869 and 1876. It was a correct construction because it gave effect to the intent and purpose of the people of Texas to own every estate that might or could be in their lands and homes; to own such estates in fee simple, subject to no contingency.

The organic law of this State, from 1866, as interpreted by the Supreme Court in the Parker case, expressly provided that in all lands granted, sold and conveyed by the State of Texas, such grant, sale and conveyance carried with it the mineral estate as well as the surface estate.

The Legislature tried to change this policy of the government in regard to the sale of its lands. The Constitution of 1876 had set apart large areas of the public domain for the use of the school, the university, and asylum funds. The Legislature, in providing for the sale of the lands set apart to the schools, provided for the sale of the surface estate, retaining title in the State to the mineral estate for the use of the school fund. This was an attempt to forsake the principles of the common law and to adopt those of Spain and Mexico. This attempted sale of the surface, reserving the minerals, was in direct violation of the Constitution, which, as interpreted by the court in the Parker case, expressly relinquished to the owner of the soil the minerals in all lands that had, prior to the adoption of the Constitution, been sold, or that might thereafter be sold.

The purchaser of school land was required to sign a paper wherein he purported to make and enter into an agreement with the State as follows: "... That said land has heretofore been classed as mineral land, and, believing there to be no minerals thereon, and hereby waiving all right to the minerals on said section to the State of Texas, should there be any mineral deposits of any character hereafter found in or on said land, and in the event of a sale to me of the foregoing land it is expressly understood that I acquire no right, title or interest in or to any minerals that are now or may hereafter be found to exist in or on said land."

This agreement was null and void because the Constitution itself, as interpreted by the Supreme Court, provided that the State relinquished the minerals to the purchaser of the lands. This being true, the men who purchased the school land were presumed, as a matter of law, to know the law; therefore, these purchasers knew the law was, as declared by the Supreme Court, that when they purchased land from the State they acquired by such purchase the mineral estate in the land.

Then, what happened?

A man by the name of A. A. Cox had purchased some school land situated in Culberson County. In due course he paid all the purchase money due the State and became entitled to a patent. He applied to the Land Commissioner for a patent. This was refused, unless he would accept a patent wherein the State reserved and retained the mineral estate. Cox applied to the Supreme Court for a writ of mandamus commanding the Land Commissioner to issue to him an unconditional patent. (Cox vs. Robison, 105 Texas, 426.)

The court refused to grant the writ of mandamus. In the course of its opinion, the court referred to that part of its opinion in the Parker case where it was expressly declared that the Constitution released to the owner of the soil the minerals in the land "whether the grant was made before or after" the time the Constitutional provision became effective; then the court said: "That part of the opinion, however, referring to subsequent grants was *dicta*, as the land there involved had been granted in 1847, and a determination of the effect of the provision upon the title to minerals in lands granted after its adoption was not necessary to the decision of the case ..."

The court then held that the above quoted provisions of the Constitutions of 1866, 1869 and 1876 were retroactive and without effect except as to land sold prior to the several times such provisions were adopted. Cox vs. Robison was decided in 1912.

Prior to the decision by the court of the Cox case, every man who purchased school land from the State had the right to believe, as a result of the clear and unambiguous language used by the court in the Parker case, that he had acquired the minerals in the land sold him by the State. If there had been no Parker case, he would have rightly been entitled to the same belief because the sale of land by a government with a reservation of any minerals, except gold and silver to be used for coinage purposes, is contrary to the principles of the common law. The Texan is familiar with the principles of the common law because it has been the law of his race for more than a thousand years. The State of Texas cannot coin money. In selling its lands the State had no right to even retain the gold and silver that might be in the land it sold.

To recapitulate, the battle in Texas between the civil law and the common law had, up to 1912, been as follows:

The court in the Delesdenier case decided in 1851 applied the principles of the common law in interpreting the Act of June 3, 1837; this meant that lands known to contain minerals could not be sold to anyone. This was a victory for the common law.

In 1862 the court, in the Cowan case, held that the person who thought he owned land in Texas had no interest in the land except that of possession of the surface, and that this right could be taken away at the will of the State in order to develop its reserved mineral estate in the land. This was a sweeping victory for the civil law, and also a reversal of what the court had held in the Delesdenier case.

In 1866, 1869 and 1876, the people took matters in their own hands and in the organic law of the State declared that the State "releases" the minerals in the lands to the owners of the land. Victories for the common law.

In 1884, the court, in the Parker case said the release or relinquishment of the minerals by the State as provided for in its Constitution applied to lands sold after the Constitution became effective, as well as to those sold prior to such time. A victory for the common law.

In 1912, Cox vs. Robison was decided. In that case the court held that the Constitutional relinquishment of the minerals to the owner of the land did not apply to lands sold after the Constitution was adopted, and that the State could thereafter sell and had sold its lands, classified as mineral, with a reservation of the minerals. A victory for the civil law.

CHAPTER XXVIII:
DID THE STATE OR LANDOWNERS
OWN THE OIL?

The next battle between the civil and the common law was in Greene vs. Robison, 117 Texas, 516. It is necessary, before we consider Greene vs. Robison, to give some attention to the events preceding the submission and decision of that case.

It is apparent that the citizen who purchased school land from the State after 1876 and prior to 1912 had received treatment most unjust. He bought his land believing that he acquired the mineral estate. The Supreme Court of his State had said so. The purchaser of this school land was a Texan of the Anglo-American breed of men. He knew that it was the law of his race for the government not to retain any mineral estate in the land it sold, except gold and silver. He knew that for one hundred years it had been the policy of the American Government to foster the settlement and development of its Western lands. This was true of the Northwest Territory, of Kentucky, of Tennessee, and of all the lands included in the Louisiana Purchase. He knew this was true of the lands ceded by Mexico to the United States. For a few cents an acre, the United States had disposed of the public domain, in order to bring about a settlement and a development of these lands.

By 1876, and certainly by the time the Legislature first provided for the sale of State land with a mineral reservation in 1883, East Texas was settled. The State had parted with its title to the land. The owner had acquired, as under the common law, a title in fee simple to every estate in the land. No more of the rich soil in East Texas, situated in a salubrious climate, could be obtained. The Anglo-American, true to his heritage, desired land, a home of his own. Immigration to the semi-arid West began. In covered wagons the pioneer men and women of West Texas trekked across a roadless country. In due course of time they located for themselves homesteads on the bleak and barren prairies. There was no timber here for building purposes, or for fuel. A hole was dug in the ground, and this hole was sanctioned with the holy name of home.

Buffalo chips were used as fuel. These pioneers were not accustomed to the climate or the soil of West Texas; what crops could be successfully planted, grown and harvested could be determined only by experiment. A determined effort was made to subdue the soil and to endure the climate. Sod was broken, crops were planted; but the wind blew, and the sand drifted. Everything happened, except rain. Crops failed. There was no water for the stock. Fall came, and the disappointed man and his weary, discouraged wife loaded their few "belongings" and their children into the covered wagon. The return trip to the abundance of East Texas began. This is a part of the heroic history of West Texas.

The brave men and no less heroic women who settled West Texas were not of the breed that accepts defeat. They tried again, not once but many times. By the laborious process of trial and error they learned what crops could be raised in West Texas. It was found that in many sections of that vast empire good water in abundance could be secured at a reasonable depth. Eventually it became possible to make a living in West Texas. Homes were erected, courthouses were built, and provision was made for schools. These men and women stood as a barrier between the prosperous and happy people of East Texas and the cruel and merciless Comanches of West Texas.

The doctrine announced by the Supreme Court in the Cowan case, that the State owned all the minerals in the land that it had sold to its citizens and had the right when "it should become necessary to use the whole of the land, timber and water upon the tract" in mining operations, is a monstrous doctrine. It is destructive of every principle upon which our government was founded. The foundation of our government is home ownership. In 1866, 1869, and again in 1876, the people repudiated the doctrine announced by the court in the Cowan case. In three different Constitutions the people declared that the minerals should be relinquished to the owners of the land. It was not the intent of the people that the State should use the "whole" of the land it had sold to a settler in order that it might develop for the use and benefit of the school fund the mineral estate in the land.

Picture, if you can, in your imagination, the sheriff removing by force the farmer, his wife and their children, from their home when "it should become necessary to use the whole of the land, timber and water upon the tract" in order to develop the mineral estate owned therein by the State of Texas. Then picture, if you can, in your imagination, the duly constituted officer of the State, acting under the compulsory school law, gathering up the homeless children and taking them to the public school maintained in whole or in part, by the money derived from the sale of the minerals underlying the once prosperous and happy homestead, from which the children and their parents had been driven in order that the State might obtain the minerals in the land. These things could have happened, and probably would have happened, had the people permitted the doctrine announced by the Supreme Court in the Cowan case to have remained the law in Texas.

The picture I have drawn is not an exaggerated one as is established by what the Supreme Court, referring to the Act of 1913, said: "Under the terms of that Act the holder of a prospecting permit is given the right of eminent domain for all purposes necessary either to the development of minerals or to the use of minerals found within the area of the permit—for buildings and works essential to mining operations, even railroads. The character of the land as a farm, the purpose for which the State sold it, may be destroyed. The surface rights may be rendered no longer of use to the owner. *It is possible for the surrender of his possession to be compelled.* No such results to settlers of agricultural land could, in our opinion, have been within the contemplation of the legislation of 1883. That was not the policy of the laws of the State at that time." 109 Texas, 367. (*Emphasis is the author's.*)

The history of our people, of the Republic of Texas, and the State of Texas, clearly indicates that it was the intention of those who drafted and by their votes adopted the Constitutions of 1866, 1869 and 1876, that the State should sell its lands without a mineral reservation, and according to the time-honored custom of the common law. The Legislature provided, however, in 1883 for the sale of the school lands with a reservation of the minerals. This law was upheld in 1912 as valid in Cox vs. Robison.

Following the decision in Cox vs. Robison, the Legislature in 1913 enacted the first mineral permit law. Very few permits were obtained on school lands under this law. Oil had not been discovered in West Texas at that time, and was not discovered in paying quantities until 1917. The mineral permit law was amended in 1917. By the terms of this law, the permittee was authorized to enter upon the land of the citizen, upon his homestead, and drill for oil. If oil was discovered, tanks were erected and the ground was covered with machinery and pipes. The Act provided for the payment of ten cents an acre to the owner of the surface. If this amount was accepted by the landowner, it was to be in lieu of all damage to the surface estate. The Stamp Tax of George III was no encroachment upon individual rights at all compared to the encroachment upon a man's land and home authorized by the mineral permit law. The descendants of those who fought and won the War for Independence were not without courage. Rebellion was the inevitable result. Winchesters and pistols were used to drive away the invading army of permittees. This rebellion is also a part of the heroic history of West Texas.

The permittees came to Austin and appealed to the Attorney General to protect their rights by instituting legal proceedings in a district court at Austin against the landowners. These gentlemen asserted that it was the duty of the

Attorney General to do this in order to protect "the sacred school fund." The Attorney General sent me to investigate the situation. I went to Pecos and Toyah where I attempted to advise the landowners that the State owned the minerals in their lands and necessarily had the right to enter upon their lands in order to reduce the minerals to possession and to remove them from the land. I further advised that under the very terms of the mineral permit law, the State recognized that the landowner owned the surface estate in the land, and that this surface estate could not be taken and destroyed without payment therefor; that it was optional with the landowner as to whether or not he would accept the ten cents an acre in lieu of all damage to the surface, but that when and if the landowner did accept the ten cents an acre, the permittee then had the legal right to go upon the landowner's land and prospect for oil and gas and to remove the same, if found. If, however, the landowner did not accept the ten cents an acre the permittee had no right to go upon his land, unless and until he made arrangements for the purpose satisfactory to the landowner, or by condemnation proceedings acquired the right to use the surface estate. There was no danger to the landowner in condemnation proceedings because in such proceedings his neighbors, other landowners, would assess the amount of damages done to the surface estate.

The advice that I gave to the landowners was based on the principles of the common law. Under the law as declared in the Cox case the landowner could not develop the minerals in his land because the State owned the minerals. Under the Constitution of Texas, which follows the principles of the common law, neither the State nor its permittees could develop the minerals without compensating the landowner for the damage done to his surface estate. This situation created a stalemate. The mineral estate could not be developed by either the landowner or the State. Thoughtful men sought a solution of this problem. Within six months after my visit to Pecos and Toyah the Legislature enacted the Relinquishment Act.

The Relinquishment Act constituted the owner of the soil the agent of the State for the purpose of making oil and gas leases upon the land the State had sold with a mineral reservation. To the landowners the State relinquished fifteen-sixteenths of the mineral estate. This relinquishment of a part of the mineral estate was in consideration for all damage to the surface estate and for the services of the landowners in acting as agents for the State. This law could not, of course, affect the vested rights of the permittees. There was nothing, however, to prevent a permittee from making arrangements with the landowner whereby the permit would be allowed to expire and a lease then obtained by the permittee from the landowner.

The Relinquishment Act was drafted by State Senator C. R. Buchanan of Scurry County, Representative Bryan of Midland, and Land Commissioner J. T. Robison. These men believed it unjust for the State to relinquish, as it had done, to the landowners owning land in East Texas the minerals in their land, and to take from the settlers of the land in West Texas the minerals in their land. Confronted as they were with the decision of the Supreme Court in Cox vs. Robison, they proposed to reduce as much as it legally could be reduced the unjust discrimination against the landowners of West Texas. Under the Relinquishment Act, the landowners would receive something for the use of the surface estate of their lands in the event oil was discovered; the State would receive the cooperation of the landowners in leasing and developing the mineral estate which the court in the Cox case had held the State owned in the West Texas school land.

If the people of Texas were as determined as I have indicated they were that the landowners should own the mineral estate in their land, then why, it may be asked, did the people not amend the Constitution after the court's decision in the Cox case, and relinquish to the landowners the mineral estate that the court had held the State owned in their land? Before answering this question, a bit of explaining is necessary.

The cause of a future illness may be present in a person's body for a long time before the person is aware of the fact. The decision of the court in the Cox case cost the landowners of West Texas hundreds of millions, possibly billions, of dollars, but they were not made aware of that fact until years later. The Cox case was decided in 1912. There had been very little, if any, oil discovered in West Texas prior to 1912. Very few people paid any attention to the court's decision in the Cox case at the time the case was decided. It was probably thought by the few who gave it any thought at all that the whole thing was an abstract question of law, because it was not believed that there were any minerals in the lands of West Texas except some silver and quicksilver near Alpine and Marfa. However, as was generally believed in 1912, if there were no minerals in the land, then there was no cause for worry.

Under the amendment of 1917 tens of thousands of mineral permits were obtained from the State on the mineral estate of privately owned land. The mineral permits were valid because of the construction placed on the Constitution by the court in the Cox case. When the great oil fields were discovered in West Texas, beginning about 1917, the holders of the mineral permits had vested rights in the mineral estate in privately owned land that could not be taken from them by an amendment to the Constitution of Texas, because the people of Texas are prohibited by the due process clause of the National Constitution from depriving anyone of his property without compensation therefor. When the people of West Texas woke up to the fact that the court in the Cox case had taken from them the mineral estate in their lands, an estate that in many instances had a value a thousand times greater than the surface estate, it was too late to do very much about it. The Relinquishment Act recognized, as it had to do, the validity of the mineral permits acquired under the Mineral Permit Law of 1913, as amended in 1917.

The situation after the decision of the Cox case was entirely different from what it was after the decision of the

Cowan case. From the time the Cowan case was decided in 1862 until the adoption of the Constitution of 1866, which released the minerals to those who had theretofore or might thereafter purchase land from the State, the State had not parted with its title to the reserved mineral estate. The State, therefore, at the time the Constitution of 1866 was adopted, still owned the mineral estate which the court in the Cowan case had held belonged to the state and could release that estate to the persons who had theretofore or who might thereafter purchase the land from the state. This was not true when Senator Buchanan and others tried, by the enactment of the Relinquishment Act, to save something for the landowners of West Texas. Those of us who participated in the litigation and legislation that followed the enactment of the Relinquishment Act were not trying to overturn the court's decision in the Cox case, because subsequent conditions made that impossible. What we did try to do was to save something for the landowners from the general wreck caused by the decision in the Cox case.

The records of the State of Texas disclose that the people of West Texas, in direct taxes, have paid to the State far more in money for school purposes than has been returned by the State to the West Texas counties to be used in its counties for school purposes. It is only human nature that the West Texas landowners feel and believe that they have been, without evil intention on the part of anyone, wronged and unjustly treated in regard to their lands, and have been handicapped tremendously in their efforts to settle and develop the West Texas territory.

The State and its school fund profited hugely from the Relinquishment Act. For about nine years the Relinquishment Act had been in force and effect prior to the decision of the Greene case. During all this time, with the consent and approval of all governmental agencies whose duty it was to construe and enforce the terms of the Relinquishment Act, the landowners had been paid and had retained the bonus received for making oil and gas leases.

The Relinquishment Act became effective October 30, 1919. In an opinion of January 21, 1921, the Attorney General assumed the Act to be constitutional, as he did in another opinion of January 4, 1922. Then, in an opinion of February 17, 1922, it was expressly held by the Attorney General that the Act was a valid enactment. In no one of these opinions was it suggested that the State was entitled to one-half the bonus. I wrote all of the opinions mentioned above. Two of these opinions were approved by the Honorable C. M. Cureton, then Attorney General. The last opinion was approved by the Honorable W. A. Keeling, Attorney General. These opinions were approved after a conference of all the lawyers in the Attorney General's Department. To the best of my recollection, no one even suggested, during the course of the conference on these various opinions, that the State was entitled to any part of any bonus that might be received.

CHAPTER XXIX:
THE LANDOWNERS WIN & LOSE

The issue involved in the case of Greene vs. Robison, 117 Texas, 516, and the companion cases, was one of the most momentous ever decided by the Supreme Court of Texas. I was of counsel in the case of Buvens vs. Robison, 117, Texas, 541, one of the companion cases to Greene vs. Robison. I there appeared as attorney for Transcontinental Oil Company and Mid-Kansas Oil and Gas Company, the latter company being the company that I appeared against when I was in the Attorney General's office when the issue before the court was whether an oil and gas lease conveyed to the lessee a taxable interest in land.

The attorneys appearing for the Relators, that is, those who were attacking the constitutionality of the Relinquishment Act, were Messrs. Charles L. Black of Austin; John J. Hines of Fort Worth; Dodson and Ezell, John Boyle and J. D. Wheeler of San Antonio; and Ward and Ward of Houston. Mr. Claude Pollard was at that time Attorney General, and he and his assistant, Mr. C. W. Truehart, filed briefs as *amici curiae*, attacking the constitutionality of the Relinquishment Act.

Mr. J. T. Robison, as Land Commissioner, appeared in defense of the law and was represented by Judge R. L. Batts of Austin, Texas. Landowners and oil companies holding leases made under the Relinquishment Act were represented by, among other lawyers, Hill, Niell and Hill of San Angelo; F. A. Williams, former Associate Justice of the Supreme Court, of Galveston; Nelson Phillips, former Chief Justice of the Supreme Court, of Dallas; G. B. Smedley, now on the Commission of Appeals of the Supreme Court, of Wichita Falls; Koerner, Fahey and Young of St. Louis; Harris, Harris and Sedberry of San Angelo; Underwood, Johnson, Dooley and Simpson of Amarillo; and me.

Briefly summarized, the contentions of those attacking the validity of the Relinquishment Act were as follows:

1. The mineral estate which the State owns in the public free school land is as much a part of the school land as is the surface estate. Section 4, Article 7, of the State Constitution provides that the public school land "shall be sold" and the "Legislature shall not have power to grant any relief to purchasers thereof." The Relinquishment Act vesting in the owners of the surface estate fifteen-sixteenths of the mineral estate for their services in leasing the mineral estate is not a sale of the land, but an attempt on the part of the Legislature to grant relief to the purchasers of the surface estate.

2. The public school land, including the mineral estate therein, is the source of the permanent school fund of the State. Section 4, Article 7, of the State Constitution provides that "the proceeds of the sale" of the school lands shall be invested in bonds of the State of Texas and of the United States. Section 5, Article 7, of the Constitution provides that the money so invested "shall be the permanent school fund" and may not be used for any purpose. Therefore, it was argued, the Relinquishment Act necessarily impaired the permanent school fund, and did so in direct violation of the Constitution.

In answer to these contentions some of my associates and I argued that as a matter of right the landowners owned the mineral estate as well as the surface estate, the mineral estate having been released to them under the Constitution at the time they purchased the land from the State. This argument could not prevail, for as previously stated, vested rights had been acquired by private individuals under the Mineral Permit Law since the court had decided Cox vs. Robison. Our arguments to the effect that the landowners owned the entire mineral estate under the Constitutions of 1866, 1869 and 1876 were made for the purpose of directing the attention of the judges to the fact that the landowners of

West Texas had received most unjust treatment. If we could convince the judges of the court of this fact, then it was believed that the judges would be in sympathy with our efforts to sustain the validity of the Relinquishment Act. Lawyers learn that judges are men with emotions and sentiments like those of other men.

We then pointed out that when the landowner, acting as the agent of the State, leased the mineral estate in his land that the lessee would receive seven-eighths of the oil produced, the State one-sixteenth, and the landowner one-sixteenth; that the one-sixteenth of the mineral estate ultimately received by the landowner would not constitute any relief to the purchaser of the school land, but was a grant made by the State to the landowner in "aid" of the State's effort to sell its reserved mineral estate in the land. The landowner had the right, we argued, to the undisturbed possession of the surface of the land, and, without his consent, neither the State nor its lessee could go upon the land for the purpose of prospecting for oil or other minerals, and if found, could not, without the consent of the landowner, erect the necessary machinery and equipment upon the landowner's surface estate necessary to develop the mineral estate in the land. In this argument we were fighting against the principles of the civil law and trying to uphold the principles of the common law.

Our contention that the grant made by the Relinquishment Act of what amounted to one-sixteenth of the mineral estate to the landowner was in aid of the power of the Legislature to sell the land, was, we believed, supported by two prior decisions of the Supreme Court.

In Central Railroad Company vs. Bowman, 97 Texas, 417, the court had held an act of the Legislature valid that granted a perpetual easement to railroad companies to use, without cost, the public school lands for right-of-way purposes. In this case the court said: "The purpose for which the school lands are required to be sold is the raising of money to support the schools, and this may be promoted in many ways by the exercise of other powers of the Legislature. Such powers are left in that body by the Constitution, and may be employed upon this land whenever the attempted exercise does not conflict with, and especially where it promotes the power to sell to advantage. To the advancement of the purpose of selling the land advantageously, by settling up the country, bringing them into demand and thereby increasing their value, the Legislature might well regard the granting to railroad companies of rights-of-way over them as a legitimate means."

In Imperial Irrigation Company vs. Jayne, 104 Texas, 395, the court held a law valid which granted to irrigation companies a perpetual easement to use, without cost, school land for reservoir purposes. This law was held valid on the ground that the grant by the Legislature of school land for reservoir purposes "is wholly in aid of the power of the Legislature to sell the public school lands for the best price and to the best advantage."

If, we argued, the Legislature could grant a perpetual easement to railroad companies and irrigation companies to forever use, without cost, the public school land for right-of-way and reservoir purposes, because such grants were in aid of the power of the Legislature to sell at the best price and to the best advantage the remainder of the public school land, then clearly the Legislature had the right to grant to the landowners one-sixteenth of the mineral estate in their land in order to obtain the active cooperation of the landowners in selling for the State at the best price and to the best advantage the remainder of the State's reserved mineral estate.

Personally I am convinced that the court was wrong in holding that the Legislature could give away any part of the school land to a railroad or an irrigation company as an aid to the power of the Legislature to sell the remainder of the school land. The people had declared in their Constitution that the school land should be sold. They had not said that the Legislature might give away a part of it in order that the remainder might possibly be sold to better advantage.

It is also my personal opinion that the Relinquishment Act was a relief act enacted by the Legislature for the deliberate purpose, of attempting to give some relief to the landowners. This action on the part of the Legislature was, however, in my opinion entirely justified because the landowners under the Constitution owned all of the minerals in their lands. The mineral estate in their lands had been taken from them by the Supreme Court in the Cox case in direct violation of the constitutional provisions declaring that the State releases to the owners of the land all minerals therein.

It was also, of course, our contention that when the landowner purchased the land from the State he acquired the right to use the surface of the soil, and that the State could not deprive the purchaser of this use by making a ranch or farm into an oil field and depriving him of the use of the surface without adequately compensating him for his right to the undisturbed possession and use of the surface of the soil.

The several cases involving the constitutionality of the Relinquishment Act were submitted to the Supreme Court on oral arguments at the same time. Among those who made oral arguments in defense of the law were three great lawyers, men whose fame will endure as long as the present government of Texas shall exist: Nelson Phillips, formerly Chief Justice of the Supreme Court of Texas; R. L. Batts, formerly United States Circuit Judge; and F. A. Williams, formerly Associate Justice of the Supreme Court of Texas.

The arguments were made before a great court. On the bench, seated in the center, was Chief Justice C. M. Cureton, a large man, with clear blue eyes and gray hair, handsome, dignified, calm, a profound scholar not only in the law but in all literature. Occasionally he directed a searching inquiry to one of the lawyers that went directly to the point. Seated on the right of the Chief Justice was the Senior Associate Justice Thomas B. Greenwood, a man of medium weight and height, endowed from birth with a fine mind, and a man of great determination. Judge Greenwood is a gentleman of the old

South. To the left of the Chief Justice sat the Junior Associate
Justice, William Pierson, tall, slender, brown-eyed, entirely
bald, friendly and kind and destined to write the opinion of
the court in this case, an opinion that saved hundreds of millions of dollars for the landowners of West Texas.

Possibly a hundred people can be seated in the Supreme
Courtroom. Few people attend the ordinary sittings of the
Supreme Court. On this occasion, however, all the seats
were occupied, and many additional chairs were brought in
to accommodate those who desired to hear the great lawyers defend the Relinquishment Act. Many women were
present.

Judge Garwood was ill at this time, but he and Mrs. Garwood came up from their home in Houston to hear the
arguments. Judge Garwood greatly enjoyed the arguments.
They were a feast to his mind and soul. Each night during the
three days the arguments lasted I went to the Driskill Hotel
and listened to the reminiscences of Judge Garwood, Judge
Phillips and Judge Williams. I enjoyed hearing these men
talk almost as much as I enjoyed hearing the arguments.

Judge Batts made an argument of force, power and great
learning, and back of the argument was the dominating
personality of the man. He was followed by Nelson Phillips,
a man of striking appearance, immaculately dressed in the
fashion of a gentleman of the old South. The only question
involved was one of constitutional law. In discussing this
question, however, Phillips exercised all his power as an
orator, and he was a great orator, and all his learning as a
lawyer, and he was a great lawyer. He made one of the finest
orations and one of the greatest arguments ever delivered
before the Supreme Court of Texas. There are those who
enjoy above all things good music, vocal or instrumental,
but there is not anything that affords me pleasure equal to
a great oration or a finely reasoned legal argument. Phillips
and Batts furnished a splendid combination of both.

The third argument was made by Judge F. A. Williams,
quiet, gentle, veteran jurist and legal logician. At the time he

made his argument in this case Judge Williams was seventy-seven years old. He did not speak long, but he said much. Perhaps there are those who will disagree with what I am about to write, but I am expressing my opinions in this book with malice toward none and with love for all lawyers I have known. It is my opinion that of the lawyers I have known, Judge F. A. Williams ranks second to none in the ability to think clearly and speak concisely. He is truly a great lawyer and was, when on the Supreme bench, a great jurist, one of the greatest that Texas has ever had.

Among the many able lawyers who appeared for those who sought to persuade the court to hold the Relinquishment Act unconstitutional was Charles L. Black of Austin, one of the truly great lawyers of Texas. In the Relinquishment cases he made a forceful argument in support of the proposition that the Relinquishment Act was an attempt on the part of the Legislature to grant relief to purchasers of school land, something which the Constitution, in no uncertain terms, expressly prohibited the Legislature from doing.

At the conclusion of the three-day oral argument in the Relinquishment Act cases, all the lawyers who had defended the constitutionality of the law, with one exception, were confident the court would sustain the law. The one lawyer, and he was a great lawyer, who feared the court would hold the law unconstitutional returned home and prepared a supplemental brief which he later filed with the court. It was in this supplemental brief that the suggestion was first made that the State should receive all the bonus money paid to the landowners for executing oil and gas leases on their lands. This bonus money amounted to many millions of dollars. Those attacking the validity of the Relinquishment Act had not even suggested that the State was entitled to any part of the bonus money if the law was constitutional.

The Relinquishment Act cases were decided on June 28, 1928. The court held that the law was constitutional. The principal opinion is in the Greene case, 117 Texas, 516. This was a great victory for the landowners—one that was worth hundreds of millions of dollars to them. By this decision the landowners who had purchased land from the State, in which the State had reserved the mineral estate and which reservation the court had held in the Cox case was valid, received one-sixteenth of the oil produced from their land.

In deciding the Greene case as it did, the court rectified to some extent the great wrong done the landowners in the Cox case. The opinion in the Greene case was in one respect a great opinion, because it upheld the principles of the common law against those of the civil law. In its opinion the court wrote: "The State had sold the land, the soil with all that goes with it, to the purchaser thereof, and was under obligation to protect him in the use and enjoyment of what it had sold him."

The court unfortunately was misled by the supplemental brief filed by the lawyer mentioned above and held that the State, while not entitled to all the bonus money received by the landowners for executing oil leases on their land, was entitled to receive half the bonus money. The Relinquishment Act did not provide that the State should receive any of the bonus money. There was no reason in law or in logic to support the holding of the court that the State should receive half of the bonus money. This part of the court's decision in the Relinquishment Act cases resulted in further legislation and litigation, the story of which will be told in a subsequent chapter.

The next incident to be related in this story of the struggle between the landowners and the State is the controversy between the majority of the Board of Regents of The University of Texas and the men who discovered the oil field on the lands belonging to the University permanent fund.

Chapter XXX:
The University & Its Oil Lands

In 1925, the Legislature enacted a mineral leasing law providing for the sale of mineral leases on University lands to the highest bidder, when the lands were in demand. The constitutionality of this law was attacked in the case of Thiesen vs. Robison, 117 Texas, 489.

The people of Texas provided in the Constitution of the State for a "University of the first class," and by a vote of the people, the "University of Texas" was located at Austin. For the support and maintenance of this University, the Constitution set apart two million acres of land as "a permanent University fund." It was further provided that "the land herein set apart for the University fund, shall be sold under such regulations, at such times, and on such terms as may be provided by law," the money received from such sales to be invested in bonds of the State of Texas, or bonds of the United States.

In 1913, the Legislature enacted a law providing for the leasing of University land for oil and gas purposes. This law was amended in 1917. Under the law of 1913, as amended by the law of 1917, the lessee was required to pay to the State, for the use of the University fund, two dollars an acre in cash, plus the value of one-eighth of the oil and one-tenth of the gas as the same was produced.

A number of citizens obtained mineral leases on University land in Reagan County. The story of how these men persevered in their efforts to find oil on this land is an interesting one. In this group of men were a number of men of wealth. Month after month, they labored on. Their finances became exhausted. It appeared that ruin could not be avoided. Money was borrowed, new efforts made to discover oil, and eventually oil was found in enormous quantities.

The new mineral leasing act of 1925 provided, among other things, that mineral leases on University lands should be sold to the highest bidder, plus a nominal rental and one-eighth of the oil and one-tenth of the gas produced.

George Thiesen complied with the provisions of the mineral leasing act of 1913, as amended by the Act of 1917. In due time his application for a mineral permit was presented to the Land Commissioner. The Land Commissioner refused to issue the permit, because it was his contention that by the terms of the Legislative Act of 1925, oil and gas leases on University lands must be sold to the highest bidder.

Thiesen instituted suit in the Supreme Court against Mr. Robison as Land Commissioner for writ of mandamus, to compel him in his official capacity to issue to him a permit under the terms and conditions of the mineral permit law of 1913, as amended in 1917. S. Rosa Frank filed application for a permit on the same land as applied for by Thiesen. Thiesen had filed on the land with the County Clerk as surveyed land. Frank filed on the land with the County Surveyor as unsurveyed land. Hence these two applicants had a controversy as to which one was entitled to the mineral lease, in the event the court determined that either of them was entitled to it. The Land Commissioner refused Frank's application for the same reason that he refused the Thiesen application.

While Thiesen and Frank were fighting each other, they were united in the contention that the Act of 1925, providing for the sale of mineral leases on University land, was unconstitutional because that act did not fix a definite time for the sale of oil and gas leases, but provided that such sale should be made when "land was in demand."

The Board of Regents of The University of Texas intervened in these suits and asserted that it was "invested with the sole and exclusive management and control of all mineral lands within the domain appropriated, set aside or acquired by The University of Texas, which includes the five sections in controversy, and is empowered and authorized by law to sell, lease and manage and control said mineral lands belonging to said University as may seem best to said

Board for the interest of the University, and such power and authority over said mineral lands including the oil and gas therein is exclusive."

The majority of the Board of Regents contended that the law of 1913, as amended by the act of 1917, was unconstitutional, because the lease gave to the lessee seven-eighths of the oil and nine-tenths of the gas in the land, and that the oil and gas in the land was a part of the land, and that no part of the land could be given away, because Section 13 of Article 7 of the Constitution commanded that said land "shall be sold." It was also the contention of a majority of the Board of Regents that the act of 1925 was unconstitutional for the same reason and for the further reason that it attempted to authorize the Land Commissioner to determine when the land should be sold, when Section 12 of Article 7 of the Constitution expressly provides that the land "shall be sold...at such times ... as may be provided by law."

In the Thiesen and Frank cases the attorneys were Ward and Ward of Houston, and R. L. Batts of Austin for Mr. Thiesen. The Attorney General; Goree, Odell and Allen of Fort Worth; and Cockrell. McBride, O'Donnell and Hamilton of Dallas represented the majority of the Board of Regents. Frank was represented by Messrs. W. A. Keeling and W. W. Caves of Austin, and G. B. Smedley of Wichita Falls. Other attorneys who had obtained leave to file briefs and make oral arguments as *amici curiae*, and whose clients were interested as owners of oil and gas leases on University lands, were T. R. Freeman, S. W. Marshall, John L. Young and Nelson Phillips of Dallas; Charles L. Black of Austin; Judge Hiram M. Garwood and C. R. Wharton of Houston; Thompson, Knight, Baker and Harris of Dallas. In this lawsuit I represented the men who had discovered the great oil field on the University land situated in Reagan County.

Because of the importance of the cases and the immense property values involved, the court granted an extension of time for oral arguments. Oral arguments were made by Messrs. Ward and Batts for Mr. Thiesen, by Messrs. Caves and Smedley for Frank, by Mr. Robison for himself, and by Messrs. Wharton and Black, and me as *amicus curiae*, and by Odell and Hamilton for the Board of Regents.

If the contentions of the Board of Regents were sustained, every oil and gas lease on the University lands would be invalidated. The owners of oil and gas leases on these lands stood to lose millions of dollars. My oral argument before the court in this case was as follows:

MAY IT PLEASE THE COURT:

Mr. Hamilton in his argument said that property rights of great value are involved in these cases. That is true, but there is something of greater and of much finer value involved. The good faith of the State of Texas and the high moral standing of its great University are also involved in these cases.

Mr. Hamilton seemed to be haunted by the thought of these moral values, for he stressed the point that we say in our briefs that the position of the majority of the Board of Regents in these cases is unconscionable. We do say that, emphatically. The history of this State and the records in these cases prove it. We say the position of the majority of the Board of Regents in these cases is morally wrong, economically unsound and legally indefensible.

The Constitution of this State declares that the Legislature shall provide how University land shall be sold. The exact language of the Constitution is that the "University lands shall be sold under such regulations as may be provided by law." Mr. Hamilton argues that the constitutional provision that the "land shall be sold" is mandatory. If that part is mandatory, then the remainder of the sentence is equally mandatory, that the "sale shall be under such regulations as may be provided by law." When any group of men are commanded to do a thing under such regulations as they may provide, such men have unlimited discretion in determining how the thing shall be done. This Court has repeatedly held that the manner and method of selling the Public Free School land of this State is left to the discretion of the Legislature. The cases are cited in our briefs. The constitutional provision affecting Public Free School lands is not dissimilar from those affecting University lands. We find then that the Constitution expressly declares that the Legislature shall provide how the University land shall be sold.

The Constitution of this State does not prohibit the Legislature from providing for the sale of the University lands, or the mineral estates therein, as similar land, or similar estates in land, are usually and customarily sold.

This Court has repeatedly held that oil and gas in place is a mineral and that the mineral estate in land is subject to severance, sale and ownership, separate and apart from the other estates in the land. This Court is entirely familiar with its decisions to this effect in the cases of Stephens County vs. Mid-Kansas Oil and Gas Company, Humphreys-Mexia Company vs. Gammon, Davis vs. Texas Company, Hatcher vs. State, Jacobs vs. Robison, Munsey vs. Marner Oil and Gas Company, Stalcup vs. Robison, Sawyer vs. Robison, and many other cases. These decisions are but a further development of Benevides vs. Hunt, and Texas Company vs. Daugherty. If the doctrine of *stare decisis* still obtains in this Court, and it does, then the question of severance, sale and ownership of the mineral estate in the land, separate and apart from the other estates in the land, is definitely and for all time settled in this State.

The manner and method of selling the mineral estates in University land provided for by the Legislature in the Act of 1917 is called in the Act a lease, but the

Court is not concerned with the name. The Lessee, by the terms of his lease, obtains the right to permanently remove a part of the land, to-wit: the oil and gas, which is a mineral and a part of the land. The Court, in the Stephens County case held, that a commercial oil and gas lease—Form 88—constituted a sale of a part of the land; namely, the mineral estate. The lease provided for in the 1917 Act is not unlike the usual commercial oil and gas lease. The words "ownership of land" would be meaningless if the term did not carry with it the thought of certain legal rights. These legal rights consist of the right to exclusive possession, enjoyment and use, with the right to sell or otherwise dispose of the land. The Lessee, under the 1917 Act, has the exclusive right to the possession, enjoyment and use of the mineral estate in the land described in his lease, with the right to permanently remove a part of the land and sell and dispose of the same. Ownership in land can vest no further or greater legal right.

The method of sale of the mineral estate in University land, as provided for in the 1917 Act, is precisely the same in principle with the method that has always been followed in selling the mineral estate in land under the common law. In fact, the method is older than the common law. In the tin mines of Cornwall, the oldest mines in England, and which were first worked by the Romans, the miner paid the owner or lord of the soil dish or toll tin, usually in an amount equal to one-fifteenth of the mineral mined. The mineral estate of the tin miner in the old Cornwall tin mines was that of fee simple and descended to his heir at law, in like manner as other lands or estates in land. The estate of the miner in the land could be sold and demised, and was liable to the payment of debts or legacies. The authorities for this and other statements that I am going to make to the Court are cited in the briefs.

Mr. Hamilton argues that a custom prevailing between private parties is irrelevant and without force because here we are dealing with a relationship between the government and its citizens. This is begging the question...It is foolish to say that the men who drafted the present Constitution in 1875 when they declared that the Legislature should provide how University land should be sold, intended to prohibit the sale of this land or the estates therein in the manner usually followed and under a custom which is as old as and older than the common law. However, I shall presently show that this custom was followed by the government of England. The method of selling the mineral estate in land, first adopted in the tin mines of Cornwall, was gradually extended so that in the course of time the custom included the lead, iron, zinc and other mines in England.

This establishes the fact that the custom under the common law was to sell the mineral estate in land for a purchase price to be determined by the value of a percentage of the minerals after they were mined. The purchase price of the mineral estate in University land under the act of 1917 is two dollars per acre, plus the value of one-eighth of the oil produced. This is the "proceeds" of the sale that the Constitution, Section 11, Article 7, declares shall be invested in Texas, or United States bonds. The "proceeds" to be invested could not be more than the purchase price fixed by the Legislature and obtained from the sale of the land or the mineral estate in the land. This disposes of the question of a part of the permanent fund of the University being diverted—the land is not the permanent fund, it is the "proceeds" received from the sale of the land that becomes a permanent fund to be invested in bonds. Land is never invested in bonds. It may be sold and the money "invested." The Legislature had the power to sell this mineral estate for two dollars an acre, or for any other price per acre it wanted to fix. But it did not choose to do this. Instead, it followed the custom that the passing centuries had found prudent and fixed the purchase price at two dollars an acre plus the value of one-eighth of the oil produced.

But Mr. Hamilton says the custom between individuals is without weight. All right. Centuries ago the custom between private parties of selling the mineral estate in land for a purchase price, fixed at a portion of the mined ore, was adopted by the government or crown of England. One desiring to acquire the right to mine coal, iron and other minerals on land belonging to the crown or government, would apply to the Gaveler of the Forest, or, as he was some times called, the Commissioner of the Woods, and if his application was granted, he would be given a permit to mine the land—they even called it a permit back there hundreds of years ago.

The miner acquired a fee simple estate in the land, an estate that descended to the heir of the miner in like manner as other lands or estates in land. The grant by the government was conditioned that non-payment of the royalty or failure to comply with the rules would work a forfeiture of the mineral estate. Here we have the determinable fee. The fee simple estate of the miner was good so long as he continued to make payments and comply with the rules. This is precisely what this Court held with reference to the commercial oil and gas lease before it in Texas Company vs. Davis. The owner of a lease under the 1917 Act has a determinable fee in the mineral estate subject to be forfeited for failure to make the payments and comply with the other provisions of the law. The purchase price paid to the crown was usually one-thirteenth of the mineral produced in the mine. We find that the crown, or the government of England, disposed of the mineral estate in crown lands on precisely the same principles that the government of Texas sells the mineral estate in its land.

As far back as 1873, the House of Lords, in the case of Gowan vs. Christie, speaking through Lord Cairns, declared that "what we call a mineral lease is when properly considered a sale out and out of a portion of the land."

It is interesting to note that when the King of England granted to Sir Walter Raleigh an immense tract of land in North America, the grant expressly provided that one-fifth part of all gold, silver or other precious minerals mined from the land should be paid to the crown. Again the purchase price or a part of the purchase price was to be paid by a portion of the mined ores.

We cross the sea and come to this country and we find that it has always been the custom of the United States Government to sell the mineral estate in the public lands for a purchase price of so much of the minerals mined or the value thereof.

In this country—I make the statement without fear of successful contradiction—between private parties the mineral estate in land is universally sold in like manner as provided in the 1917 Act for the sale of the mineral estate in University land. The purchase price is a portion of the minerals, usually one-eighth of the value thereof.

We come to Texas. Here we find that in 1883 the Legislature enacted two laws. One of these laws provided for the sale of public land but expressly provided that the sale should not include the minerals. By this law the Legislature carved out two estates in the land: the soil estate to be sold, the mineral estate to be reserved. If the soil estate could be separated from the mineral estate and sold, then, of course, the mineral estate can be separated from the soil estate and sold. The other law passed by the same Legislature in 1883, in fact, introduced only one day later than the Act just mentioned, provided for the leasing, that is to say, the sale of the mineral estate. What was the purchase price? Five per cent of the ores mined. We find then that Texas for almost fifty years has been selling the mineral estate in its land under precisely the same plan as that provided for in the 1917 Act, and that our fathers before us were following the age-old custom of selling the mineral estate in the State-owned land for a purchase price of a portion of the minerals mined or the value thereof.

And this is not all.

The two Acts just mentioned were enacted in 1883, which was but eight years after our present Constitution was drafted and but seven years after it was adopted by the people. Several men who had been members of the Constitutional Convention were members of the Senate and House when these two laws were passed. Fortunately, the Senate and House Journals show that these men, who but eight years before had served in the Constitutional Convention, voted for both of these laws. Who can better know what was meant by the provisions of the Constitution relied on by the Board of Regents than the men who wrote them? Was there ever a more perfect case of contemporaneous constitutional interpretation than this?

The great Chief Justice, John Marshall, in that history-making decision of his in Cohens vs. Virginia, declared that great weight always has been attached, and very rightly attached, to contemporaneous exposition of the Constitution by the men who wrote it. Again, in Fairbanks vs. United States—I believe this is the style of the case, the cases are cited in the briefs— the Supreme Court of the United States declares that "laws enacted during the period when the framers of the Constitution were actively participating in public affairs may be treated as clearly approved by those who as members of Congress or of a State Legislature were in effect giving a practical construction to the Constitution which they had helped to establish." Courts give great weight to the interpretation of a Constitution by the men who helped to write it because as said by Judge Cooley in his work on Constitutional Limitations, "The contemporaries of the Constitution have claims to our deference on the question of right, because they had the best opportunities of informing themselves of the understanding of the framers of the Constitution and of the sense put upon it by the people when it was adopted by them."

And this is not all.

Since 1913, citizens of this State have acquired thousands of permits and leases under the 1913 and 1917 Acts. Controversies have arisen between citizens as to their respective rights to these permits and leases. Cases of this kind have been before this Court. This Court has adjudicated these private controversies, and neither the parties to the litigation, nor this Court, have ever questioned the constitutionality of these Acts.

And this is not all.

Since 1913, the Attorneys General of this State have repeatedly construed the provisions of the Acts of 1913 and 1917. The administrations of Looney, Cureton, and Keeling did this. These lawyers did not question the constitutionality of these laws. They assumed their constitutionality—of course.

And this is not all.

Citizens who were refused permits and leases by the Land Commissioner for various reasons under the Act of 1913, as amended by the Act of 1917, applied

to this Court for writs of mandamus to compel the
Land Commissioner to issue them a permit. The extraordinary writ of mandamus will never issue except
upon a clear showing of right. Certainly this Court had
no power to compel the Land Commissioner to issue
a permit or lease under these laws if they were unconstitutional. As a result of these suits, this Court has
caused to be issued writs of mandamus commanding
and compelling the Land Commissioner to issue permits and leases under the Act of 1913, as amended by
the Act of 1917. This amounts to a judicial declaration
of the validity of these laws.

And this is not all.

In the case of Bowman vs. Railroad, this Court in an
opinion by Judge Williams—that great judge—declared that an Act of the Legislature was valid which
expressly provided that railroads should have, without
cost, a perpetual easement over the public school lands
of this State. Here was what amounted to an outright
gift of a part of the public school land. This Court held
that the act was valid because it promoted the power to
sell to advantage these public school lands and to the
advancement of the purpose of selling the land advantageously by settlement because it would bring them
into demand thereby increasing their value.

To the same effect is the opinion of this Court in the
Imperial Irrigation Company vs. Jayne, opinion
by Judge Dibrell, where the validity of an act of the
Legislature was upheld which granted to irrigation
companies a perpetual easement without cost to use
public school land as a reservoir, because such use of
the land was in furtherance of the value of such lands.
Again the Legislature made what amounted to a gift
of the public free school land. This act was held valid
because as Judge Dibrell declared, "The construction
of the Constitution here given is wholly in aid of the

power of the Legislature to sell the public school land for the best price and to the best advantage."

Citizens of this state, knowing this history that I have briefly sketched, and relying on the good faith of the State of Texas, have accepted the invitation extended by these laws, expended millions of dollars in developing the great natural resources of this state, brought in great oil fields on University land that resulted in the building of cities and directly and indirectly furnished employment to thousands of men whereby they were enabled to provide for their families and educate their children. These citizens, by the discovery and development of the natural resources of the state, have paid and are paying hundreds of thousands of dollars in taxes every year to the State of Texas. This has increased the value and promoted the power of the Legislature to sell the University land for the best price, and to the best advantage. If for these reasons this Court could, as it did in the Bowman and Jayne cases, uphold Legislative Acts which for all practical purposes made absolute gifts of the public free school land, how, in these cases, can it be argued that the act of 1917 is invalid where the land is not given away but is sold for two dollars an acre plus the value of one-eighth of the oil produced?

At this late date, fifteen years after the first of these laws were enacted, a majority of the Board of Regents of our State University seek to destroy the labor of the pioneers who risked their fortunes in an effort to develop the University land—the search for oil is among the most hazardous of ventures. The majority of the Regents insist that the University lands should be sold as one estate. A hasty examination of their contention discloses economical weakness. Suppose that in 1913 the Legislature had interpreted the Constitution as the Board of Regents desire this Court to now interpret it, what would have been the result?

It was not known in 1913 that there was any oil in West Texas where all the University land is situated. The major portion of this land is located in semi-arid country. The value of the land ranges from one to four dollars an acre. The State has never sold any of it for as much as four dollars an acre. The average price is about two dollars an acre. Let us assume that it could have been sold for four dollars an acre in 1913, at which time the lands set apart for the University were something less than two million acres. Counting two million acres and at four dollars an acre, the total purchase money that would have been received by the University of Texas for the sale of all its land would have been, under the Constitutional interpretation insisted upon by a majority of the Board of Regents, about eight million dollars. Under the wise and age-old custom adopted by the Legislature for selling this land, the University has actually received more than eight million dollars from only five sections of the land in Reagan County, and month by month the payments continue to be made.

Brave, adventurous men have developed by their initiative those great oil fields and thereby enriched the University. Are these men, at this late date, to be deprived of their honestly gained and hard-earned fortunes? The statement may sound harsh to the ears of my learned friends, Judge Hamilton and Mr. Odell, but I repeat what I said in the beginning, that the position taken by the majority of the Board of Regents in these cases is morally wrong, economically unsound and legally indefensible.

This is a case in which I could talk for a week, but it is not necessary. I believe that I have demonstrated historically and judicially the validity of these laws.

The court held the Act of 1913, as amended by the Act of 1917, a valid law. This established my clients' title to their oil field. The court also held that Land Commissioner Robison had acted correctly in refusing the permits to Theisen and Frank. This was true because the court held the Act of 1925 constitutional, and this Act superceded the Act of 1913 as amended by the Act of 1917.

Chapter XXXI:
Attempted Impeachment
of the Land Commissioner

The attempt to impeach Honorable J. T. Robison, Commissioner of the General Land Office of Texas, is a part of the history of the controversy between the West Texas landowners and the State of Texas. I may be mistaken, but it is my belief that Mr. Robison's support of the Relinquishment Act and his opposition to the majority of the Board of Regents of The University of Texas in the Thiesen case had much to do with the effort that was made to impeach him.

The Mineral Leasing Act of 1925, which the Supreme Court held to be a valid law in the Thiesen case, provided for the sale of mineral leases on University lands "when the lands were in demand." The law provided that the leases were to be sold by the Land Commissioner, after the sale had been duly advertised, to "the highest bidder."

In November, 1928, the Land Commissioner, Honorable J. T. Robison, duly advertised for sale mineral leases on all the University land, the sale to be made on January 2, 1929. Those desiring to submit bids on one or more tracts of land were required to submit their bids in sealed envelopes. Each bid had to be accompanied by a certified check for a certain percentage of the amount of the bid.

Prior to January 2, 1929, when the bids were to be opened and the leases sold, the Attorney General brought a suit against the Land Commissioner in the name of the State of Texas in one of the District Courts of Travis County, Texas. In this suit the Attorney General asked the court to grant a temporary restraining order pending a trial of the case on its merits, restraining the Land Commissioner from opening on January 2, 1929, the sealed envelopes containing the bids, and restraining the Land Commissioner from selling leases on the University land pursuant to the advertisement offering the same for sale on January 2, 1929. The court granted the temporary restraining order as prayed for.

Before the case could be tried on its merits, the Legislature convened in regular session in January, 1929. One of the first things the Legislature did was to enact a law on January 11, 1929, by the terms of which the Land Commissioner was prohibited from selling leases on University land.

The Attorney General is the legal adviser of the Land Commissioner and ordinarily acts as his attorney in all litigation in which the Land Commissioner, in his official capacity is a party. In this suit the Attorney General and the Land Commissioner were not in agreement, and the Attorney General was the attorney for the State, and the State was seeking to enjoin its own officer, the Land Commissioner, from opening the sealed envelopes containing the bids and from selling any leases on University land.

A client of mine had submitted bids on many tracts of land believed to contain oil, and his bids were for very large sums of money. He had obtained from his bank the certified checks that had to accompany his bids. He had, as I recall the facts, about $200,000 on deposit with the Land Commissioner in certified checks. He did not know and could not find out whether he was the highest bidder on any of the land he had bid on, because the Land Commissioner was restrained from opening the envelopes containing the bids. My client could not withdraw his bids or obtain his certified checks.

In this suit the State was represented by Honorable C. W. Truehart, Assistant Attorney General and an expert land lawyer. The Land Commissioner and those who had submitted bids were represented by former State Senator Lloyd E. Price of Fort Worth; the late Judge C. A. Wilcox, Mr. J. Harris Gardner, and me, all of Austin.

When the case was tried on its merits, the State contended:

1. That there was no "demand" for oil and gas leases on University lands in November, 1929, such as jus-

tified the Land Commissioner in advertising for sale leases on all the University lands.

2. That the Land Commissioner had not complied with the law in advertising the leases for sale.

3. That the Legislature had, by the Act of January 11, 1929, prohibited the Land Commissioner from selling any leases on University lands.

To these contentions my associates and I answered:

1. That the Land Commissioner had received many requests, oral and in writing, requesting him to offer leases on University land for sale.

2. That the Land Commissioner had complied with the law in advertising the leases for sale.

3. That the Land Commissioner, as the duly authorized agent of the State, acting under the authority of the mineral leasing law and in the name of the State of Texas, had offered the leases for sale. Our clients, in response to that offer, had submitted bids for certain tracts of land, and if their bids were the highest bids, they were entitled to oil leases on the land for which they had bid.

4. That the Legislative Act of January 11, 1929, was null and void insofar as it attempted to prevent the Land Commissioner from selling leases to those who had submitted the highest bids pursuant to the offer made by the State to sell the leases to the highest bidder; that the State could not make an offer to sell oil and gas leases on University land and withdraw the offer after it had been accepted.

The case was tried before Judge J. D. Moore in the 98th District Court of Travis County. Judge Moore held that there had been a sufficient demand for land to justify the Land Commissioner in offering the leases for sale, and that the Land Commissioner had complied with the law requiring the sale of leases to be advertised. He then held that the State, through its duly authorized agent, the Land Commissioner, had offered the leases for sale, and that those who had submitted the highest bid for any tract of University land had accepted the offer; that this offer and acceptance constituted a contract between the State and the highest bidder which the Legislature could not nullify. He then held the Legislative Act of January 11, 1929, unconstitutional insofar as it attempted to prohibit the Land Commissioner from selling leases to those who had submitted the highest bids on January 2, 1929.

The State appealed from the judgment entered by Judge Moore in favor of the Land Commissioner and those who had submitted bids. In due course the case reached the Supreme Court of Texas, and about eighteen months after my client had submitted his bids, the Supreme Court affirmed the judgment entered by Judge Moore. (State vs. Robison, 119 Texas, 302.) When the bids were finally opened, it was found that my client was the highest bidder on many tracts of land.

This was the only lawsuit in which I ever participated where my client, by winning his lawsuit, lost a fortune. My client believed that the lands he bid on were oil-bearing lands, and they were. At the time he submitted his bids the country was very prosperous; oil was in demand and was selling at a high price. When the lawsuit was decided by the Supreme Court and he could obtain his leases, the country was in a financial depression; new oil fields had been discovered and the price of oil was a few cents a barrel.

In the meantime and long before the Supreme Court had decided the lawsuit, an effort was made to impeach the Land Commissioner. This attempt had its beginning at the regular session of the Legislature, which convened in January, 1929, and was continued and finally concluded at a special session of the Legislature held in the summer of 1929. The effort of the Land Commissioner to sell oil leases on the University land caused certain powerful groups to become very hostile toward him. I believe Mr. Robison was trying to serve the best interest of the State and the University in offering the leases for sale.

The Supreme Court held that he did his duty under the law in offering the leases for sale at the time and in the manner that he did. I do not question the sincerity of many of those who sought to impeach Mr. Robison. Subsequent events proved that the University would have received more money from the sale of the leases in January, 1929, than it could have sold them for at any time since 1930. Many of those who submitted bids and whose bids were the highest bids at the January 2, 1929, sale forfeited to the State the money represented by their certified checks in preference to buying the leases at the high prices they had offered for them.

The Senate and the House appointed a joint committee to investigate the affairs of the General Land Office and the controversy that had arisen between the Land Commissioner on one side, and the Board of Regents and the Attorney General on the other side. I represented Mr. Robison before this committee. The investigation lasted for many weeks. Mr. Robison had been Land Commissioner for more than twenty years and had been re-elected for another two-year term at the November, 1928 election. During these years Mr. Robison had sold for the State hundreds of thousands, perhaps millions, of acres of land. He had forfeited thousands of sales for non-payment of interest on the deferred purchase money obligations of those who had bought land from the State. As Land Commissioner, Mr. Robison had decided hundreds of contests between claimants for the surface estate or for a mineral lease on the same tracts of land. As a result of these actions on his part there were men who had what they probably believed were just grievances against Mr. Robison as Land Commissioner. Some of these men came to Austin and told their petty stories to the committee.

After hearing an immense amount of testimony, the committee made its report. In this report a brief summary was

made of the facts, and the Legislature was left to form its
own conclusions. A resolution was introduced in the House
of Representatives in which thirteen charges were made
against Mr. Robison, and providing for a hearing on the
charges by a committee of the whole House. This resolution
which was adopted further provided for the employment by
the House of attorneys to represent the committee of the
whole House. Judge C. T. Freeman, of Sherman, and Judge
Robert Allen, of Dallas, were employed by the House. Mr.
Robison was allowed counsel of his own selection. He selected former Senator Lloyd E. Price and Dayton Moses, of
Fort Worth, and me.

I shall not discuss the details of the hearing before the
committee of the whole House. The entire proceedings, including the arguments of the lawyers, are a matter of record
in the House Journal. During the hearing hundreds of West
Texas landowners came to Austin to do what they could to
assist Mr. Robison. These men had not forgotten that Mr.
Robison had helped to write the Relinquishment Act and
had assisted in defending that Act when it was under attack
in the Supreme Court.

During this hearing I became well acquainted with that
fine American citizen and Texan, Judge J. C. Hunter, now
of Abilene. Judge Hunter was, many years ago, the County
Judge of a West Texas County. He entered the oil business,
and, I understand, has prospered. He deserves all of the
good things of life. For years he fought the battles of the
landowners of West Texas. His fight was an unselfish one
and was made without thought of personal reward. Judge
Hunter fully appreciated the great wrong done by the State
to the landowners of West Texas. He came to Austin during
the hearing on the impeachment charges and remained in
Austin until the hearing was concluded. His services on behalf of Mr. Robison were invaluable.

The hearing before the committee of the whole House
lasted about two weeks. A table was arranged near the
Speaker's desk. A microphone was placed on each side of the

table. The lawyer examining a witness would sit on one side of the table and the witness on the other side. The lawyer questioned the witness by speaking into the microphone on his side of the table, and the witness answered the questions by speaking into the microphone on his side of the table.

One witness, whom I shall refer to as Mr. Tom, although that was not his name, was called to testify against Mr. Robison. This gentleman was well and favorably known and was a man exercising a tremendous influence over the members of the Legislature. He had the reputation of saying what he thought and of using strong and forceful language. Personally, I feared his testimony more than I did that of any other witness that was called to testify against Mr. Robison. I was afraid that if we pressed him on cross-examination he would make some wholly irrelevant answer, but one that would hurt our cause and hurt it badly. He had a reputation for making caustic and cutting remarks. Judge Garwood once said to me, referring to this gentleman: "Tom had rather say something mean about his opponent in the trial of a lawsuit than to win the case."

When this gentleman was called to testify, Senator Price, Mr. Moses and I were sitting together at our table. Senator Price was in front, for he had been cross-examining most of the witnesses. Senator Price did not need a loudspeaker, for he had a magnificent voice, and the 150 members of the committee had no difficulty in hearing any questions he asked a witness. Mr. Tom was questioned at great length on direct examination and his direct testimony had not, in my opinion, hurt our cause. When it appeared that the direct examination of the witness was about complete, I whispered to Mr. Moses that we should waive any cross-examination. Mr. Moses agreed and asked me to make the same suggestion to Senator Price. When I whispered the suggestion to Senator Price, he agreed that we should waive our right to cross-examine. I then whispered to Mr. Moses that Mr. Price had agreed to our suggestion. Mr. Moses then left our table and went to some other place on the floor of the House.

When the direct examination of Mr. Tom was concluded, Senator Price began to cross-examine him. Mr. Moses came back to our table and wanted to know why Senator Price was cross-examining Mr. Tom. I told him I did not know. The cross-examining of Mr. Tom was a fearless one and brought out some facts which I think helped our cause. When his cross-examination had been concluded, there was a few minutes recess, and I said to Senator Price: "I thought we were agreed that we would not cross-examine Mr. Tom. What happened to cause you to change your mind?"

"Not a thing in the world," the Senator replied. "I simply decided that I would show the old hellion that I was not afraid of him."

When the evidence had all been introduced, Judge Allen made the opening argument and it was a good one. I followed Judge Allen, and by agreement with my associates, my argument was limited to a discussion of the legal propositions upon which we relied. Senator Price and Mr. Moses both made what I thought were great arguments. Senator Price has a marvelous memory, and he is a great reader of the poets. His argument was a poem in prose. Some of his best points he illustrated with quotations from some well-known poems. Mr. Dayton Moses is one of the famous trial lawyers of Texas. He was at one time a district attorney; then for years he was the attorney for the Texas Cattle Raisers Association. In this latter employment one of his jobs was to assist district attorneys in prosecuting those charged with crime. He has in his private practice been employed for the defense in many famous criminal cases. Judge Freeman made the closing argument against Mr. Robison, and his argument was an excellent one.

The closing argument was finished at about 9:00 o'clock at night. The House gallery was crowded with people when the vote was taken. The final vote on the charges of impeachment was thirty-seven for and eighty against. When the vote was announced, the friends of Mr. Robison who were in the gallery came downstairs and on the floor of the House.

Mrs. Robison was with her husband. Hundreds of people crowded around them to shake their hands. Many were crying with joy. It reminded me of the old-time revivals when men and women became so happy that they shouted.

Not long before the investigation into the affairs of the Land Office began, Mr. Robison had a serious illness which necessitated a major operation. The long strain of the investigation was too much for him in his weakened condition. In a short time he died. He was not alive when the Supreme Court placed its judicial approval upon his acts in offering the oil leases on University land for sale.

I shall never forget the naive statement made by Mr. Robison when he was on the witness stand before the committee of the whole House. He said: "I have perfect confidence in my own honesty." Those of us who knew, respected, and loved Mr. Robison believed that his confidence in his own honesty was not misplaced.

Chapter XXXII:
The Landowners Lose Again

The Relinquishment Act took the place of the Mineral
Permit Law, insofar as the school lands which the State
had sold and reserved the minerals were concerned. Under
the Permit Law, the State was paid no bonus but a rental of
ten cents an acre. The Relinquishment Act, in the form in
which it was originally introduced, did not provide for any
rental to the State. In the Senate, Senator Dean offered an
amendment requiring a payment of ten cents an acre rental
to the State so that the State might receive, under the Relinquishment Act, the same revenue that it was then receiving
from the school lands under the Mineral Permit Law. If it
had been the intent of the Legislature that the State should
participate in any bonus received by the landowner, the
Legislature would, of course, have made express provision
in regard to the bonus, fixing the amount to be paid to the
State, and by whom it was to be paid. No such provision was
made.

In many sections of West Texas, oil was found in paying quantities. The price of oil was high. Oil leases were in
demand. Oil companies paid large bonuses for oil and gas
leases. It never occurred to the able attorneys representing
these companies that the State was entitled to any part of
the bonus. The Land Commissioner never demanded or
suggested that any part of the bonus be paid to the State. No
such demand was made by any of the several distinguished
lawyers who served the State as Attorneys General during
the period from 1919 to 1928 that any part of the bonus belonged to the State.

During the oil boom period, thousands of landowners
received bonuses for oil and gas leases executed by them under the Relinquishment Act, and the amendments thereto.
The money so received was used by them in the payment of
debts, in many instances to pay the State the balance due on

their lands, to make improvements on their lands, thereby increasing the taxable values, and indirectly but very substantially adding to the revenues of the State.

It will be recalled that one of the distinguished counsel in the Greene case filed a supplemental brief wherein he made an argument in support of his thesis that the Relinquishment Act was a valid enactment to the effect that the State was entitled to all the bonus money paid to the landowners for executing oil and gas leases on their lands. In this supplemental brief for the first time a suggestion was made that the State was entitled not to one-half of the bonus money but to all of it.

The case of Greene vs. Robison, 117 Texas, 516, was decided June 25, 1928, and in the course of its opinion, the court said: "If a bonus is paid…the State and the owners of the soil receive equally in like amounts."

There was no issue before the court over the bonus money. The only question before the court was the constitutionality of the Relinquishment Act. There was no necessity for the court in deciding that question to say anything about the bonus money. After the decision in the Greene case the landowners would not pay the State half of the bonus money they had collected for executing oil and gas leases on their own lands. Many of them could not do so for they had long since spent the money. It was the opinion of the Attorney General that the lessees and the landowners were jointly liable to the State for the payment to the State of the bonus money. He accordingly brought a test suit against the Empire Gas and Fuel Company, as the lessee, and the landowner that had made the oil and gas lease to the company to recover one-half of the bonus money that the landowner had received for making the lease to the Empire Gas and Fuel Company. The District Court followed, as it was bound to do, the holding or suggestion made by the Supreme Court in the Greene case. The Court of Civil Appeals at Austin affirmed the judgment of the District Court on the authority of the language used in the Greene case.

The Supreme Court granted writ of error in the Empire Gas and Fuel Company case because of the importance of the question involved. Clearly the court would have been justified in refusing to grant the writ of error, because of the language used in the Greene case, except for the fact that the bonus money question was not before the court in the Greene case, was not discussed in the many voluminous briefs filed in that case and the companion cases, nor was it discussed in the oral arguments. The only mention made of the bonus money in the Greene case was made in the supplemental brief filed with the Supreme Court after the oral arguments before the court had been concluded.

While the Empire Gas and Fuel Company case was pending in the Supreme Court, the Legislature, being fully advised of the existing situation and convinced that a great injustice was about to be perpetrated against thousands of Texas citizens, landowners and homeowners, enacted Senate Bill 310. The Governor of Texas, Honorable Ross S. Sterling, being in sympathy with the laudable motive actuating the Legislature in the passage of Senate Bill 310, promptly approved the bill and it became the law.

Senator Clint C. Small and Senator Walter C. Woodward, aided by others, were responsible for the passage of this bill in the Senate. In the House, Senate Bill 310 received vigorous support by leading members from every section of the State. Among those who made speeches favoring its enactment may be named R. M. Hubbard of New Boston, W. E. Pope of Corpus Christi, R. M. Wagstaff of Abilene, and Coke Stevenson of Junction. These men on the floor of the House made it clear that one of the purposes of Senate Bill 310 was to give effect to the intent of the Relinquishment Act, which intent was that the State by the terms of that act intended to sell the reserved mineral estate to the lessee for the rental named in the act and the one-sixteenth royalty, and that any money, bonus or otherwise, paid by the lessee to the surface owner for the right to take and use the surface estate should belong to the surface owner. This is the legislative construction of the Relinquishment Act, as is apparent from the language used in Senate Bill 310. This law also authorized the sale of the State's reserved mineral estate to the owners of the surface estate. Thousands of landowners complied with the provisions of Senate Bill 310 and believed that they had finally regained the title to the mineral estate in their lands. The landowners were destined to suffer another cruel disappointment.

That the members of the Legislature, in enacting Senate Bill 310, were not actuated by any spirit of sectionalism but were motivated by the desire to do justice, which always has a universal appeal, is disclosed in no uncertain terms by the votes cast for and against Senate Bill 310. In the House the bill received one hundred and eight votes, while twenty-one votes were cast against it. In the Senate the bill received twenty-nine votes, while one vote was cast against it.

The Supreme Court in the Empire case held that the State was entitled to one-half of the bonus money, and that Senate Bill 310 in its entirety was unconstitutional. The court did this, notwithstanding the fact that the validity or invalidity of Senate Bill 310 was not before the court at all.

Lightning from a clear sky could have been no more surprising, and not nearly so disastrous, to the West Texas landowners as the decision of the court in the Empire case, striking down as it did, in its entirety, Senate Bill 310. Those vitally affected by the provisions of the bill were not even aware that the court could or would consider the constitutionality of that bill in a case filed long before its enactment, and in which no attack was made on Senate Bill 310, and none could be made because the bill had not been introduced in the Senate at the time the suit against the Empire Company was filed.

With the exception of the dicta therein to the effect that the State was entitled to one-half of the bonus money paid to the surface owner, the opinion of the court in Greene vs. Robison is a great opinion. The court, in that opinion, rejected the principles of the civil law, principles utterly repugnant to home ownership, which has ever been the cornerstone of Anglo-American civilization, and reasserted the doctrine of the common law in the following language: "The State had sold the land, the soil with all that goes with it, to the purchaser thereof, and was under obligation to protect him in the use and enjoyment of what it had sold him."

In its opinion in the Empire case the court repudiated the doctrine of the common law which it had once more reasserted in the Greene case, and quoted with approval the language used by Chief Justice Wheeler in the old case of Cowan vs. Hardeman, decided in 1862, that the State "must have the easement of going upon" privately owned land for the purpose of developing its mineral estate "and if to the full enjoyment of the right of the State, it should become necessary to use the whole of the land, timber and water upon the tract, the right of the State to an easement to that extent cannot, I apprehend, be questioned."

The Supreme Court quoted with approval the above language from the Cowan case notwithstanding the fact that the people of Texas, four years after the Supreme Court decided the Cowan case, had repudiated the doctrine there announced by writing into the Constitution of 1866 a provision declaring "that the State of Texas hereby releases to the owner of the soil all mines and mineral substance that may be on the same." After the Supreme Court had decided the Empire case, I was employed by the landowners of West Texas to file in the Supreme Court a written brief in support of the oil company's motion for rehearing. The court very kindly gave me sixty days in which to prepare my brief. In my brief, I reviewed the land history of Texas and pointed out to the court that the people in the Constitutions of 1866, 1869 and 1876 had declared that the minerals in the State lands should be relinquished to the purchasers of those lands, and that the Supreme Court itself, in 1872, had held that these constitutional provisions applied to lands there after sold; that while the court could not overrule its erroneous decision in the Cox case it could and should, as a matter of law, hold that the State was not entitled to half the bonus money received by the landowners for executing oil leases on their own lands; that the court could not lawfully pass upon the constitutionality of Senate Bill 310 in the Empire case because the validity of that law was not before the court for decision. If, I argued, the court insisted upon deciding the validity of Senate Bill 310, it should hold the law constitutional because there were no provisions in the law that were contrary to or in conflict with any provision or clause of the Constitution. The court refused to follow the law as it had declared it to be in the Delesdenier, Parker, and Greene cases, and overruled the motion for rehearing.

The long controversy, lasting for almost eighty years, between the government of Texas and the citizens of Texas over the mineral estate in the lands of Texas, has apparently been finally determined. The landowners in East Texas obtained all the minerals in their lands and all the bonus money that they have received or may receive for executing oil and gas leases, because they had purchased their lands from the State prior to the adoption of the Constitutions of 1866, 1869 and 1876. From the landowners of West Texas the State took one-sixteenth of the mineral estate, plus one-half of the bonus money which the landowners have received or may receive for executing oil and gas leases on their own lands.

CHAPTER XXXIII:
A HYMN OF PRAISE

Law is a system of principles and rules of human conduct, prescribed by the supreme power in the state. This supreme power under our form of government is lodged in the people. Subject to the limitations upon their power contained in the Constitution of the United States, the people of any state may change the rules governing human conduct in either of the following ways: They may adopt a new constitution or amend their present constitution; or the representatives of the people in the legislature, the lawmaking branch of the government, may make new laws or amend old laws, provided such new laws or changes in the old laws do not conflict with some provision in the state or national constitutions.

The courts are not authorized either to make new laws or to change old laws. In deciding a lawsuit, the court must declare what the law is as applied to the facts of the case being decided. In determining what the law is, the Supreme Court of Texas may look to the Constitution of the United States, the Constitution of Texas, the statutory law of the United States, and Texas, and in the absence of any constitutional or statutory law upon the subject may be guided by the common law. In some cases the law is determined by the custom of the people. Sometimes in Texas the civil law is the law of a particular case.

If the question before the court is one of constitutional law, the court must interpret the pertinent provisions of the Constitution. If the language used in the Constitution is clear and definite, there is nothing to interpret, and the court must give effect to the language used. If the language used is ambiguous, then the court is at liberty to consider "the prior state of the law, the subject matter and the purpose sought to be accomplished, as well as to consult the proceedings of the convention and the attending circumstances," to the end that the court may determine the intent of the people who adopted the Constitution or the amendment to the Constitution. The same general rules are applicable in the interpretation of a legislative enactment, except that in interpreting a statute, the thing sought to be ascertained is the intent of the Legislature that enacted the law, and no interpretation should be given to a statute that will bring it into conflict with the Constitution, if any other interpretation of the statute is reasonable, because it will not be assumed that the Legislature intended to enact a law in violation of the Constitution.

In the absence of any constitutional or statutory law to guide the court, it may be governed in its decision by the law of custom. Custom may be general or it may be local. A general custom is one that everyone knows and of which the courts will take judicial knowledge, and, therefore, a general custom need not be proved. A local custom has to be proved in like manner as any other fact.

If the case is one that should be controlled by the civil law, then the court must determine what the civil law is. While the civil law has influenced the common law in many instances, it has done so in a very peculiar way in Texas. Louisiana is the one state in the Union that has never adopted the common law. The civil law in Louisiana is different from the civil law of Mexico. The Code Napoleon is a modification of the civil law of Justinian. As a French province, Louisiana adopted and has continued to use, with modifications, the Code Napoleon as its basic system of law in like manner as the other states in the Union have adopted and continued to use, with modifications, the common law of England as their basic system of law. The civil law of Spain is the civil law of Justinian, with modifications. The civil law of Mexico is, with modifications, the civil law of Spain. Both the civil law of France and the civil law of Mexico have influenced the law of Texas. Perhaps the best way to describe the influence of these two different modifications of the civil law upon the law of Texas is to say that the common law has in some instances been modified or altered in Texas by the civil law of Louisiana and by the civil law of Mexico.

Using one of the methods suggested, the Supreme Court of Texas in deciding a lawsuit declares what the law is. If the people are dissatisfied with the law as declared by the court, they may change the law by amending the Constitution, or their representatives in the Legislature may change the law as declared by the court by a new statutory enactment, or by amending an old statute. When the law as declared by the court is set aside by the people in either of the two methods suggested, the court is thereafter bound to follow the law as made by the people directly, if the Constitution is amended, or as made by the law-making branch of the government, if a new statute is enacted or an old statute amended.

When the Supreme Court of Texas, in deciding a lawsuit, declares what the law is, and this is the only authority the court has, for it may not rightfully either make or change the law, the people may and generally do accept the court's declaration of what the law is. When the court has declared what the law is and there has thereafter been a session of the Legislature, and no constitutional amendment has been submitted to the people, and no legislative enactment changing the law as declared by the court, there has been an acceptance by the people of the law as declared by the court. This law as declared by the court has become a part of the laws of Texas.

The rule of *stare decisis*, which means to stand by and uphold the decided cases, is a rule that should always be respected by the court where the law as declared in the decided case has become a part of the laws of the state. This is true because when the law as declared by the court has been acquiesced in by the people, it is their law, and the court may not thereafter rightfully change the law as it has declared it to be, for it has no more authority to change the law of decided cases than it has to change the law as declared in the Constitution or by the Legislature in statutory enactments.

While I have referred to the Supreme Court of Texas in the above discussion, all that I have said about the doctrine of *stare decisis* is equally applicable to the Supreme Court of the United States, and to the courts of last resort in all the other states, as it is to the Supreme Court of Texas.

The Act of June 3, 1837, provided, "that no land granted by this government shall be located on salt springs, gold or silver mines, copper or lead, or other minerals, or on any island of the Republic." This law prohibited any individual from acquiring any estate in any land located on an island or that was known to contain minerals. It was as simple as that. It was so decided by the Supreme Court in 1851 in the Delesdenier case.

In deciding the Cowan case in 1862 the court refused to stand by its decision in the Delesdenier case. Instead, the court in the Cowan case held that an individual could acquire the surface estate in land containing minerals. The State, however, owned the minerals and had the right to use the "whole" of the surface estate in developing its mineral estate in the land.

In the Delesdenier case the court followed the principles of the common law, which had been adopted as the law of the Republic of Texas by the Act of January 20, 1840. In the Cowan case the court refused to be guided by the principles of the common law, but followed the principles of the civil law of Justinian.

Four years after the court decided the Cowan case, the men of Texas, having returned from the War between the States, wrote the Constitution of 1866. In this Constitution and in all subsequent Constitutions of Texas, including the present Constitution, the people of Texas refused to acquiesce in the law as declared by the Supreme Court in the Cowan case. To the contrary, the people declared in the Constitutions of 1866, 1869 and the present Constitution, which was adopted in 1876, that the State releases to the owner of land purchased from the State all the minerals in the land. This was as complete a repudiation of the law as declared by the court in the Cowan case as it was possible for the people to make.

There is no better established principle of constitutional interpretation than that all the provisions of a Constitution are intended by the people to operate *in futuro*, unless language is used indicating a contrary intent. When the people in the Constitutions of 1866, 1869 and 1876 declared that the State releases to the owners of land all minerals therein, it was their intention that the minerals should be released to those purchasing lands from the State after these several Constitutions were adopted, as well as to those who had purchased land before the adoption of these Constitutions. There was no language used in these Constitutions indicating that it was the intent of the people that these constitutional provisions releasing the minerals in the lands to the purchasers thereof should not operate *in futuro*. The history of the English-speaking people make it certain that it was the will and intent of this English-speaking people in Texas to acquire from the State all the minerals in the land they purchased from the State. In 1884, when the Supreme Court decided the Parker case, the court placed the same interpretation upon these constitutional provisions that I have and held that they applied to land bought from the State after the adoption of these constitutional provisions, as well as to land bought from the State prior to their adoption. The people acquiesced in the law as declared by the court in the Parker case.

The declaration by the court in the Parker case that those who purchased land from the State after the adoption of the Constitutions of 1866, 1869 and 1876 acquired all the minerals in the land, having been acquiesced in by the people, became a part of the laws of Texas. If thereafter the court had followed the rule of *stare decisis*, and had upheld its own decision in the Parker case, the people who purchased land from the State after 1876 would have acquired title to all the minerals in their land. The court refused to follow the rule of *stare decisis*. Twenty-eight years after it decided the Parker

case the court decided the Cox case, and there held that the
State retained the minerals in the land that was sold after the
adoption of the Constitution of 1876. What the court did in
the Cox case was to change the law, and this it had no right
to do. This unauthorized act on the part of the Supreme
Court of Texas cost the landowners of West Texas hundreds
of millions of dollars. In the Empire Gas and Fuel Company
case, the Supreme Court of Texas actually cited and quoted
with approval from its decision in the Cowan case decided
in 1862, a decision which the people had emphatically repudiated and rejected as not being the law in the Constitutions
of 1866, 1869 and 1876.

The status quo can no more be maintained in the law than
it can in anything else. Change is inevitable in everything.
The law must be changed to meet changing and changed
conditions. Where some of our judges fall into error is in
believing that they have the power to change the law to meet
changing and changed conditions. I have often heard judges
declare that the law of decided cases should not be followed
by the courts if conditions have changed so as to make the
law of decided cases unjust. Judges who make statements
like this frequently acquire reputations as being liberal men.
When judges set aside the law of decided cases they are doing
something which they have no right to do. When changed
conditions make a law unjust, the law should be changed;
but the change should be made by the people adopting a
new constitution or by amending the old one, or by the law-
making branch of the government, the Legislature.

Under our form of government the people in their national
and state constitutions reserved to themselves certain powers
and rights. They then authorized the legislative branch of the
government to make laws not contrary to the provisions of
the Constitution, the judiciary to interpret and declare what
the law is in deciding lawsuits, and the executive department
to enforce the law. If the members of the several branches of
our government could be content to limit their activities as
the employees of the people to doing what the people have au-

thorized them to do, we would indeed have a marvelous government and the kind of a government that the people have provided for in their written constitutions. Whenever the law of a decided case becomes unjust, the law-making branch of the government, or the people themselves, may change the law. Courts should not usurp the power of the law-making branch of the government or exercise power which the people have reserved to themselves. It is as necessary under our form of government for the courts to obey the Constitution as it is for members of the executive department and of the legislative department to obey the Constitution.

In recent years, as I have watched events at home and abroad, I have wondered if my ideals of democracy, the sovereignty of the people, and the freedom of the individual were obsolete. Do the people really want to be free, if to be free means personal responsibility and personal sacrifice? Are we, the people, willing to surrender our sovereignty, our liberty, and freedom of thought and action for a promised personal financial security? If we make the surrender, we will be horribly disappointed. The promised financial security will be a mirage devoid of any semblance of reality. By our surrender, we will not alone lose our liberty, but the security that we now have or that we have reason to believe we may attain by individual effort under a free government.

What, after all, is the goal that we, the people, are striving for? Is it not individual happiness? Possibly men in other countries can be happy without freedom. If they can, then let them have their dictators. It is no concern of mine what kind of a government the Russians, Germans, and Italians have. I want them, however, to keep what I consider their pernicious doctrines in their own countries. It is hard for me to believe, and I refuse to believe, that a majority of the American people can be happy unless they are free. Liberty and freedom are the heritage of the American people, a heritage and a right originally procured for us by the heroism of our forefathers under the unselfish and devoted leadership of the immortal Washington.

The men who wrote the Constitution at the Philadelphia Convention, the convention over which Washington
presided, made the purpose of the American people clear.
I think our purpose today is the same as it was then. The
entire question of liberty and freedom for the individual
under the Constitution, the supreme law of the people, was
covered completely by the late Chief Justice C. M. Cureton
in an address which he made at a dinner in Austin given in
his honor.

Judge Cureton said: "The Constitution declares in its
preamble that one of its purposes was to 'establish justice';
and that another was to 'secure the blessings of liberty to
ourselves and to our posterity.' By 'liberty' was meant not
only political liberty, not just some liberty, but all liberty—
political liberty; freedom of trade and commerce and travel;
the freedom to own and use property—to plant, to sow, and
to reap; personal liberty, freedom of speech; freedom of
religion; freedom in all righteous things. In short, liberty
meant then, as it means now, the right to do anything on
earth you desire to do, so long as you do not impinge upon
or restrict the equal rights of another."

The banker thinks he would be happier if he were a doctor; the doctor regrets that he did not study law instead of
medicine; the office lawyer envies the trial lawyer; and the
trial lawyer, by the time he is fifty, has suffered so many
losses, disappointments, and heartaches that he sometimes
wonders why he ever wanted to be a lawyer. To the trial lawyer come those in trouble, and they bring their troubles with
them and leave them on the trial lawyer's desk. He lives in
an atmosphere of controversy, conflict, ill-will and hate.
Always there is consciously and subconsciously present in
his mind some legal problem for which he is trying to find
a solution. He tries a lawsuit in the district court, and wins
it. The Court of Civil Appeals affirms the judgment, but the
Supreme Court grants a writ of error. Perhaps four years after he filed the suit in the district court, the Supreme Court
reverses the judgments of the Court of Civil Appeals and the

district court and remands the case to the district court for a new trial. After four long years he and his client are back where they started. The work must all be done again.

Why, it may be asked, should the lawyer worry about how many times he has to try the same lawsuit; it means more fees for him, does it not? The answer is that the real lawyer makes his client's case his own, and keenly feels the loss and disappointment suffered by his client. The real lawyer is not so much concerned about his fee or the amount of it as he is with winning the lawsuit. Trial lawyers will understand me when I say that the greatest compensation that comes to a trial lawyer is in winning his case and in having a happy and an appreciative client.

Once I was employed in litigation that involved an estate. The estate was worth more than a million dollars. If my client lost, he would lose, under one construction that could be placed on the law, all of the estate; under another construction that could be placed on the law, he would lose half the estate. The claim that my client had in the estate was about all that he owned in the world. If he lost the estate, he would be a poor man. If he won all, or even half of the estate, he would be a wealthy man. After prolonged litigation, the controversy was settled. Under the terms of the settlement my client received approximately ninety-five per cent of the estate.

I had worked almost constantly for a year on this one case. I was delighted with the settlement that I had been able to make, for I knew it was a dangerous case. When the case had been settled, my client came to the office and wanted to know how much he owed me. I suggested a fee that I considered fair. My client insisted on paying me more than I had asked. I was, of course, glad to receive the additional sum of money, but what made me very happy indeed was the knowledge that my client appreciated the services that I had been able to render him.

The law has been good to me. The practice of law can be and sometimes is made into a business, and sometimes, but not often, it is converted into a criminal racket, but to most lawyers it is a profession, a learned profession and a noble one.

In my heart there is a song, a hymn of praise, because I was born a citizen of the United States. Where else but here could a boy, situated as I was, have dreamed of some day being a lawyer and had his dream come true? It is my prayer that our country may ever be the land of equality, where every boy and girl may have the opportunity of making life what they want it to be, if they are willing to pay the price. Everything of value that we desire has a price tag attached to it. Those unwilling to pay the price must do without.

In my opinion there is no hope for those who accept as true the doctrine that America is finished; that the individual is either too incompetent or too dishonest to be trusted; that his life must be planned by men who have never succeeded in anything except politics; that the only honest men in the nation and the only ones competent to plan their own lives and ours are the officeholders. If a majority of our people believe in this erroneous doctrine long enough, there will be no hope for any of us; for no empire, whatever its natural resources and advantages, can long exist if the people have lost confidence in their own ability and integrity.

For our country and for every boy and girl in it there is a marvelous future, if we, the people, are willing to begin now the task of saving our country. There must be years of labor and sacrifice. We must produce, produce, and produce, until there is an abundance of everything so that there will be plenty for all. To do this we must work harder than we have ever worked before. We must live economically and save, and save, and save, until our debts are paid. The longer we put off this sacrificial effort, the more difficult it will be to do that which we know must be done if we are to survive as a great nation and as a great people. If we wait too long to begin this task, it will be come so great and we will have grown so weak and cowardly as a people, that we will be unwilling to make the attempt. When that time comes, our country will become the victim of a sterner and hardier people than we will be.

Our country is yet in a position to go forward. We can achieve a standard of living in this country incomparably higher and better than our highest standard of the past. A high standard of living is a valuable thing, but to this valuable thing is attached a price tag. Are we willing to pay the price in order that we may live in a country where men are free, where all men and women of good will may plan their own lives with reason to believe that their plans, if reasonable, can be made into realities; where the limitations on personal success are only those inherent in the personality of the individual? The price that we, the people, must pay is self-reliance, hard work, thrift and integrity.

We are all Americans and we should have no room in our minds for forming class, religious or race hatreds. If there is injustice, remove the cause. If an individual sins, punish the individual, but do not destroy the group to which the individual belongs.

One of the many important things that all Americans have in common is individual freedom. This is a priceless thing, hard to obtain, easy to lose, and once lost difficult to regain. It alarms me when any public official continually seeks grants of power to be exercised by him at his discretion. Such grants of power are a threat to our freedom. We should, I think, avoid such risks.

In this book I have pointed out some of the mistakes that I believe the courts have made. The fact that the courts sometimes err is no reason why we should lose confidence in them. The courts have an enviable record for protecting the rights of the individual. The mistakes of our judges to which I have referred have been honest mistakes.

There will be some able lawyers who will disagree with some of the statements I have made in this book. Judges disagree as to what is the law. What the law should be and how it can best be administered is a matter of opinion. I have no quarrel with those who differ with me in regard to these matters. In writing this book I have tried to avoid being offensive to anyone in my expressions of opinions and in my criticisms.

CPSIA information can be obtained at www.ICGtesting.com
Printed in the USA
LVOW091603101111

254413LV00003B/2/P